# RETURN TO SAIGON

# RETURN TO SAIGON

From high school in Saigon
to his return as a wounded naval aviator,
Vietnam shaped his life

A Memoir
by
## Larry Duthie

OK-3
PUBLISHING
Annapolis, MD

Published by OK-3 Publishing,
26 Williams Dr., Annapolis, MD  21401

Library of Congress Control Number: 2020921622

Library of Congress Cataloging in Publication Data
Duthie, Larry.
Return to Saigon


First Edition
Second printing November 2, 2020

Cover Design: Don Purdy
Cover photo by Quang Nguyen Vinh

Printed in the United States of America

ISBN:  9798680692028

To Roz,
light and inspiration,
my brilliant wife and partner in all

# CONTENTS

**PROLOGUE**                                    1

PART I:   **SAIGON**

1. *Paris of the Orient*                        7

2. *On the Fringe of War*                       23

3. *Do That Tomorrow*                           31

PART II:   **TRAINING FOR WAR**

4. *Accidental Navcad*                          41

5. *Three Must-Pumps*                           55

6. *To Childplay*                               67

7. *Over the Beach*                             75

PART III:   **VINH**

8. *Mortality*                                  91

9. *Blame Robert*                               97

10. *Vinh*                                      103

11. *White Canvas Casing*                       107

12. *Dick Hartman*                              115

13. *Iwo Jima*                                  121

## PART IV:  **CO TRAI**

14. *Portent*                                    131

15. *A Quiet Breakfast*                           139

16. *Man 'em Up*                                  147

17. *Flying Through Water*                         159

18. *That Rattlesnake Sound*                       163

19. *On the Karst*                                171

20. *A Hillside*                                  177

21. *Barking Like Dogs*                           183

22. *Jolly Green 37*                              191

23. *The Shack at Lima 36*                         197

## PART V:   **SAIGON REDUX**

24. *It's Not Water*                              207

25. *Earthquake*                                  215

26. *Oak Knoll*                                   225

27. *Tissue-Thin Letters*                          233

28. *Airborne Again*                              245

29. *One More Try*                               251

## PART VI:  **RETURN TO SAIGON**

30. *See the Caverns*                             263

31. *Incense and a Prayer*                         271

**AFTERWORD**                            281

There are certain things that are too painful for people to even write about sometimes, and there are certain things that are too hard to read about again.

— *V.S. Naipaul*

---

# *Prologue*

They say a massive shot of adrenaline accelerates the brain, that this explains why we experience exhilarating events—car wrecks and such—as if in slow motion. Mine is rocketing, for I no longer have any control.

My airplane banks past 135 degrees and the nose falls through and points steeply down at the earth. I take in a mental picture, a snapshot of the green foliage covering the slope of the karst mountain now filling my windscreen and then I glance at the instrument panel.

All this in slow motion. I brace flat against the seatback and jam my head tight in the V of the headrest, for there are plenty of stories of compressed vertebrae when guys aren't positioned right. With both hands I grasp and pull straight out, then sharply down on the yellow and black D-ring above my helmet. A nylon curtain, meant to protect me, unfurls and follows the D-ring down to cover my face. That slow-motion thing. I hear the canopy go, feel the

1

rocket ignite under my seat-pan, a big slam as the seat smacks against my butt, and then the high-speed blast upward. All unfolding in a distinct sequence, yet this happens in a quarter of a second, the length of time it takes to say, "Oh!"

The rocket blasts me clear of Alpha Hotel Four One Five, the crippled bird with my name stenciled under the canopy rail. I shoot up at thirteen Gs of vertical acceleration to 103 feet-per-second. Exactly one second after pulling that D-ring, a tiny charge blows my harness free of the ejection seat while bladders inflate behind my back to pop me clear. The seat and I now fall separately. I've slowed some, but I'm still going way too fast and flail violently in the fierce slipstream. This continues for another full second, when the parachute snaps open. Somewhere in these two seconds, I'm knocked unconscious. When I revive, it's quiet. I am awake and see only blackness.

I've been blinded.

I reach for my eyes. But my hands are blocked by the glossy surface of my flight helmet. In the blast and the flailing, it rotated forward to cover my face. I push it into position on my head and am hit with the vivid light of a clear morning in Vietnam. For a second or two, I take in the lush view. It truly is beautiful. Sweet fresh air replaces the oily smoke I'd been breathing. It's odd how this registers right now, how I'm taking in a vista when I'm facing capture. Death even.

I revert to what I'm trained to do. First on the list is to look overhead. Excellent. I'm hanging under a good parachute; no ripped panels. The ejection has gone as my Navy training said. Except for a strange sensation. A strong breeze is flowing up my body, a cool stream of air coming straight up from my feet. In all our training, no one has ever mentioned this.

It seems as if I am suspended, although I am in fact falling. For another second or so I allow myself to marvel at this new experience, the fresh air coming from my feet, the sunshine. How interesting. This relative wind, this cool zephyr blowing straight up from my boots, is the only indication that I'm plunging rapidly toward earth. Then off to my right, at the base of this karst formation

I hope to land on, something catches my eye. It's my airplane, burning.

This, after a day that started so peacefully. Before daylight, in the formal and quiet wardroom aboard CVA-34, Oriskany, the aircraft carrier with the radio call-sign Childplay, my flight leader for the past seven months and I met for breakfast. Dick Hartman and I sat across from each other, and any thought that our day would go so terribly wrong—well, the idea was unthinkable.

Now I've ejected from my A-4E over Vietnam—North Vietnam—where we have been bombing for five straight days. The cold center of my gut informs me I'll have only a slim chance of rescue. Fear envelops me, for I know if I'm captured this far north I can expect to be severely beaten, killed even, during my first moments on the ground.

I've survived this high-speed ejection, but I understand it's only the beginning.

# PART I

## SAIGON

I had given up some youth for knowledge, but my gain was more valuable than the loss.

—*Maya Angelou, I Know Why the Caged Bird Sings*

In the Saigon villa rented by his parents, the author, (white shirt) stands with Joe Christensen. He and Joe returned to the States together. Seated are four other expats—an American, two Frenchmen and a German.

## CHAPTER ONE

# *Paris of the Orient*

T his is not my first waltz with death in Vietnam. I've been terrified here before when I—improbably—spent my senior year of high school living in Saigon with my family. Eventually I would come to love the warm people of the great city, but initially my few buddies and I looked upon Saigon as an alien playground, one custom-made for arrogant American teenagers. And although I eventually came to love much of my new life in the exotic country, I felt I was stagnating. We all did. My clique of friends and I countered ennui with frenetic activity—swimming daily and parties every weekend. Afternoons I'd join buddies in downtown cafes, where we'd imagine ourselves beatnik intellectuals as we sipped coffees from tiny demitasse cups—all sad substitutes for the good and exciting life I imagined my peers were enjoying back in the States.

Certainly my high school fell short. In early September—this was 1959—I began studies at the American Community School, a series of low buildings near Tan Son Nhut Airport at the edge of the city. Although that word, *studies,* is too generous for my dawdling over correspondence-course lessons in pulp-paper workbooks. My coursework from Texas Technological College quickly became boring, and with no one monitoring my progress, I fell behind.

The school had been created five years earlier to serve dependents of the handful of Americans who rushed into the little country to support the new South Vietnamese government shortly after the French were defeated. My entire high-school was twenty-eight students, all in a single classroom. Six of us, the seniors, clustered in one corner. Because there were no formal classes, we were free to wander about. And we did, meeting in the restroom to smoke or leaning on a parapet in a breezeway connecting the buildings as we gazed across a rice paddy. I was academically adrift.

We were all adrift, one way or another, so we compensated, quickly discovering we could be served in Saigon's bars, no IDs required.

About nine of us, most from school but also including a couple ex-pat Frenchmen and several Vietnamese guys, formed a clique that came to be called The Clods. Our Chinese-Vietnamese buddy, Domino, had earned the *Mr. Saigon* title in a weight-lifting competition. Very cool. So he was a Clod.

The Olympic, a joint in the waterfront district, became a favored Clods' hangout. There was nothing fancy about the place. At the back was a long bar, rather plain, made of tropical wood. Placed around the room without any discernable plan were three small tables and a few chairs arrayed beneath harsh fluorescent-tube fixtures. In a corner was a juke box that we fed, playing and then replaying Hank Locklin's "Geisha Girl."

Not a chance we'd be spotted by our parents at the Olympic, a risk in the open-front bars downtown, because our parents never came into this district. For good reason. To get to it we crossed the Khanh Hoi Bridge, and our folks understood the other side of the bridge was one dangerous place. After my frightening night, I learned that the Viet Minh raised their flag over Khanh Hoi every night. And there was solid reason to fear the Viet Minh.

Dad had occasionally tried to warn me—always rather obliquely. On one occasion he casually mentioned that his tiger-hunting ambition had been thwarted. I knew he'd gone through a long application process to import his hunting rifle—a beautiful 30-06 with a custom stock and telescopic sight.

"I'm being told it's too dangerous," he said. "The guerillas control the countryside. They can be brutal."

He mentioned that communist cells came into villages, killed the village chief—to make a point—and then conscripted young men of fighting age to join their forces. "They don't give a choice," he added. "Join with the communists or die." In his telling, this was no problem for us. We simply wouldn't be going into the countryside.

Another time, Dad told me about a Frenchman's family, members of the Saigon Yacht Club that Dad had applied to join. The family had chugged up the river in their boat, and while still in sight of downtown Saigon, their motor quit. The boat, slowly twisting in the current, drifted to shore. As it touched the muddy bank, two or three armed Viet Minh came out of the jungle and boarded the little vessel. The guerrillas forced the man ashore. In front of his family, while his wife and two children watched from the boat, the guerillas assassinated their captive.

"They tossed his head into the boat," Dad said. "They can be savage." After my shock subsided, Dad added, "They didn't hurt his wife, because she's Vietnamese. He was French, the Viet Minh hate the French." He said nothing about them hating Americans. And he failed to mention that this had happened recently.

For the Clods, the Olympic was calm and fun. Bar girls, one across from each of us, poured Ba-Mui-Ba beers from bitter-cold bottles into chilled glasses. We'd pay with a *mot-dong* note, and they'd place coins, our change, onto the bar. The girl across from me slid a coin next to my glass and kept her index finger on it. It was as if we were playing chess, and the way she looked into my eyes, I understood she had a power position. I set my hand on top of hers. Gently. "Ceci est pour vous," I said. Joe looked down the bar and smiled. He had been trying to teach me French phrases. Thick frost formed on my glass in the tropical night-air and it sloughed down the side. "Cam on," she said in soft Vietnamese. She giggled.

That night we tried to dance with our assigned bar-girls, urging them onto the empty concrete dance floor. But they didn't understand Hank Locklin or country music, so they stood as still as soft statues while we erratically bopped about like fools. They found it hilarious. We laughed with them.

We'd roared over the Khanh Hoi bridge that evening on motorcycles—Paul behind his brother Joe on their little Moto Guzzi; Domino and I on his powerful Yamaha. The only other patron that night was a British ordinary-seaman off a tramp freighter. We related to him, because he was seventeen. In short order he was regaling us with tales of his adventures at sea, relating one escapade after another. He told us about the great ports his ship had visited and how it felt to stand a graveyard-watch on a black night.

"A life at sea, man, all a bloke should ever want," he said. We showered him with questions, and after a couple more beers he asked, "You blokes like to see my vessel? She's anchored near."

So, sure. Paul settled behind Joe on the Moto Guzzi and I straddled the backseat of Domino's big Yamaha. Our new friend, the British deckhand, hailed a taxi, and we fell in behind, following the little blue and white Renault snaking through dark backstreets of Khanh Hoi. The taxi turned onto a long gravel road leading to the water, and it was darker yet. We stopped at a muddy bank of the Saigon River.

"Lock your bike," Domino told Joe.

Four landlubbers clambered into a skiff at the bank. Our new friend pushed it off, and at the last possible moment, he casually stepped in. Impressive.

The Brit began rowing powerfully, angling across the current on a course that carried us arrow-straight to a steep ladder on the port side of his old freighter. On deck, rust, crumbly and bubbling corruption, was everywhere. Old tools and partially dismantled equipment lay scattered about the scaly deck. It was shocking, not at all what I expected. In his little room he handed out bottles of

English beers. Sticky, hot foam flowed down the bottles. I understood that the English drink beer at room temperature, but this was hot and bitter. As he rowed us back to the motorcycles, he again made seamanship look easy. That part of life at sea, picking up skills, seemed okay. But not the rust, hot beer and musty odors.

Domino, the muscular body-builder, had always come off as confident and at ease, so I was taken aback when he gasped as he approached his motorcycle. Then I saw; both his tires had been slashed. I turned to see that Joe's tires were also cut open.

"Viet Minh!" Domino said in a loud whisper. Then in a higher-pitch and a little louder, "They want to kill us. Leave now!"

With his powerful right leg, Domino gave his kick-starter one fast stroke, the motor sprang to life and he was moving. But I wasn't on. Without a glance back at me, he picked up speed as he turned onto the dark gravel road leading away from the river. His tires made a flopping sound as he ran through the gears. I turned then to see Paul on the back of Joe's small Moto Guzzi. He, too, was turning for the road to follow Domino. With its flat tires and feeble engine, Joe's bike was struggling. There was no room for a third rider.

A glimmer of light spilled from a nearby warehouse yard. I had been abandoned by my buddies and left in darkness. I thought about that Frenchman in his disabled boat.

A cold fear shuddered through my body, my stomach churned, breathing came shallow and erratic. There was nothing to do but walk to a safer area, but I was frozen with fear. I forced myself to turn for the road and begin. I hadn't made it very far when—what the hell?—I was slammed with a blast of blue-white light.

The intense light stayed on, bathing me. I froze once more. The fierce light was coming from my right, from a high place on the edge of the warehouse yard. Was I targeted?

Once, when Dad and I were in the Guadalupe Mountains hunting deer, he explained how a bullet flies faster than sound, how if I shot a buck, he would be down before the report from my rifle arrived. Was a bullet about to rip into me? Unheard but final?

11

Nothing to do but resume walking. If a bullet did come, I'd at least present a moving target. I took a step. Then, haltingly, another. The gravel crunched under my loafers, and the pool of light followed my slow progress. I could now make out that the road was bordered on both sides by steel mesh fencing topped with rows of barbed wire. I saw, too, that the light formed a disc on the road. I was in the center of a searchlight.

Someone in a warehouse guard tower was protecting me. Meaning someone else believed I was in grim danger. I trudged on, my breathing unnatural. The long bright cone from the tower followed me a quarter mile, then a second light, this one from a tower ahead, merged with the first. I was now walking in two searchlight discs. A little further on, the light from behind shut off, while the new guardian bathed me in brilliance. The road narrowed, the gravel faded and the light shut off. I was now walking on compacted-mud between rows of thatch-roofed hooches. It was very late, and there were no lights, but I found someone awake, an old woman walking toward me on the path. In my wobbly French and pitiful Vietnamese, I asked for a taxi. She nodded, then turned away from me, leaving me alone. She walked swiftly down a side street, an even narrower track, then stooped to enter one of the hooches. Standing there in the dark, it hit me—this might be where the Viet Minh tire-slashers lived. Was she alerting them? Would they cut off my head here? There was nothing to do but wait.

Eventually, however, a sleepy-eyed guy, the neighborhood taxi-owner, emerged. The old woman had—what—saved my life?

So how was it that in 1959 and '60 I would be a teenager running amok in Saigon?

It began in El Paso toward the end of my junior year, when I came upon my parents huddled, sitting on kitchen chairs pulled up beside a bookcase in the hallway of our new suburban house. They were speaking in hushed tones, and each held an open volume of our World Book Encyclopedia.

"What're you guys up to?" I asked.

Dad hesitated, then explained that he had been offered a position running a large engineering project in Asia. He'd be working

12

for an American firm with a contract awarded by the United States Agency for International Development—USAID. This was a significant step upward in his career.

It also meant uprooting our family.

Duthies had been in West Texas since 1903, three generations. Dad was now—as Texans put it—about to kick the dust from his boots and pick up stakes. My entire life had been lived in three houses, all within a couple miles of each other. Now my parents were about to make a choice that meant living halfway around the world.

"We could live in Bangkok. It's in Siam," Dad said. He was referring to a recent blockbuster musical, *The King and I,* in which Thailand was referred to by its old name.

"Or I could set up offices in Indochina." He was still speaking softly, and it felt as if I was being invited into an exotic conspiracy.

Balancing a heavy volume on his knee, my father read a short description of Saigon. He came upon a sentence describing it as "The Paris of the Orient," and he paused to glance up at Mom. "Now, that sounds nice," he said.

Mom smiled. "It does."

Dad turned to me. "If you want to stay here, you can live with my folks."

My mind wandered. I began running through options. I wasn't thrilled with high school in El Paso. Osgood-Schlatter disease, a knee condition, had kept me off the football team, so I was missing out on the sport's quintessential camaraderie. And I wasn't much of an academic, settling for Bs and Cs in courses I didn't care for, picking up As only in English and science courses. I realized, as I thought about it, that I felt no strong attachment to Stephen F. Austin High School. Or, now that I thought more about it, to Texas.

"I'm going," I said.

So it was in that moment, a splinter of time in the hallway of a suburban tract house, that my lifelong and complex relationship with Vietnam launched.

Only the last leg of our series of flights—Hong Kong to Saigon—remains vivid. At Kai Tak airport we walked out to board an Air France Caravelle—the first jet-powered airliner I had ever seen. Seating was tighter than the two-deck Boeing Stratocruiser that carried us across the Pacific, but I loved the little plane. You don't forget your first flight in a jet.

Early that afternoon, we landed at Tan Son Nhut International Airport and taxied to the small Art Deco terminal. After a few minutes on the ramp, a stairway lowered at the tail of the jet. I followed Mom and my three younger sisters off the airplane, and tropical heat engulfed me—far more intense than any dry Texas summer air. I was wearing carefully polished cordovan penny-loafers—in the '50s we dressed up for airline travel—and as I stepped onto the tarmac, my heel squished into the hot asphalt and stuck. Vietnam's hold on me had begun.

It truly is a gorgeous land, though this knowledge would come later. The order was this:

Culture shock.

Acceptance.

Finally, after months and months, appreciation.


The Majestic Hotel was on the waterfront. From our rooms we enjoyed a panoramic view of the Saigon River where only five years earlier battles had raged. Aside from the relic of a partially sunken ship on the far bank, the scars of that war had been erased. Saigon appeared calm and vital.

My own culture shock commenced. Geckos crawled on the Majestic's walls, the heat continued to stun, pungent odors wafted through our rooms. Most unnerving, people ate full meals from ancient-appearing wooden carts on street corners. What about sanitation? There was no proper way to wash utensils. But street-cart hygiene was still a step above the rice-cake vendors. Various women near our hotel were selling food from their upturned conical hats. And then there was the sidewalk medical practice. Daily, I kept an eye on a man below my room's window who squatted in front of a mat he rolled onto the sidewalk. His medical therapy seemed to involve herbs and application of heated glass jars placed upside down on a patient's bare back. It was all unsettling.

From the hotel, we moved to a small apartment on Le Loi, a slightly shabby place adjacent to a high-rise hotel. The Caravelle, jewel of Saigon, was as modern as any new building in El Paso with an elegant top-floor bar that in a few years would become the watering-hole for war correspondents.

While the Le Loi apartment was tired and unremarkable, it did offer a fine view of the Saigon Opera House across the street. This was an Art-Nouveau architectural gem—still is—built in 1897. It served as the South Vietnamese Assembly Hall, and from our balcony, I'd often watch a procession of white-uniformed policemen arrive on Harley-Davidson motorcycles. Out of the stately black limousine escorted by the motorcycle-police would pop a portly little man in a dark western suit. Hurriedly, penguin-like, he'd hustle up the steps into the Assembly Hall.

This was Ngo Dinh Diem, the president—dictator, to put it accurately—who would be killed four years later with the complicity of our CIA. I could not have imagined then how the assassination of Diem would lead to a long series of faltering and corrupt South Vietnamese governments. No one did. But soon enough I'd be asked to risk my life for several of these shaky régimes. Even then the American War was a smoldering fuse, the fizzing glow of a bomb just lit. Diem and his flamboyant sister-in-law, Madam Nhu, were pouring gasoline on it.

As was expected, my parents hired servants: Mssr. Ich and his wife, Ti Ba. The kitchen was solely the realm of Mssr. Ich. Off limits to the family.

As head of our family's service staff, Mssr. Ich was allotted a budget of ninety dollars monthly, a sum that sounds meager today. Even then it seemed low, yet with that budget, Mssr. Ich provided all our food and any added staff he needed. Whatever remained, he retained. You'd think this would result in a boarding-house diet for us all, yet that was never the case. This French system worked, and we ate very well. Until the pumpkin-pie crisis.

When Thanksgiving approached, the American holiday puzzled Mssr. Ich. My mother attempted to explain. She spoke Spanish. Mssr. Ich also was bilingual, but unfortunately his second language was French. They tried to find common meaning using their imperfect versions of the two Romance languages, mixing words from their native tongues and, at times, pantomime (on Mom's part; Mssr. Ich maintained his dignity). The mix of French, Spanish, Vietnamese and English failed when it came to this Thanksgiving business. Mssr. Ich remained puzzled. When Mom obtained a can of American pumpkin puree, probably from someone who had privileges at the military post exchange store in Saigon, the problem magnified. She showed the can of mystery-sauce to Mssr. Ich, informing him with her inadequate communication tools that she would be the one to use this to make the holiday pie.

She! She would enter his kitchen, push him out of the way and take over the important duty of a chef—a chef who had been well trained in the preparation of French cuisine! He left.

By evening he had found a translator who, in plain enough English, drafted a two-page resignation letter. Mssr. Ich, who was now wearing a suit and tie, formally handed the letter to my father. The words "lose face" were included in the text.

"No, no, no. No one wanted Mssr. Ich to leave us, certainly not Madam Duthie," my father exclaimed (using only English). Now pantomime, more efforts to communicate. It was not enough. The following day, having had the wisdom to make a formal appointment, Dad and one of the tri-lingual Vietnamese engineers from his office met with Mssr. Ich. The matter was cleared up. Madam would not be in his kitchen, would not interfere with him. And the Vietnamese engineer also clarified for Mssr. Ich that the mysterious contents of this can were meant to become the filling for a pie, an odd American pie that neither man had ever heard about. Mssr. Ich did get a general picture of this Thanksgiving business, and through the interpreter he informed my father that the oven at this apartment building was very small. More negotiations. Mssr. Ich would secure a nice duck, instead of the turkey my mother had

16

lined up, to roast for the midday meal on the coming Thursday holiday.

Whew.

The duck, served alongside potatoes and vegetables, was perfectly cooked. Excellent, we all agreed. The salad, served as in Europe at the end of the main course, was also tasty. And then the pie was brought to the table. A thin slush quivered within the confines of a lovely crust. The soupy filling was greenish brown and it was hot, fresh from the oven. I don't remember who cut it and managed to transfer the messy affair onto our dessert plates, but I do clearly recall my father's evenly delivered command.

"We will all eat every bite of this pie. We will smile. And we will enjoy it."

The information that eggs and sugar were also ingredients to be used in conjunction with the mystery-ingredient had not been properly conveyed to our chef and head-servant. But by now we were all aware of the important concept of losing face. And indeed we all did smile and fuss over the delicious pie.

"Bon. Tres Bon!"

Sometime after Thanksgiving we moved again, this time into a lovely French-style villa on quiet Phon Dinh Phung Street, not far from a roundabout, in the center of which stood a beautiful cast-bronze statue of the Trung Sisters. These were Vietnamese heroes—women, mind you—who a thousand years earlier had acted as generals and defeated an overpowering force of invading Chinese. There was a message for Americans in this monument, if anyone had paid attention to the long history of this little country, and it was that the Vietnamese value autonomy so greatly that they'll take on, and defeat, far stronger armies. They always have. The two sisters represented a powerful nationalist legacy that our government's leaders were ignoring.

By now, I was entering the acceptance phase of that three-stage process. Culture shock was fading and I was beginning to feel more at ease. I began to relate to our servants; I was moving from the acceptance stage to the cusp of appreciation—which had been accelerated by Mssr. Ich's honorable stance Thanksgiving week.

Indeed, Mssr. Ich, who with his knowing eyes and sunken cheeks resembled a clean-shaven Ho Chi Minh, remained proud and a touch aloof. But at times, he'd let his sense of humor seep through. Ti Ba, however, was quick to smile, flashing her gold-capped teeth, and she was eager to teach me a few words in both French and Vietnamese. I soon learned she had a terrific sense of humor, and I found her wonderfully entertaining.

Ti Ba and Mssr. Ich had a daughter, who was fifteen, and a granddaughter, my age, and the pair helped Ti Ba around the house. Both girls were pretty and shy. Mornings, when the two girls walked out our driveway on their way to school, they wore white ao dais, the national garment of Vietnamese women. Tailored of satin material and form-fitting, the ao dai was said to cover all and hide nothing. Chaste, yes, with a high collar and long sleeves and panels of light fabric that floated almost to the ground in front and back. When a breeze caught the fabric panels of an ao dai, it was like watching white butterflies lifting.

A handful of us would meet on Rue Catinat, the main downtown street, in those days tree-lined, clean and quiet. At various sidewalk cafes we'd sip coffee, discuss art, literature and sex with the gravitas only teenagers can affect. At one of these sessions the talk turned to our futures. Richard assured us he would become an artist, and Paul vowed he'd be a poet. Joe already was a musician, and we knew he'd continue. That left writing for me. "I'm good at English," I said.

This was before the lovely trees lining Catinat were ripped out to accommodate war machinery—tanks and trucks—and some years before American soldiers would flood the city and cause sedate bars to morph into rough dives braying rock-and-roll music out into the street. This time of sipping coffee from demitasse cups was way before victorious Northerners would roar down Rue Catinat—the South Vietnamese had renamed it Tu Do by then—in their victorious battle tanks.

By now I had forgiven Joe and Paul for deserting me in Khanh Hoi. Domino, too. I had to; there were too few of us to divide into cliques any smaller than the Clods.

I had a more serious problem. In the tiny ex-pat community, the few girls I found attractive were taken. The sense that I was missing something important intensified, and I began to believe that had I stayed in El Paso, I'd by now have a lovely girlfriend, one with a soft West Texas accent.

At the Cercle Sportif, where I swam daily at the club's pool, there were always a number of French girls. But they would never enter into conversations; they'd merely say hello and continue walking on by. "You meet them at the Sunday Tea Dances" someone explained to me.

That Sunday, I approached a girl named Annie. She spoke English, and when I attempted a few words of French, she was nice, she didn't laugh. We danced to several of the fast pieces, and then to my great surprise, when slow music began, she took my hand. We remained on the dance floor, and, swaying with the music, she snuggled in closely. I told her I'd see her there next Sunday.

Two days later I was at the Sportif, hanging around the cantina next to the pool while I waited for Richard to show up. I ordered a Segi Cola. As I sipped at it, I noticed Annie at the other side of the pool. Her bikini was small and revealing. But sitting next to her was a glowering French boy. I knew of this guy; his name was Alain.

With his dark eyes fixed on me, Alain stood, dived into the pool and swam aggressively directly toward me. He pulled himself powerfully from the water and in two strides was next to my table. He reached up to his dripping hair and flicked water onto me.

I stood.

As I did this, Alain picked up a heavy glass ashtray from the center of the table. He cocked his arm back as if he were a quarterback.

"Do you seek a fight?"

"No," I answered, "but if you were to throw that at me, you'd be a coward."

Using a complex sentence-structure, with a conditional clause in Alain's second language, was a poor choice. To him, it sounded as if I had called him a coward.

The ashtray weighed a pound or so, and it crashed into my forehead a quarter-inch above the hairline, knocking me back. The fight was on. By the time it was stopped, Alain had two broken ribs and my blood was everywhere.

Richard arrived about then. From the backseat of his Lambretta motor scooter, I directed him out Cong Ly Street to Rue Lacaut where I knew of a Seventh Day Adventist medical clinic. It was housed in an old French villa. Feeling wounded and holding a handkerchief to my head, I climbed the concrete stairway to the entrance.

Inside, I was astonished at a scene of actual suffering. There were thirty or so dreadfully ill people crowded into what had once been the front parlor. Because Vietnamese peasants sought Western medical treatment only when their ailments became dire, almost always after exhausting traditional folk-medicine remedies, there was no one here with a malady as trivial as a cut scalp. For most, this was last resort.

A man in the final stages of malaria convulsed on a couch, while members of his family tried to comfort him. A hollow-eyed old woman sat on one of the few chairs, wheezing so deeply and irregularly I worried her next breath might not come. In another chair a young woman gently rocked an infant, a baby with pale, dry skin and a glassy stare.

Near where I found a place to sit on the tiled floor, was a young boy, his thin forearm askew. The broken radius stretched his skin thin and white.

An American woman came into the room from time to time, briefly interviewing new arrivals to perform triage. She took a quick look at my head, then turned to help the family lift the malaria man into a wheelchair. She returned for the wheezing woman. Then the boy with the broken arm, and a train of others went back. At some point she handed me a gauze pack and said, "Press it tightly on your cut," adding, "It will be a while."

The afternoon wore on. All this acute suffering around me was sobering; I'd never seen such quiet anguish, so many people near death.

The American woman came into the room at another point and spoke in Vietnamese to the woman with the baby. They went back. And others followed, one after another, until after sundown when the room was cleared of the truly sick, finally, my turn.

She wore a print dress, not a uniform, so I was slow to comprehend that she was a nurse. She began closing the wound with widely-spaced stitches. "It's in your hairline," she explained, as she tied off a knot. "I'd use more if it would be seen." In a few minutes I was done. "Five days from now, put some hydrogen peroxide on it, then cut each stitch and pull it out."

"I'll come back for that," I said. I'd never heard of anyone removing their own stitches.

"You can do it," she said. This was a directive; the clinic wasn't there to coddle ex-pat teenagers.

I stepped out the front door into the cool air of evening. The sun was well down, the horizon hazy and mauve. On the top step sat the woman with the infant, the young mother who had been on a chair near me. She was rocking slowly back and forth, moaning— the most doleful moaning I had ever heard. I stepped near her—I had to in order to move down the steps—and as I did I understood that her baby was dead. In the arms of this young woman was the first death I'd ever looked upon.

I stood there, near her, quiet and respectful...until I grasped there was nothing I could do, nothing anyone could. I stepped around her with care, wishing I could float silently down the stairs, so I wouldn't disturb her. I said nothing. Even in English I had no words.

I walked into the mauve gloaming, and as I descended those concrete steps—shedding the ethnocentricity of a narrow Texas life—I entered that third stage.

I felt empathy for this young woman, for the others in that room. I understood. That evening, for the first time, I fathomed the truth of that old expression: "It broke my heart."

## CHAPTER TWO

# *On the Fringe of War*

Because his father was with the State Department, Joe had lived in Lebanon and Paris, and because he had an affinity for languages, he spoke both French and Arabic. He attempted to teach me French, and I'd test it on Ti Ba. She was generous. Leaning on her little broom, she'd interrupt her sweeping and struggle to figure out what I was trying to say, then smile and correct me. As time went on, I got better at it, and we'd communicate in our argot of French, English and Vietnamese—with our words generously supported by hand gestures and smiles. No complex thoughts were ever conveyed, but we did keep each other informed on a basic level—such as that I was going swimming or that Mssr. Ich was at the market hoping to source boeuf for dinner. We found it easy to make each other laugh.

I was fully acclimated and enjoying Vietnam by now. Yet something important was under way, and I was clueless. While I was so pretentiously sipping coffees on Rue Catinat with my Clod buddies, I could not guess that I was on the fringe of war, one that would change the lives of millions. And my own.

Equally clueless was MAG, The Military Assistance Group, the U.S. Army's advisors to the South. Hamlets in the countryside outside Saigon were falling under Viet Minh rule—because a village chief had been assassinated, because the Viet Minh offered the remaining peasants free medical aid and free education classes, and because the Viet Minh promised protections. The Vietnamese Army was prone to use the new howitzer cannons the MAG folks had trained them to fire. They'd shell the hapless village, and in the process make solid communists of terrorized folks who before had no political beliefs whatsoever. Clueless: the South Vietnamese Army and their MAG advisors.

There was, however, someone who did have a clue, a sharp understanding of what was at stake. He was born Nguyen Sinh Cung in a tiny hamlet near Vinh. Early in life, Cung attended a prestigious lycée in Hue, but he didn't relish the mandarin life his education was preparing him to follow. He dropped out of school.

Cung then worked on a French ship and after that, as a kitchen boy at the Parker House in New York. Later he was a house-boy in a Boston home. He worked as a sous chef in London under the famous chef, Auguste Escoffier, and from there moved to Paris, where he was employed retouching negatives for a photographer.

By the summer of 1919, when he was twenty-nine, this guy with the menial jobs was calling himself Nguyen Ai Quoc (Nguyen the Patriot) and he showed up at the Versailles Peace Conference wearing an ill-fitting suit. There he petitioned for civil rights for the Vietnamese in French Indochina, passing out his demands on leaflets. He was ignored.

Then he disappeared into the Soviet Union, only to resurface in China during World War II, where he rescued at least one of General Claire Chennault's Flying Tiger pilots. And for this, the American OSS helped arm his little band of fighters.

It was not until he turned fifty-five, when he was pictured with a wispy beard and thin white hair, that he began using a new name:

Ho Chi Minh. By then his vision for unification and self-rule for his little country had cemented his standing as Vietnam's natural leader.

It was this picture—Old Ho with the thin beard—that we pilots fighting in the air war would know as the face of the enemy. But we knew nothing of his ideas. We thought we were fighting communism. I don't recall anyone ever explaining it was a nationalist we were fighting. I'd never heard that he vowed his fighters could lose ten lives for each one our side lost, that he was willing to make such a sacrifice. It turned out this wasn't hyperbole.

Robert McNamara, our smug Secretary of Defense, kept a body-count ledger. He and General Westmoreland bragged to the press how we won every battle, how we killed more of their combatants than we lost. What they ignored was that Old Ho's fighters were never killed at anywhere near that ten-to-one ratio he had vowed to endure.

How could I know then that my war started while I was drinking beers at the Olympic Bar? But it did.

Some 900 miles to the north, at the same time I was downing Ba-Mui-Ba beers in chilled glasses, Ho Chi Minh ordered the 559th Engineering Group, 6,000 fighters, to begin moving south down a spiderweb of trails. This was the first escalation.

A few years later, Americans would misname the web of jungle paths that the 559th was slogging down as The Ho Chi Minh Trail, as if it was only a single supply line to sever. Six years after we Clods were affecting our phony beatnik lifestyle in Saigon, I would be dropping tons of bombs onto those very trails. I'd no longer be on the fringe.

Dad's work on the USAID contract was as a tele-communications engineer, a new field. He was proud to have come up with a way to construct a microwave system to serve the civilian population of the country for far less taxpayer money than previously estimated. It could be built in increments, rather than all at once as envisioned by the project's specifications, saving millions. He was outlining his beautiful plan at a briefing, when a man from the embassy interrupted.

"Let's take a break." The man pulled Dad into a hallway. "You will build this the way we want it, and you will go back in there and brief it that way," the embassy man said in a hissing whisper.

In that moment Dad understood. This man was no embassy functionary, he was CIA. (I'm certain today that he was William Colby, a senior CIA agent working under cover of the embassy in Saigon at the time. Thirteen years later, Colby would be named CIA Director by Richard Nixon.)

After his embarrassment in the hallway, Dad got it: although the massive upgrade was indeed far too ambitious for a developing nation's citizens, it was about right for a large military buildup. And this was not the only robust infrastructure development underway across South Vietnam at the time. The huge construction firm Johnson, Drake & Piper, was throwing up massive new concrete bridges and upgrading roads throughout the South, all built to specifications stout enough to accommodate fifty-ton Patton battle tanks. (Ironically, on an April day fifteen years later, it would be across a sturdy JDP concrete span that North Vietnamese T55 tanks would rumble on their way to the Independence Palace to complete the fall of Saigon.)

Some historians pinpoint the beginning of our war in Vietnam as October of 1957, when thirteen Americans were wounded in bombings in Saigon. One of the blasts had been at the Military Assistance Group building where a year-and-a-half later Joe and I, trying to build up our pecs and biceps, lifted weights in the MAG gym. We worked out to look good at the Cercle Sportif.

The 1957 bombings, though, had been merely another iteration of a Vietnamese war underway in one form or another since World War Two, when the Japanese controlled the country. During my family's stay, the war outside of Saigon escalated to a point where some 100 village chiefs were murdered monthly—news downplayed by our embassy for American civilians in Saigon at the time.

In the late '50s, communism was the big fear, and my own ramped up when Dr. Tom Dooley, a famous writer, visited our school. He arrived with an embassy entourage. All twenty-eight of us in the high school had been encouraged to find and read the doctor's best-selling book: *Deliver Us From Evil*. I hadn't, but it wasn't necessary. The friendly guy in khaki pants and a white short-sleeved shirt sat on the edge of a desk, and in conversational tones, detailed for us the same horror stories that made up his book.

He painted a vivid image of thousands of North Vietnamese fleeing to South Vietnam, all frightened for their lives. A provision of the agreement between the French and the North Vietnamese, signed in Geneva, allowed residents to choose which half of their new divided country they wanted to live in. Most went south, Tom Dooley said, especially the Roman Catholics. Why? Because the communist government of the North was so very evil. Communism forbids the worship of God, the doctor reminded us. The Viet Minh method of preventing children from hearing priests recite prayers was to pound chopsticks into their ears, he told us. "That rendered them deaf for life, you know."

What he left out was that he had not seen any of these atrocities. The stories had been fed to him by his employer, the CIA, so that he could spread propaganda. The idea was to make a coming war, one just beyond the horizon, palatable.

Almost as an aside that morning, Dr. Dooley mentioned he was on his way back to the States to have his own disease treated.

"I have cancer."

He said this casually, cocking his arm out in front of his white shirt so we could see where the disease had attacked him. "I've got a melanoma here." It was as if he was showing us his watch. I was in college when I read a newspaper story about his death at thirty-four.

Now I was fully in the appreciation stage—all traces of culture shock behind me.

Joe loved the Vietnamese, and he nudged me to abandon the last remnant of my West Texas ethnocentrism. On sidewalks, Joe and I would chat with street vendors or cyclo drivers, teasing out their wonderful sense of humor. We wandered the central market, bargaining with merchants. Once, Joe insisted I go with him to meet his favorite mechanic, a smiling fellow who set up shop each morning on a busy thoroughfare. Squatting at a curb with a few beat-up tools arranged on a greasy cloth roll, here was the artist who could infuse hot-rod life into Joe's tepid motorcycle.

By summer, 1960, my backsliding during the school year had caught up with me, and my parents were now monitoring my daily progress. I had to finish high school, they said, if I wanted to fly to California to begin college. I was at home, putting in long hours with my Texas Tech workbooks, when one of the Clods came up our gravel driveway on his motorbike.

"Did you hear about Joe's wreck last night?"

He told me. Joe and Paul had been on the Moto Guzzi, flying down a busy thoroughfare in Cholon. A man with a trash can on his shoulder stepped off a curb. Joe swerved to duck behind him. Suddenly, the man turned back.

At impact Paul was thrown free, and he landed on his feet. Joe went down with the bike, sliding along the asphalt. He looked back, and saw the man on the pavement. Not moving. Joe came away with a scraped arm. For the man, the accident was fatal.

Saigon's English-language newspaper, in both a news story and an editorial, characterized Joe and Paul as "hoodlum American cowboys." The next day the American ambassador called Joe's house. Paul remembers listening to his father's end.

"Yes sir. He'll leave. Out within the week."

So Joe and I traveled back to the U.S. together. One of our stops was Oslo, where an intoxicated man stopped us on the street our first night there. The fellow was aggressive. Standing in the pink light, the drunk said, "You Americans want to bring our country into war. You like war." Left to me, we'd have walked on, but Joe wanted to know what he meant.

The drunk guy was referring to a spy-plane and its CIA pilot, Francis Gary Powers. A few months back, this had been big news, and I recalled a few details. The aircraft, a U-2, had been secret until this incident. It could fly so high that no Russian fighters could reach it. The mission was to fly from Pakistan to Norway, while the U-2's sophisticated cameras took high-resolution photos of Soviet defense sites along the route.

But near the Urals, Powers had been shot down by a surface-to-air missile—a SA-2, the same model SAM I'd see a few years later over North Vietnam.

"Your spy plane was going to land in our country, it was headed here," the drunk heckler said. "We don't want any trouble with the Soviets."

From Oslo we flew into New York, and I continued west, making a stop in El Paso. With a long-time buddy, I attended a party, but as I chatted with old friends, I came to understand that the senior year I imagined my peers had enjoyed, lacked luster. My year in Saigon took on a glow; I'd had an adventure and hadn't missed a thing.

The next day I met with my former principal, the man who promised a diploma in exchange for completing the correspondence courses. Still seated, the principal reached into the top drawer of his desk. Without offering so much as a congratulatory handshake, he handed the document across his desk. "There you go."

## CHAPTER THREE

# Do That Tomorrow

Four months later, I was done with college. Didn't like it, didn't like San Diego Junior College at all. I informed my folks. The response letter was written by Dad—on another topic. There had been an attempted coup d' etat, he wrote. A group of South Vietnamese officers marched their troops down Cong Ly, the street in front of their house. Foxholes were dug into Cong Ly and side streets, machine-gun-fire and explosions were heard nearby. The rebels wanted Diem, the little dictator, out—along with Diem's brother and his brother's wife, the hated Madam Nhu.

"We are all under 'house arrest' by Ti Ba," Dad wrote. "She told me very emphatically that none of us were to leave the house until she told us it was all right." I pictured TiBa leaning on her little broom, and this time her gold-filled smile was gone. She was sternly protecting people she served and cared for.

In the margin of that letter, and dated three days later, Mom wrote that the city was now calm. She and Dad were packing to come home. They planned to live in Scottsdale, Arizona.

"There is a good college," Mom wrote. "Arizona State. For me, will you please give that a chance? It's a university. I think you would like it."

So at ASU I declared a major in metallurgy, which was the single course I'd liked at the junior college. But once more, I found myself agitated and lonely. And I had no concept of what a metallurgy degree might do for me. I drove from Tempe up to Scottsdale, where my folks had bought a house. "I'm quitting at the end of the semester," I told Mom.

"And?"

"Going to Alaska," I answered.

We talked it out. Both of my parents were from blue-collar backgrounds, the first in their families to attend college. Higher education was sacred to them. At the end of our chat, I agreed to try another major. I declared as a pre-dentistry student, and attended summer school to catch up. Microbiology was a required course, and I loved the classes, loved the labs. That summer I formally changed my major. I'd become a microbiologist, not a dentist. During a lab, I asked the TA, a graduate student, what I might do with a degree in microbiology.

"Oh," he said with some enthusiasm, "you can work in a brewery. Or at a sewage-treatment facility."

I finished summer school and firmly announced to my folks that I intended to drive to Anchorage.

What was the matter with me? Why couldn't I find anything of interest like the guys in my fraternity? The answer, I'd realize many years later, was that nothing in my life offered the excitement, the electric surge, of running free in an exotic Asian city. I packed my car.

The diminutive Austin Healey Sprite sported a thin canvas top, frog-eye headlights and an anemic heater. I could not have found anything more unsuitable. The mud, gravel and fist-size rocks of the Alcan Highway would have eaten the car. I made it as far as San Francisco, where I stalled.

After a few weeks, I landed a job at Macy's downtown department store and found a cheap place to live in North Beach—the heart of the beats of San Francisco.

The Golden Eagle Hotel was on Broadway—it's still there—a couple blocks from Lawrence Ferlinghetti's bookstore. I paid forty dollars monthly for a single fourth-floor garret space furnished with a chair, a lumpy bed and a grubby little washbasin on the wall. A short walk down the hall was an always-filthy men's restroom, and beyond that, a community kitchen—which I entered only once and left in disgust.

I was living in North Beach with real Beatniks. I wrote to Richard. "I'm right up the street from City Lights Books," I bragged. Somehow, though, the thrill of a beatnik life evaded me; I did not feel cool at all. Something was missing in my life.

Then, to my bewilderment, in January I learned I had been hired only as holiday help; Macy's laid me off. Living in a cold city, jobless and shaken, I began to see myself as a failure. I was a college drop-out who couldn't even hold an entry-level job. The feeling intensified after I botched a dexterity test placing washers on rivets and lining up dominoes. I wasn't fast enough for an assembly-line position at a General Motors plant near Oakland.

Finally, in early February, with my savings falling toward zero, I was grateful to land a job as an apprentice PBX telephone installer with Western Electric Company. With better pay, I relocated to a rooming house at 1780 Fell Street, leaving behind the fading beat scene. My new residence was a lovely old three-story Victorian on the Golden Gate Park Panhandle. Across the Panhandle and a block up was a convenience store, an easy walk for snacks and milk. It was at the corner of Haight and Ashbury Streets. I had left the fading beatnik scene and found the nascent hippie movement. San Francisco was vibrant, yet I remained unsettled. Miserable, at times. I was often cold, nearly always too broke to eat well. My life had no purpose or direction.

I returned to ASU, vowing to become a serious college student. I declared a major, my fourth, English Literature. That lasted a single week. Reading, and then, my God, discussing in detail, *Sir*

*Gawain and the Green Knight* did it. The nice clerk in the registrar's office by now knew me by my first name. Major number five was architecture, which I liked.

I quit school a final time one crisp October morning in 1962. The idea darted into my mind as I stared at the fuzzy blue-gray image of John F. Kennedy on our fraternity's new twenty-three-inch television. The president seemed to be talking directly to me. U.S. spy-planes flying over Cuba had discovered and photographed ICBM missiles. I thought about that guy in Oslo and Francis Gary Powers in the U-2. This could lead to war.

If there was to be a war, I wouldn't miss out. I'd screwed around at two colleges, drinking, partying, missing classes and declaring major after major. Once I had switched majors twice in a single semester. I was into my junior year at Arizona State University, architecture was okay, but I still had no solid idea what I was doing there. I was rudderless.

But now! President Kennedy provided an objective.

(Such an archaic notion: leave college to go to war. College boys did this in 1916 and '17 and in hordes after December 7, 1941.)

I walked into Tempe and trooped smartly into the Army recruiting office, where I was given a simple written test.

"You got a really good score, here," said the sergeant, a short man with an intense expression. The crease in the sleeve of his broadcloth shirt was sharp and impressive. "You can be anything you want in the Army, go to any of our training schools." I was still seated at the test-taking table.

"Got some papers here." The sergeant laid documents onto the table and, slick as a used-car salesman, he slipped the pencil from my hand, replacing it with a pen. I began reading.

"For two years?" I asked.

"A full enlistment. Four."

"The draft is two," I said. "I'll go for two."

"Let's get these signed."

I explained I wasn't going to go into the Army for any four years. When you are twenty, four years is forever. Then we were both standing, and a weathered hand jutting from the crisply ironed sleeve was poking me in the chest, jabbing with each word he spoke, stabbing with a bony index finger.

"You won't sign these papers? Come into the Army when it needs you?"

Jab, jab, jab, jab.

"You. Are. The. Most. Unpatriotic. Puke. I have ever seen!"

After dinner that evening, my roommate—he was flummoxed by my craziness—drove me to the western edge of Phoenix. Alone and shivering in the cold desert air, I stood facing traffic with my hand out, thumb up. I had a new plan.

By mid-morning I was in the Selective Service office in San Diego, where almost two years earlier I had registered for the draft. Now I'd volunteer.

"Yes, certainly," said the lady in the large office. "Your board will meet in January. They'll reclassify you as 1-A."

"January? I'm volunteering. For now." To underscore the urgency, I said, "There's going to be a war. They'll need me."

Although she seemed to care about my predicament, the clerk was not persuaded. No deal; the draft board had to meet on this.

In a calmer voice, I asked when I might be called up. Her answer I remember clearly. "Oh, June or July, I'd think."

I was screwed. I had hitchhiked all night to my draft office, where I intended to volunteer. For two years. Now, like my visit to the Army recruiting office the morning before, my new scheme had gone awry.

My grandparents—Anne and Pop—lived just a short drive from downtown San Diego. Pop would gladly come pick me up. I simply needed to make the call. My room from the semester I lived with them when I gave college a first try would still be ready for me. I could sleep until supper. No. Standing in front of the Selective Service office, I again stretched my arm toward traffic, thumb up. There was no plan at all now. I would work my way up the coast and come up with something. Hitchhiking was easy then, very common in 1962. Without a strategy for life, my outstretched thumb carried me to Northern California. My father by this time had been recruited to a new engineering position in what was to become Silicon Valley, so my folks now lived in Palo Alto. It was early November when I made my way to their house.

Dad was quiet after arriving home from work that first evening. He was steamed, a mix of anger and disappointment on his face. No shouting, no sarcasm. Merely a quiet burn and a scary darkness in his deep brown eyes. Without speaking, he swept past me on his way to his bedroom, where he changed out of his suit and tie.

At dinner, Dad finally spoke. His tone was soft; it was clear he was working to keep it that way.

"What are your plans?"

This was neither a time for a long explanation about an Army sergeant who called me a puke, nor an occasion for talk about a nice lady at a draft board office. And unquestionably this was not a moment to suggest I hang around home while working out a next step.

"Maybe go in the Navy," I answered.

"Tomorrow," Dad said. "Do that tomorrow."

# PART II

## TRAINING FOR WAR

When you go to war as a boy, you have a great illusion of immortality. Other people get killed, not you. Then, when you are badly wounded the first time, you lose that illusion, and you know it can happen to you.

*—Ernest Hemingway, Men at War*

The author in his flight gear stands before an A-4E. He has at this point completed his training and is ready to begin flying combat missions. The bulky vest contains survival equipment, including a handheld radio.

CHAPTER FOUR

# *Accidental Navcad*

The Navy took me right away. By Thanksgiving I was in boot camp in San Diego, a few long blocks up the street from that Selective Service clerk's office and not far from where I first attempted college. I scrubbed my clothes every evening on a huge outdoor concrete table along with all the other recruits and I learned to march and say YES SIR!

In boot camp no Army sergeant yelled at me or called me a puke; that was a chief petty officer's role. I learned to keep my head down and speak up only when quizzed. Boot camp went by quickly, and from there I was sent to a thirty-eight-week electronics-technician school in the Bay Area. Treasure Island, a man-made island wedged between San Francisco and Oakland, is where I attended classes and on piercing cold nights it's where I stood four-hour watches.

I found the school interesting enough, and began to visualize myself maintaining and fixing elaborate electronic equipment. I even wondered if later I might return to college to study electrical engineering—a major I'd not yet tested.

While at Treasure Island, mainly as a lark and with no real hope of success, I applied to a new program designated OCAN— officer candidate airman. If selected, I'd train as bombardier-navigator and potentially fly in the back seat of fighter-bombers. The program would lead to a commission as an ensign. I completed several written tests and a physical examination, and then I was scheduled for the final step in the application process: an interview by a five-officer selection board.

The interview was still several weeks off when Boggs and I drank far too much beer at the enlisted-men's club. During this time, the Navy actively encouraged drinking, and for around a dollar each, Boggs, a fun guy, and I made an evening of it. Well into the ten beers a buck would buy, we agreed we'd teach our barracks master-at-arms a good lesson. The poor man, a second-class petty officer, had been tasked with overseeing a barracks packed with 1,200 testosterone-stoked young sailors. He was tough on us, had to be. All those beers told us he was cruel. We'd deliver retribution.

It was after midnight. On the stair-landing, we quietly freed a firehose, folded accordion-style in a case behind a glass door, and I hauled it by its brass nozzle down the stairs, then crouched near the man's office. Boggs stood by on the landing.

"Turn on the water, Boggs!" I shouted, and then I tossed the heavy brass nozzle over the bottom half of a Dutch-door into the tiny office. Hose followed it in.

Boggs had a moment of clarity, a dot of responsible thinking. He did nothing. Thank God. But the petty officer caught a good look at me before I fled up the stairs to my sleeping bay.

I was not home free. The master-at-arms, accompanied by a pair of shore-patrolmen, came into the sleeping bay and began shining a penlight onto the faces of sleeping sailors. The trio was clearly looking for me. They headed in a direction away from my rack. Good, but soon they would turn a corner and come my way.

I had recently seen the James Bond movie *From Russia With Love*. It struck me that, like James Bond, I could craft a slick escape.

I'd tip-toe over to the window near my rack and, I imagined, lower myself until my feet somehow would find the moveable sash of the window below and...with Bond-like magic, I would somehow be lowered to the ground.

I fell two stories.

Such falls don't kill drunks, they say, but sharp rocks in the asphalt below punctured my hip and the fleshy palms of both hands. Otherwise okay, I staggered off to another wing of the barracks. I found an unassigned rack without a mattress and flopped onto the lattice of steel bands.

When I awoke, maybe an hour later, lights were on and Navy men surrounded my rack. Closest were four corpsmen. Apparently, I had been moaning and wiping my bleeding palms on my white t-shirt.

There appeared to be lots of blood, so medics had been called. Right behind them stood the aggrieved master-at-arms and three shore-patrolmen.

"That's him! That's him!" the master-at-arms chanted. He was bouncing up and down.

Behind him, awakened by the excitement, were some ninety guys who lived in this wing. I was taken to sick-bay, my hands and hip were bandaged, and from there driven to the brig, where I was written up. A few days later I stood at attention before the captain of the base for a legal proceeding called a Captain's Mast. He consigned me to fourteen days of restriction, a non-judicial-punishment in which I would live under strict regulation in a barracks for miscreants. As required, I sewed the white band of a restricted sailor onto the left arm of my jumper, and two weeks later I was done—properly punished.

Good thing, because two days after I unstitched the armband-of-shame, I was looking shipshape in my dress-blue jumper as I reported for the OCAN officer-selection interview. My service record, with the Captain's Mast paperwork neatly clipped into it, was passed from officer to officer. I assumed my misbehavior disqualified me, yet I answered questions as if I had a chance. I was not informed of their decision, and I put it out of mind.

A few weeks after the OCAN interview, I received orders to report aboard USS Sellers in South Carolina as an electronics technician. This was a new guided-missile destroyer tasked with protecting an aircraft-carrier battle group from air attack.

I arrived at the Charleston Naval Base and found Sellers tied side-by-side with sister destroyers on the muddy Cooper River. My first day, I was shown around by a young petty officer. When we arrived at the aft end of the ship, he proudly showed off the guided missile launcher. The mechanism, with a launching-rail taller than me, was empty. I tried to visualize a missile in place. Below the launcher was a magazine intended to house twenty-four Tartar missiles. A slight problem. My young guide explained that shortly before I arrived, a little mistake had caused the magazine to flood. When the damage was repaired, he told me, we'd put to sea.

The Tartars were surface-to-air missiles—SAMs—with a range of almost nine miles. At the time this seemed like a long way away to find and destroy an aircraft. I could not have imagined as I viewed the missile-launcher in 1964 how a little more than three years later I would be frantically dodging Soviet SAMs with almost three times the range and flying nearly twice as fast as the Tartars aboard Sellers.

I was assigned one of the bunks lining the side of the ship far up in the bow. My rack was a piece of white canvas stretched and laced tightly to a metal frame. Identical racks stacked tightly above and below. That first night I found I was unable to turn from one side to the other without jamming my shoulder against the sagging form of the man in the canvas above.

Taking up most of our berthing-space in the ship's bow was the below-deck portion of a naval gun, a 5-inch-54, a weapon more prosaic than the Tartar system. Its shrieking scream during early-morning testing woke us all well before reveille. This was something to get used to.

I had another difficulty. I had been denied advancement as a result of the misbehavior with the fire hose, so I arrived with the rating of E-3, a lowly seaman. The electronics department had expected an E-4, a third-class petty officer. It was as if I came aboard waving a flag proclaiming *screw-up*. I was marked. I'd have to behave for a while.

Yet with all this, my attitude soared. I had a job to do, and my ship was set to put to sea. *Join the Navy and See the World*, recruiting posters had advertised. Sellers would soon fulfill the promise.

I had been aboard the ship only a few weeks, when the division officer came to me. He was an LDO Lieutenant, what we called a Mustang, signifying he had earned his commission the hard way, working up through the enlisted ranks.

The salty Mustang stood quietly before me, puzzled, I think, by the orders he clutched. "You're going to the Naval Academy," he eventually said.

My own puzzlement showed. "These orders say NAVCAD," the Mustang lieutenant went on, "and that means Naval Academy." I politely corrected him. NAVCAD stood for the Naval Aviation Cadet pilot program, which I knew about. While still at ASU I had tested for it. I had been told I didn't qualify. Although my vision was 20/20, something was not quite right, a corpsman had said.

But these new orders meant I did meet the OCAN program requirements. Evidently, I had passed the selection board interview. Somehow the wrong orders, clearly wrong, were in my division officer's hands.

By this time, I had learned it was best to keep one's mouth shut if things seemed to be going well. I'd report to the Naval Air Station at Pensacola, and there the mix-up would be sorted out. I was due in Florida in two weeks.

A few days later, Sellers slipped her lines and glided down the brown Cooper River toward the blue waters of the Atlantic. Our nearly new destroyer was to be part of a display at the 1964 World's Fair. I would ride the ship to New York, then fly to Pensacola.

I no longer had duties at my electronics technician job, so I wandered the ship, marveling at the ocean, at flying fish spooked by our sonar blasts and at all the phosphorescence shimmering on the face of waves at night. It was as if I were on a cruise, all expenses paid. Join the Navy and see the world, indeed.

We steamed south and circumnavigated Cuba (surveillance, I believe), and then we turned north for New York.

I left the ship as soon as it tied up, got a room at the YMCA and saw a few Broadway shows, including a young Barbra Streisand in *Funny Girl*. I went up Fifth Avenue to admire Frank Lloyd Wright's new masterpiece, the Guggenheim Museum. And I made my way to Flushing Meadows to take in the World's Fair. At the end of a fine week in the Big Apple, I caught a flight to Florida.

I have enjoyed good luck throughout my life. It was lucky that Boggs didn't turn on the water the night of our misbehavior. Lucky, I escaped serious injuries when I fell from the window. And I was exceptionally lucky to receive the wrong orders to the NAVCAD program. It no longer exists, but the program had been around, in one form or another, for a long time, permitting college dropouts like me to earn aviator wings and commissions as officers. President George H. W. Bush earned his wings in an early version; at eighteen he was the Navy's second youngest aviator.

On a warm, clear day in June, I checked in at NAS Pensacola. Historic and beautiful, this was the Navy's first air station. Broad lawns and parade grounds were surrounded by graceful architecture. Building Sixteen, built in the 1850s, is a nearly perfect example of a briefly popular architectural style called Octagon. Others are elegant samples of Greek Revival. Yes, truly I was a lucky young man.

I was assigned to Class 24-64, a designation reflecting the week in 1964 our training began. My orders, these bogus orders to flight training, had not yet been questioned. Was there a chance I could become a naval aviator? If somehow they allowed me to continue, I wouldn't screw up. I'd apply myself this time, work diligently.

We cadets were mixed in with commissioned officers, guys who had finished college at the Naval Academy or at elite schools such as Princeton, Marquette and UCLA, schools with Naval ROTC programs. I was pleased and surprised that I was able to keep pace academically with guys who had not changed their major even once or ever dropped out of college.

One afternoon, the NAVCADS were separated from the others. Our sketchy educational backgrounds would hobble us, we were told. Although we were training alongside men already commissioned as officers, and doing well, too, we'd nevertheless climb only part way up the ladder—to lieutenant commander, perhaps a step higher. The tradeoff, we were promised that afternoon, was that we'd enjoy plenty of time in the cockpit. We'd fly, fly a lot. Every Blue Angels pilot to that point, we were told, had been a NAVCAD or the Marine Corps equivalent, MARCAD. This was all fine with me. Flying: that's what I wanted.

Most NAVCADs in the classroom that day didn't care about rank or career, and I was with them. We left that classroom promising ourselves we'd become very good at the two traits that define naval aviators: skill in the cockpit and raising hell with panache.

We pressed on with our classwork; the prospect of flying into combat was too far in the future to give much thought. Who in 1964 could envision that an air war bubbling just over the horizon would launch careers—careers even for NAVCADs? Who would have predicted that one of the cadets in our class, a nineteen-year-old NAVCAD with two years at a rural Alabama community college, a guy who spoke with a drawl so heavy we could barely understand him, that he would soar up the ladder and retire as a three-star admiral? And I certainly never imagined that a little over a year later, he and I would become friends and rent an apartment together.

It happened that during the time we were still limited to classrooms and marching fields, a U.S. destroyer was attacked off the coast of North Vietnam. In that skirmish on August 2, 1964, USS Maddox suffered a single bullet hole, while one Vietnamese PT-boat was claimed to have been sunk. Two days later the Maddox and a second destroyer were supposedly once again engaged by PT-boats (this attack turned out to be imaginary). The next day, in retaliation, President Johnson initiated Operation Pierce Arrow sending the first air strikes into North Vietnam. Richard Sather, an A-1 pilot, was killed, and Everett Alvarez, an A-4 pilot, was the first aviator to become a POW. The entire operation totaled 64 strike sorties—a partial day's work a couple years later.

Alvarez appeared in newspaper photos the Vietnamese released wearing sandals and striped prison garb. Later his photo was in Life Magazine. Sobering. I wondered how many months it would be until he was freed. Through a prisoner exchange, I imagined. As it turned out, he would be imprisoned more than eight years.

Primary training followed pre-flight and was the first phase we did any actual flying. This was where numbers of guys decided flying airplanes wasn't what they anticipated. They suffered continuing airsickness, they found leaving the earth frightening or the whole package too stressful. So they DORed—dropped-on-request. A handful of others had no aptitude for airplane flying and were bounced out. All of it required a surprising amount of study—bookwork—and for once I pushed myself. The hell-raising, that other naval-aviator trait, came so naturally that I toned it down a notch. Here, finally, was an opportunity to make my parents proud.

In a group of some thirty students who completed that week, I finished primary training ranking sixth. I had requested jet training, but this was a week in which there were jet-training slots for only the top five; I missed by one. Instead of orders to jet training at Meridian, Mississippi, I was sent a few miles north to Milton, Florida. I was devastated. I had worked so hard. I saw myself as a jet jock. That evening I drank, and drank more until I became knee-walking drunk. But I had improved, matured. There were no fire hoses, no second-story window escapes.

The T-28s at Whiting Field in Milton were robust propeller-driven craft with massive 1,425-horsepower radial engines that pumped fire and thunder from huge exhaust pipes below the cockpit rail.

I completed nine training flights with an instructor, and then I took one up solo. Alone, I looped and intentionally entered a spin, knowing the big bird had no bad habits, knowing I could handle it. When I landed and parked the big bird, I felt accomplished; I was exhilarated by my solo-flight in such a powerful bird. I felt wonderful.

Over the next seven months, it was in T-28s that I learned to fly next to another aircraft in close military formation, to fly and navigate at night, to recover from any situation the instructor might put me into—including a simulated engine-failure—and I was introduced to instrument flying. Then it was time to learn the skill that separates naval aviators from all others; it was time to learn how to land on the tiny deck of an aircraft carrier.

With several other students, on August 9, 1965, I flew out to sea from the coast of Florida to USS Lexington. Eight times I flew down the glideslope, making tiny adjustments as I had been trained, and eight times the tailhook on my aircraft snatched one of Lexington's arresting cables. After each arrested landing, I lined up, added power and flew off the bow: deck-launches. Catapult shots would come later. I had recently turned twenty-three and had accomplished something few pilots ever do in a lifetime; I'd landed aboard a moving ship.

From Whiting Field I was ordered to advanced flight training at Corpus Christi, Texas. Most graduates from the Corpus Christi pipeline could expect to fly multi-engine, prop-driven airplanes. But I had kept my grades up and had hopes of being assigned to fly A-1 Skyraiders—attack aircraft. I checked in, then was taken into an office. I was offered a transfer to advanced jet training. Jets!

"Expect to play catch-up," the lieutenant commander said. "Everyone else has 150 hours in jets."

"Oh yes sir," I answered the officer. "I'd love the opportunity, thank you sir. I'll work very hard." But to myself, I thought, there'll be no catching up. After all, I've got 150 hours in a complex airplane. Jets have a throttle and a control stick. Unlike the T-28s, jets have no supercharger to manage, no constant-speed prop to tend to, no manifold-pressure gauge to monitor, no carburetor mixture control.

The next day I reported to advanced jet training at Kingsville, Texas, to begin training in the Korean-War-era F-9F Cougars. Jets. As a kid I had glued together a plastic model of a Cougar and thought it the coolest-looking airplane on earth.

I considered this opportunity another example of my fantastic good luck. But in reality it was driven by the Navy's needs. Six months earlier President Johnson had initiated Operation Rolling Thunder, a campaign of bombing North Vietnam. The Navy was losing jet pilots. It now needed more—many more.

Flying jets indeed did require less cockpit work. But the head-work required, the thinking, was more intense. Learning to think faster, to anticipate further ahead, didn't come easily. As the officer in Corpus Christi predicted, I was behind the guys who'd trained at Meridian.

I worked harder than ever, and slowly I began to catch up and again have fun. On one of my training hops I was to take the F-9 supersonic, which for this airplane was a stretch. It was capable of breaking through the sound barrier. But only in a dive. With full power, from a very high altitude, it was a sort-of-supersonic air-plane.

With my instructor seated behind me, I climbed to 40,000 feet, seven-and-a-half miles above East Texas. The F-9's jet-powerplant spooled to 100 percent and I pushed over the nose, diving steeper and steeper, until we were pointing straight down at the desert. The Mach-meter climbed through 0.90, past 0.96, 0.97, 0.98 until it reached 0.99. Where it froze.

The speed of sound increases as air density increases. This damn aircraft, screaming toward the earth, wouldn't nudge through the sound barrier that morning, because the speed re-quired do so increased as I plunged through denser and denser air. I'd fly another three and a half years in the Navy and never reach the magic Mach 1.0.

When bad weather curtailed flying in Kingsville, a group of us flew F-9s cross-country to a Marine Air Base at Yuma, Arizona. Be-cause my flight grades had improved, I was among students se-lected to fly one of the single-pilot airplanes. Piloting a jet solo across Texas, New Mexico and on to Yuma without an instructor monitoring my decisions gave me time to think. The Navy had changed me. I felt better about myself than ever before. Even today I can pull up those positive feelings, that pride of accomplishing something very difficult.

At Marine Corps Air Station, Yuma, we were introduced to aerial combat maneuvering—dog-fighting. We pulled heavy Gs, we learned to yo-yo, to get inside an opponent's turning radius, we learned to think in three dimensions like fighter pilots.

Then we flew back to Kingsville to learn how to bring a high-performance jet aboard an aircraft carrier.

Near the end of advanced flight training, in early 1966 on a drizzly Texas day with a low overcast that appeared way too ugly for flying, six of us waited at NAS Corpus Christi for a weather report from USS Lexington, which was operating off the coast. Word came, and we launched. Five student-pilots on the wing of an instructor flew low out over the gulf. The weather deteriorated, but on we went, skimming above choppy, wind-blown waves and scudding beneath angry clouds, at times no more than 600-feet above whitecaps. The weather improved as we arrived overhead the ship.

Our instructor circled Lexington like a worried mother quail, watching as his untested students attempted to bring high-performance jets aboard a small aircraft carrier. At the boat, there are many ways to screw up. A young pilot might come in with too little power and hit the ramp, sending fire and debris down the deck. Or near the ramp he might feel he is too high and push the nose over in an effort to salvage the pass, setting up a sink rate and smacking onto the deck so hard metal parts shatter. And there are many other ways, in the vernacular, to bust your ass at the ship.

A future roommate would one day usher a group of young pilots out to this same ship, and he would die. Mike was an excellent pilot and a good guy who had survived over 200 missions on two combat cruises. That day, as a training-command LSO, Mike circled overhead, watching his students car-qual. Did he worry for his charges? Certainly. But it was Mike who died.

Some say he got slow and stalled. But why? Did a young novice bolter, that is, miss the wires and, at full power, have to fly back off the carrier and go around? Did this distract him? Or was Mike's attention disrupted when he heard Lexington's LSO call for "POWER, POWER!" Perhaps Mike's own bird lost one of its two engines, and without enough thrust, his aircraft quickly stalled. I never heard for certain. Only that Mike bought the farm. All of us can recall a time or two when a few seconds of inattention could have been deadly.

Mike might have saved himself had he ejected as soon as he felt his aircraft began to shudder as it stalled. Yet I understand why he didn't, why he tried a risky save and attempted to recover from the stall before smacking into the water. You want to avoid embarrassment. You don't want to explain why you lost an airplane. So you hang it all out, hoping you can pull it off. And most of the time it goes your way. After, and only to yourself, you'll mutter, "Yeah, way too close."

I made two practice touch-and-go landings with my hook up at Lexington. Then I was cleared for an arrested landing, and I dropped my hook. The landing was far more violent than those in the slower T-28. I was thrown forward in my harness. The airplane was snatched to a stop. A director in a yellow jersey, with a hand-signal, told me to lift the tailhook, then with another signal, he indicated I was to taxi forward. Not many seconds after the landing, I was positioned on the catapult and running power up to 100 percent. The acceleration slammed me back in the seat, blurred my vision, and then two seconds after it fired, my Cougar and I cleared the bow. My aircraft and I were floating—that was the sensation. Time to fly, to concentrate on what I was doing. Interspersed, sandwiched in among all the chores of flying, was a moment of exhilaration. I love this, I said to myself. This is what I am meant to be doing. I turned downwind, reduced power and came around for another trap. The precise flying, feeling the tailhook snatch up the wire, the violent deceleration—it set my heart pounding. As I taxied forward for a second and final catapult launch that day, I was smiling behind my oxygen mask.

Two arrested landings. That's all. The abbreviated time at Lexington was a result of the nasty weather and the long, fuel-eating flight out to the ship. The instructor led us back to Corpus Christi without incident.

If a strict reading of the regs was done, I doubt my two arrested landings were enough to meet the requirements and qualify me as an F-9F carrier-aviator. Nevertheless, a qualification certificate was inserted into my records: I was car-qualled in jets.

Qualifying as a jet carrier pilot was the final step in a year-and-a-half of intense training. I had changed. I could feel it when I woke up each day.

The screw-up who could not finish college, who drank too much and fell out of second-story windows and who had been denied promotion to third-class petty officer, was transformed into a naval aviator...and according to the Navy, also an officer and gentleman. I had stuck with and completed something.

Truly, my parents were now proud. Word from my sisters was that Dad bragged about me. To strangers, even.

CHAPTER FIVE

# *Three Must-Pumps*

My new orders: Central California. I was to report at Naval Air Station Lemoore, a place I had never heard of, to check out in A-4 Skyhawks. I would train to fly them aggressively, to navigate accurately, to drop bombs and fire rockets and cannons. And I'd learn current maneuvers designed to evade flak and SAMs.

I was thrilled. A-4s were flown by a single pilot, unlike the much larger F-4 Phantom, which required a guy in the backseat to assist in the navigation and bombing chores. No committee flying this bird; I'd be doing everything myself. What I could not know then, was that these orders placed me on a trajectory to the July morning Dick and I would both be blown from the sky.

The morning after I was handed the orders, I headed out to California, droning northwest across Texas in my newest underpowered British sports car, the vastness and desolation numbing me. Piedras-Negras, Dryden, Sanderson, Alpine—towns with interesting names that offered nothing. My home-state held nothing for me. An endless low overcast like a stratus of damp mover's blanket, purple-gray, stretched soggy and flat to the horizon. The desert was equally dull, blown down to gravel by constant wind and dotted only here and there with clumps of bunchgrass, greasy scrub and an occasional prickly pear cactus. I had once regarded this region as home. Now, glad to put Texas in my rearview mirror, I was bound for something new and wonderful.

Pushing my car's puny engine hard, rpms singing near redline, I was pleased to be cruising well above the speed limit, when a red Austin Healey 3000, the powerful big brother to my Sprite, overtook me. This was somewhere near Marfa, still in desert country. As he passed, the driver and I exchanged glances. We drove side-by-side, occupying both lanes of the thin highway, as we recognized each other.

John Allen Lockard was piloting the powerful car. At nineteen, he had been the youngest NAVCAD cadet in my preflight class. Briefly during preflight training Lockard had been an object of whispered ridicule for his thick, rural Alabama accent. A few guys wondered aloud how he managed to land among us. The guy couldn't swim; he was a sinker. Every Navy person must swim, so during Saturdays, when we might have had time to get to know Lockard, he was at the pool for remedial swim lessons.

He had poor posture, too, a result of gaining height so quickly in his late teens. And he seemed to amble. Awkwardly. The surprise, then, for our whole class came when we began flying airplanes. Instructors, we heard, were talking about the gangly young cadet who possessed a splendid natural talent. He was being compared to Chuck Yeager, the famous test pilot. Lockard was nice about it; no gloating, no posturing; but his flight grades and academic scores put him at the top of our primary flight class. He easily qualified for jets at NAS Meridian in Mississippi. He won the prize I had wanted so much. That was when I'd lost contact with him.

And now, on open road in the tedious Texas wasteland, Al Lockard was passing me. Again. This time in a more powerful road machine. We pulled over. His posture was now erect and confident, all awkwardness gone, yet he retained his smile and easy manner. We quickly discovered we both had orders to VA-125, the replacement air group (RAG) at Lemoore. We agreed to be roommates.

The next day we drove through the main gate at Naval Air Station Lemoore where a manicured grass parade-ground greeted us. At the corner, mounted on a white concrete pedestal at a rakish angle as if climbing out fast, was an A-4. Cool. This was my first glimpse of the airplane I'd be flying. I had seen only photographs until then. The whole place was cool.

Commissioned only five years earlier, NAS Lemoore was a modern and stylish attack aircraft base on 30,000 acres carved from the fertile heart of California's Central Valley. Al and I signed in at the bachelor officers quarters—the BOQ—and then we toured the base in his Austin Healey. We located the officers' club, the movie theater and other important-to-us facilities. Tucked in a quiet corner of the base, miles from the noise of the active runways, were beautiful small homes for Navy families. They had been designed by Richard Neutra, a name I recalled from my brief stint as an architecture major. Neutra was a visionary credited with developing the California Modern Style. I would later hear about quality issues when a buddy's wife objected to the fact her walls did not properly connect with the concrete slab foundation. Weeds and tendrils of Bermuda grass crept from the lawn into her living room. But as Al and I drove the base, I was thrilled that it was all so modern, so California Modern.

We doubled back to the Officers Club. There, at twenty, Al could legally drink.

The first few training days were filled with classroom work. I was issued a thick manual—NATOPS was the acronym on the cover—and told to read it cover to cover. Following a few days of classwork, and study of assigned sections, an officer handed me a NATOPS quiz. I passed, but the officer went over every missed question and assigned more study. "You'll fly tomorrow," he said. "But keep studying. Concentrate on the red pages." Those were emergency procedures, including two ways to operate the ejection seat, information I'd never need. I thought.

The next day I briefed with an instructor, a Marine Corps lieu-tenant who had recently returned from Vietnam. All his missions had been south of the demilitarized zone—the DMZ. "What was it like?" I wanted to know. "Interesting," he said, and then he went back to briefing for our hop—my first flight in an A-4. I would be solo, and he'd be in another Skyhawk.

We were to check in by radio. When cleared, we'd taxi onto the runway together. I was to place my bird in formation position on his right wing. When he nodded his head smartly forward and then back upright, we were to add power simultaneously. It would be my job to keep in position by adding or pulling off little increments of throttle. "Don't fall behind," he warned.

A half hour later, the Marine instructor's helmet nodded and his airplane began to surge forward. We were rolling. Faster and faster. I concentrated on staying with him, saw his nosewheel lift from the runway, and we were airborne. His helmet nodded and I reached for the handle to retract the landing gear, he nodded again and I lifted the flap handle, and then we were accelerating faster than any F-9F in Kingsville. It was glorious.

Such a wonderful, nimble airplane. It fit me, I loved it. My land-ing was good, on the numbers as we liked to say, and as I taxied back to the line, I was smiling so broadly my oxygen mask pulled at my cheeks. During the debrief, the Marine said I had done well. A perfect day. Others would follow.

After a couple weeks at the BOQ, Al and I rented an apartment in town, a few miles east of the base. Ours was a shabby, cheaply furnished place with two bedrooms, a tiny living room and a kitchen. Two families of itinerant farm workers shared a unit across from us. We bought a large used television set that sort of worked, after a fifteen-minute warm-up.

That night, our first supper was spaghetti. I had never cooked, so Al instructed me in the simplicity of basic bachelor meals. Hard sticks of pasta softened and slid under gravity in a boiling pan of water. Mom often fed us spaghetti, but apparently, I had never watched the process. Al hooked a single strand with a fork, lifted it from the water, then threw it at the painted wall behind the sink.

"Sticks," he said. "How you know it's done."

That bit of spaghetti remained on the wall until I cleaned the place when we moved out at the end of our training.

We advanced to meals centered on frozen meat patties, beginning with hamburgers on buns, of course. Then we branched out. Patties could be chopped up as they sizzled in a skillet, and at the right moment, a can of cream-of-mushroom soup was dumped in. Bingo—Al's stroganoff gravy.

"Ya'all make some toast,' he said to me. "We'll want to dollop this over two slices each." Accompanied by a bottle of beer, a fine meal. We did this often, sometimes adding canned vegetables on the side. We were living.

Late in the summer, I attended classes on nuclear weapons, and learned we Navy pilots did not drop nuclear weapons, we *delivered* them to a target. I was required to have a Top-Secret clearance before admittance into an isolated and windowless building surrounded by a tall fence topped with concertina wire.

The first day, on a small cart, a Mark-28 weapon was wheeled into the classroom. I found it difficult to envision this bomb's murderous capacity, equal to many thousands and thousands of tons of high explosives. The weapon on the trolley was disturbingly beautiful. Painted glossy white, finely crafted and so sleek and smooth it would have done credit to any Ferrari. Exposed titanium and aluminum fittings, machined to perfect tolerances, faired smoothly into the polished skin of the bomb. Not a bump or ripple marred its sleek shape. So pretty, it appeared harmless.

In that windowless classroom we learned how, someday, we might be called upon to fly one of these things to a distant target— a bridge, a factory, an air-base. Though it was never said, we had an uneasy sense it might well be a one-way trip.

To hone our navigation skills for such a mission, we flew low-altitude sand-blowers, hops that first took us hundreds of miles out to sea off California's coast and then back to land well north of Point Reyes. We skimmed above treetops across northern California into Nevada. Then, several miles from the target, at a bombing range, we accelerated to 500 knots and dropped down to fifty feet. Streaking over the desert this low and this fast, the scenery blurred past, and at the carefully planned initial point—a landmark—while flying at 500 knots—some 575 miles per hour—we'd press a button on the control stick to trigger a primitive computer.

When a beeping signal in our headset began, we'd pull up quickly and smoothly into the beginning of a loop, holding exactly four Gs. During that precise half loop, at 45-degrees above the horizon, the elementary computer aboard the A-4 would fire a tiny explosive charge to blast our load, a concrete shape simulating a nuclear weapon, from under our bird's belly, tossing the concrete dummy into a miles-long arc.

Once free of the weapon, once that ton of concrete was lofted toward its target, we'd continue through the half-loop until past the top and going back down, where we'd roll from inverted to right-side-up, a maneuver called a half-Cuban-eight, finishing in a shallow dive—enabling our airplane to regain some speed, speed required to dash away from a ghastly (in this case simulated) weapon still sailing through the sky in the other direction, a bomb that—if we ever had to do this—in a few more seconds would erupt into more than a megaton of unthinkable destruction. But it would never happen. We promised ourselves this.

From those first days in the windowless building of secrets, I understood that should I ever be called upon to do the unimaginable, carry a live nuclear weapon into war, I'd launch from a carrier so far from my target I'd have but a faint possibility there'd be enough fuel to return to the ship, that my chance of making it back aboard even if I did have enough fuel was decreased by realities. For one thing, after launching the attack airplanes, the ship would turn and head full-steam away to open sea. Three hours later, it would be another 100 miles farther from the launch point. And for another, to preserve the ship, an asset more valuable than the airplanes, it would adhere to electronic silence—no navigation aids, no radar vectors. I'd have about as much luck finding a wine-cork in Lake Erie.

Following this phase of instruction, a sheet was inserted into my records stating that I was now a nuclear delivery pilot qualified to carry the Mark-28 weapon, a bomb with destructive power equivalent to over a million metric tons of TNT, and qualified, too, in delivery of lesser bombs.

During the summer of 1966, Al and I flew accelerated training regimens. We were pushed hard, the fleet needed attack pilots, there was a shortage. Toward the end of our training we were working very long days, and for a time I flew six days a week. It was not uncommon to complete an early morning training hop, sit through six or eight hours of classroom work, then fly a night hop. It left few hours for sleep, and no time at all for those many beers in our refrigerator.

To keep our training moving quickly, nine of us were sent to Fallon, Nevada for a few weeks, where the Navy had thousands of acres devoted to bombing ranges. There we learned the fine art of dive-bombing, loft-bombing, strafing and aerial refueling. The weather was excellent, allowing us to fly two and sometimes three hops a day. We all lived in the Fallon BOQ and bonded as a group. The senior man among us students was Bill Searfus, a Navy commander with a brilliant smile and an upbeat attitude. He asked us to call him Bill, not Commander.

At the end of his training, he was to join a squadron returning from deployment as its executive officer, the number-two guy in seniority. It was understood that after a successful year in that position, he'd become its skipper.

We were flying two hops a day, and at times a third hop—at night—was tacked onto our schedule. This was physically demanding, but fun. The more I flew the bird, the more I appreciated the A-4. I loved its shape: simple and sexy, a delta-wing airplane with rounded tips and tail surfaces to match, and rounded intakes behind the cockpit, high, like shoulder pads. The bird was designed to be inexpensive, easy to maintain, and initially it was to have that single mission: nuclear-delivery. By the time I arrived at the RAG it was a multi-purpose attack airplane.

The initial price was $860,000. (In comparison, the specialized helmet alone for our country's newest fighter, the F-35 Lightning, costs taxpayers almost half of that.) We joked that the A-4 was dispensable, intended to fly to the target, but not home.

The A-4 wedges a single pilot into a cockpit so compact his shoulders rub the canopy rails. All navigation and bombardier duties are assumed by the guy doing the driving, which at times can be a busy task. But Al and I like it this way; we agree we don't want to fly as part of a committee.

When Ed Heinemann designed this warbird, nuclear weapons were large, and it was believed, erroneously it turned out, that future weapons would be even larger. Hence, the A-4 sits tall on spindly landing gear to accommodate huge weapons that never materialized. When parked on its stork-like landing gear, the bird lacks the brutally aggressive looks of, say, an F-4 Phantom, which on the ramp appears to be squatting, ready to lunge into the air. The Phantom was designed a couple years after the Skyhawk. Huge and angular and configured for takeoff, it weighs more than twice a fully loaded A-4. The Phantom requires a crew of two, and it is a vision of sheer brutality, a squatting monster with a pair of huge turbojet engines that gulp air through boxy intakes. And those enormous engines are equipped with afterburners—which A-4s lack—to supply the massive thrust required to muscle the monster through the sound barrier, smash through it, to more than Mach 2.

No, A-4s are not that. They are all smoothness and finesse. This airplane was intended to catapult from an aircraft carrier far from an enemy's coastline bearing a terrible weapon, then skim above the sea at some 360 knots, flying so low that it would escape the searching beams of radar. Once across the coast, the A-4 pilot would wend through hills and valleys, still cruising at the 360 or so knots, staying fifty feet, no more than a hundred, above the terrain, evading known defenses until very near the target.

Weeks before we departed Fallon, we were taken to a handgun and rifle range in Nevada. Marine instructors ran us through a shooting course, including a series of firing positions intended to teach us how to use handguns in combat situations. We ran from spot to spot, shooting from sitting positions, crouching stances and prone positions. We were timed, so a certain amount of hustle was involved. Between each station we reloaded our weapon. It was harder than I thought it would be—all this running and shooting and reloading.

At one station was a life-size cutout of a standing man, six feet from where I stood, and I was to empty all the rounds in my weapon at it. I had a lightweight .38 Smith & Wesson that held only five shots. Point blank I emptied the little toy of a pistol, the one I would fly with strapped to my chest, at a paper-covered metal silhouette of a man. It was two yards from me. When I finished the course, a rather disgusted Marine showed me my poor results. He was particularly insulted that I had failed to place even a single round in the cutout of the standing man. He shook his head and motioned for the next pilot to debrief.

This instruction, this fast-track we were on, sometimes culminated in what the Navy mysteriously called *must-pump*. When we arrived back in Lemoore, three of us in the Fallon contingent—Ken Adams, Mike Confer and I—were informed we would soon become the first must-pumps turned out by VA-125 in a while. This may have been an experiment. Customarily, we'd each have joined a squadron returning from a Western Pacific deployment, and we'd train with that squadron for six months, flying out of Lemoore. We'd have time to bond with the group, build time in the A-4 and pick up skills from pilots with carrier experience. But apparently the Navy thought we were young and resilient. Someone somewhere decided the three of us were doing well enough to be sent directly to carriers on Yankee Station—to the Vietnam war. Replacement pilots were needed.

Bill Searfus, Ken Adams, Mike Confer and I continued to be pushed hard at VA-125. The training pace became like a dash. Fatigue became an enemy. Little mistakes emerged. Ken Adams bent a fuel probe on a bird when he came in hot while practicing to refuel behind an aerial tanker. I skidded an A-4 off a taxiway late one night when I hallucinated, misperceiving far-off lights as coming from an airplane about to land on my taxiway. Damage to the airplanes in both incidents was minimal, but VA-125's safety officer urged us to get as much rest as possible. Yet the hurry-up tempo continued.

It had never occurred to me during all the formalities of my early training, that later we pilots would socialize, and that when it came to flying airplanes, rank would no longer be a great divide. Bill Searfus, a full commander, invited me to a party at his house. He said something along the line of, "We need to unwind some."

I arrived with a date at his California-Modern home that Friday evening. He greeted me by my first name and introduced himself to my date as "Bill." Rock and roll music blasted from his living room, and there was hard liquor on the kitchen counter, not beer as at some junior officer's party. He told my date that she was far too pretty to be hanging around with a guy like me. During the evening he kicked off his shoes, danced with his wife to Little Richard music, danced with her like a kid. And he danced with my date, too, bounding around like a NAVCAD. This was a Navy I had not known existed.

Four months after reporting to the RAG, I was nearly done. To prepare for carrier operations—our most difficult test—we had practiced at night, making landing after landing on a little patch of runway outlined in dim lights in the shape of a carrier deck. A landing safety officer—LSO—graded every landing. Then, with a small group, I flew an A-4E (the echo model we called it) out to USS Bennington off the coast of Southern California. This was for carrier qualifications—A-4 car-quals. Serious car-quals.

My logbook indicates that over a two-day period I trapped aboard Bennington twenty-six times. Seven of those were at night—a new and intense experience. Coming aboard a ship requires the lightest touch on the controls. The airplane is guided, with tiny changes of throttle setting and minute movements of the control stick, to bring it down a three-degree glideslope as if on a rail to the tiny piece of real estate. On moonless nights the sea is as ink-dark as the sky, there is no horizon. From a quarter mile aft, the tiny ship in the distance appears suspended on a curtain of black velvet, with the only visual references a string of faint lights down the center of the landing area and a dim yellow light on the port side of the ship. We called the dim yellow light the meatball. And through optics, the meatball appears to rise or fall in relation to the airplane's position on that three-degree glide-slope. Go a tiny bit above the path, and the meatball rises, go low and it falls. And dip too far below that glideslope—we are talking about only a couple feet, here—and the yellow glow shifts to red. And at the moment you begin to see that red glow, the landing signal officer—the LSO—will be shouting over the radio: "Power, give me some power. Power!"

I accomplished the twenty-six traps, then flew from Bennington to El Toro in Southern California, and from there a 2.2-hour flight back to Lemoore. This was my last flight with VA-125. I was now a fully qualified A-4E attack pilot. It was the end of August.

A few days later I was handed orders to VA-164, a squadron that was with Air Wing Sixteen aboard USS Oriskany, which at the time was deployed at Yankee Station off North Vietnam's coast. I was pleased with the orders. I'd be assisting the South Vietnamese. I thought of Ti Ba and Mssr. Ich, what good people they were. And their daughter and granddaughter, who likely were married and had families now, and of the Vietnamese teenagers I'd met at Cercle Sportif. The adults, too. Several times I had watched Big Minh, one of the generals we were fighting alongside, play tennis at the Cerc. Yes, communist aggression had to be stopped somewhere, and Vietnam was where I'd fight it. I believed, in other words, in America's position in this war. I was fully a son of the 1950s.

## CHAPTER SIX

# *To Childplay*

I took a week of leave to unwind at my folks' home in Palo Alto. Six days later, in early-morning darkness, my parents drove me to Travis Air Force Base, where I found Ken Adams and Mike Confer. When a public-address announcement summoned us, I kissed Mom, patted Dad on his shoulder and said goodbye. We three must-pumps headed for the gate, pleased to find we were on the same flight and excited to face adventures ahead.

In the blackness of pre-dawn, we boarded a civilian jet, a World Airways Boeing 707 chartered by the military to haul young men off to war. With flight attendants walking the aisles, it didn't feel at all martial. There was an energy on the airliner until, after a few hours, we settled into the long flight.

Our destination was Clark Air Force Base in the Philippines. Once there, we three must-pumps showed our orders around. They proved meaningless at the Air Force Base. Someone eventually suggested we make our way to the Naval Air Station at Cubi Point. Which we did. But again, since this must-pump business was a new program, not a soul we showed our orders to had any idea what to do with us. We'd get ourselves out to our carriers, we decided.

Ken somehow found transport on an oiler, a big refueling ship headed from the Philippines to Yankee Station. In the Tonkin Gulf he was transferred across to Oriskany on a highline, seated in a little cage suspended from a cable strung between two ships steaming parallel to each other. Dangling, swinging not many feet above the waves, he and his cage were pulled across by sailors hauling on lines.

Mike and I hung around the maintenance shacks at the Cubi Point Air Base until we found rides on aircraft headed to Yankee Station. Mike scored a jump-seat on a carrier-onboard-delivery airplane, a COD, riding the 600 miles to USS Coral Sea, where he joined VA-23.

I don't recall how I found Tom Maxwell, the colorful and bigger-than-life pilot of Oriskany's huge twin-engine A-3 Skywarrior, but he offered me a seat on his big repurposed bomber, now referred to as a Whale, and we flew to Yankee Station that afternoon. Whales were used for radar-jamming and as refueling tankers, and they were the largest aircraft operating off carriers.

Bringing one aboard small Essex-Class boats such as Oriskany required great skill. Tom Maxwell possessed it in abundance, I'd learn.

I wedged sideways onto a jump-seat behind the co-pilot. The three of us chatted during the flight to Yankee Station. "You're joining a great squadron," Tom told me. "Engel is a strong skipper."

My first glimpse of my new ship, the carrier with the radio-call-sign Childplay, was over the shoulder of the co-pilot. Tom brought the Whale down the glideslope, precisely minding his airspeed and line-up. As we neared the fantail, the ship seemed way too small to accommodate such a beast.

I slammed sideways into a bulkhead when we trapped. We taxied out of the cables as the big airplane's wings folded. On deck, I shouldered my big sea-bag and grabbed the strap of another bag filled with my helmet and flight gear... and I realized I had no idea where I should go.

Tom offered, and he led me through a hatch on Oriskany's island, the tall structure on the starboard side of the ship serving as a command bridge and control tower. We descended into Oriskany, wound through a maze of gray passageways and hatches until we arrived at VA-164's ready-room. It was a route I could not have retraced.

Tom dramatically announced in his baritone voice, "Ghostriders, I bring a new pilot."

My new squadron's ready-room appeared precisely as in the WWII movies I loved—and as ready-rooms remain today. Rows of comfortable padded chairs with high backs gave the room the appearance of an intimate movie theater—one with a desk near the door for a duty officer. An aisle separated the two rows. Seating was assigned by rank, so mine would be near the back. The skipper's was front row, right side of the aisle.

Cmdr. Paul Engel was seated in that number one spot. A small stack of folders and papers rested on his lap. He looked up, startled perhaps at Tom's booming announcement. My new skipper fixed his eyes on me—steely is the right word—and then he smiled.

"Welcome to VA164," he said. He patted the empty seat next to him.

I handed him the large envelope containing my orders, my personnel file and my medical records and took the seat he indicated. He turned and passed the whole batch to a lieutenant commander two rows back.

"This is Deny Weichman," the skipper said. A big man, imposing, took the envelopes, saying nothing. But Deny did smile in a broad, welcoming manner. A bit of my nervousness left.

Cmdr. Engel welcomed me aboard with a short sentence or two and immediately launched into a rather formal briefing. He explained the strategy for the air war, our reasons for bombing North Vietnam and how we pilots were going to execute this strategy with precision and dedication.

"We bring the war to the enemy," he said. "We won't let the enemy bring his war to us."

And to prevent that enemy from bringing the war to me, I was to follow rules. In other words, no cowboy antics. I was to fly over the North at least 3,000 feet above the ground. I was to make only a single bombing run at each target, for it was far more likely that our planes would take hits on second or third runs, he told me. Gunners got hits once they figured out the pattern pilots favored, he explained. We were to bomb approved military targets only and never drop near a school or other community building. And villages were not our enemy; avoid dropping ordnance near one. He explained the current strategy of denying the North Vietnamese all petroleum, oil and lubricants—POL.

The idea was to slow the North's delivery of war supplies to its troops in South Vietnam by destroying the oil-based products required to fuel a supply line. It had worked against Nazi Germany, the strategists in Washington reasoned, so why not here? We would hit refineries—in fact, the Ghostriders a week earlier had utterly destroyed a refinery and oil storage area near Vinh, Skipper Engel explained. We would take out any trucks we could find, for every Vietnamese truck was assumed to be delivering POL or other supplies. We would drop bridges to block or slow those trucks. And if we were so fortunate as to find a train on open tracks, we'd attack it.

"We aren't at war with civilians. We are not Nazis," the skipper said. I don't recall the precise wording of sentences before or after his statement, but this is a precise quote. As is another sentence he voiced as we sat together in that first briefing at the front of our ready-room: "You are not going to die."

Well I knew that. I truly believed I was invincible. Nugget pilots—so named because as ensigns we had so recently pinned new gold bars onto our collars—had to believe this. I was well trained. I flew A-4s with confidence. I would not make mistakes. And therefore, I could not be harmed.

"You are not going to die, because you will fly on my wing," he added.

Wow, I thought. This is a great honor. In reality, assigning the most junior pilots to fly with the most senior was common practice. It balanced the experience levels throughout the squadron. Nevertheless, I was thrilled.

Then from Deny Weichman: "Skipper, excuse me, but he's missing one little thing here." He stood, unwinding himself from his chair. I was looking at the tallest man in the squadron, perhaps the tallest pilot in the Navy and certainly the tallest to squeeze into an A-4. He held one of my folders open.

"What's that?" Skipper Engel asked.

"That new exercise in the JFKs," Deny answered. He was referencing a set of exercises added to the training regimen of officers and enlisted men during the administration of our previous president. Addressing me, Deny said, "You can do it now."

He was grinning. He didn't wait for a response. "Right here." He pointed to the aisle. I stood. I noticed the several pilots scattered through the ready-room were watching. All of them. This was no time to screw up.

"All you need to do is put both hands on the deck. You can bend your knees, if you want. It's pretty easy."

I did this, and it wasn't difficult.

"Now bring one leg up as high as your shoulders," he instructed. "Either leg. Doesn't matter." This was not at all difficult. But as my leg lifted, there was a chorus from everyone in the ready-room.

"Wuff, wuff, wuff."

Then laughter.

I was perplexed. I had been tricked into appearing like a dog peeing on an aisle chair. Here in the ready-room? We're at war, these are warriors, and they're playing practical jokes on the new guy?

As I stood, I turned to the skipper. He was laughing too.

"Deny's favorite joke," he said. "His call sign is Wuff One."

Deny came over and shook my hand, but he said nothing because he was still chuckling.

One of the pilots in the ready-room was Frank Elkins. Skipper Engel asked him to show me the differences between the A-4Es I had trained in and the newer version of the E-model that the squadron was flying, the model I'd be flying into combat the next day. Frank and I arranged to meet later on the hangar deck.

Then someone, I can't recall who, led me through another labyrinth of passageways and ladders until I arrived at the junior-officers bunkroom, an L-shaped space with twelve berths—six sets of uppers and lowers. I was assigned a steel drawer along the wall near the head. As the new guy, I was shown to an upper, of course, which I soon discovered had problems. These new quarters, I realized, were somewhere up near the bow of the carrier, but again I could not have retraced my steps.

I liked Frank Elkins immediately. In coming days, I'd understand that he was, in our vernacular, a truly shit-hot aviator. Maybe the best in the squadron. At twenty-eight, this lieutenant with his handlebar moustache and close-cropped hair looked as if a Hollywood studio had cast him for a fighter-pilot role.

He and Bill Johnson, his wingman, loved to push the envelope, test the limits of what could be done with an A-4—stuff others weren't doing. One day, not long after I came aboard, Bill Johnson told me that after their mission and on the way back to the ship, Frank noticed how the Tonkin Gulf was mirror-flat calm. They flew down, lower and lower, flat-hatting. Frank lowered his hook and eased down lower still. His hook found the water, touched, skipped up and banged under his fuselage. Flying that low and fast requires the steadiest hand. One quiver, one wrong breath would cause the plane to descend that last couple of feet.

Fini. All done. Bought the farm.

But if you are good, truly shit-hot, the water, hard as granite at that speed, bounces your hook up and it thumps smartly against its rubber stop. Yes, if you are truly good, your hand remains steady. *Knowing* you will sidle up this close to death, defy it...and get away with it. That defines shit-hotness.

The Navy understood this as well, that Frank was a talent. He had been selected for the Navy's test-pilot school, coveted orders.

In fact, by the time I met him he should have already been in Maryland at his new post at Patuxent River Naval Air Station. But by August, the heavy losses over Vietnam meant the Navy was running low on Yankee-Station aviators. So Frank's orders had been extended. He'd have to stay with the Ghostriders for the full cruise before checking into PaxRiver.

Frank and I met on the hangar deck after the evening meal. We climbed a ladder and stood together on a little platform at the top. I slipped into the VA-164 aircraft's cockpit. Frank showed me the instrument panel and various switches and control boxes. Most were the same as aircraft I had flown at Lemoore, but there were differences, too, in this newest version of the A-4E the Ghostriders had. The intervalometer, for instance, a little box that allowed pilots to select the time interval at which bombs would release from their aircraft, was a new version. The most significant difference was inclusion of electronic gear to sense the radars of the enemy. I had never seen such equipment. It was designed to offer a pilot warning in the event that a tightly focused beam guiding a SAM locked onto his airplane.

"Memorize this," Frank said. "I'll be back in a half hour." He disappeared. I concentrated on the unfamiliar, touching each switch, knob and instrument.

"Okay, look up at the overhead," Frank commanded when he came back. He'd name a switch or an instrument and I'd touch it. He was quite formal about this, and I took it seriously. Here, working with me, was the real thing, an experienced combat veteran on his way to becoming a test pilot.

I demonstrated familiarity with the new stuff in the cockpit, and Frank said, "You got it. You're ready."

I wasn't so sure.

The Navy's latest experiment with must-pumps fresh from the RAG had begun.

Did it work? I assume the Navy judged it did. Or perhaps there was no other choice, for the practice continued. For me the question persists. Ken Adams and I, both flying off Oriskany in sister squadrons, gained skills quickly enough to survive. But we hadn't heard from Mike Confer.

## CHAPTER SEVEN

# *Over the Beach*

I slept poorly my first night aboard Oriskany, the night before my first combat sortie. Nervousness was surely a factor, but what sticks with me was the upper bunk I had been assigned. It was beneath the flight-deck in a corner of the bunkroom, a dank spot with a permanently damp mattress reserved for the most junior officer. The previous occupant, a VA-163 Saint named Louie, had vacated it when a shoot-down freed the dry one below.

That was the grim deal: whenever a pilot was lost, bunks and staterooms would be shuffled by seniority. My moldering mattress was the result of a long-standing leak, and Louie warned me a new drip wouldn't be noticed until well after it rained.

"Shows up a couple days later. Sorry," he said.

Louie showed me how plastic sheeting had been taped into place above the bottom half of my bunk by a former occupant in a futile attempt to divert the drip away from the bedding. "Mostly works. Some'll still get through. Enough to keep your mattress damp," Louie said.

There was an odor. I clearly recall the moldy scent that first night and how Louie, below me, snored gently as I tried to settle in.

The next morning, I learned I was assigned to fly on the wing of Lt. Cmdr. Dan Strong, our operations officer, not with Skipper Engel. A surprise. Later I would understand that the ops officer is charged with ensuring all pilots are up to their jobs. Strong wanted to get to know this new nugget right away.

He and I met in the ready-room, and in a few minutes he completed his brief on what he expected of his wingie. Dan Strong was slightly built, wiry, and he was intense. He said nothing during the brief to settle the young nugget. He finished and turned to walk to the Air Intelligence briefing room, where we'd receive a formal briefing from the Carrier Air Wing staff. This was efficient—a few words about our target assignments, a listing of known defenses, a run-down on weather and winds predicted over the target area and then some general information on where our resources—such as our fighters—would be deployed.

Back in the ready-room, we suited up in flight gear. "Easy target," Dan Strong told me as he zipped up his survival vest. "In and out."

We compared charts and he pointed to a spot on the coastline, a little bay. "We'll coast-in here." I marked the place on my own chart. "Before we go feet-dry, loosen up," he instructed. "Position yourself about a thousand feet off my wing and a little aft." This was the same as the tactical maneuvering we'd practiced at the RAG. "You have the target marked?" he asked. The briefer in the aviation-intelligence (A.I.) space, a lieutenant, had pointed at it, a little bridge spanning a thin blue line representing a tributary to a river. But I hadn't thought to mark it. Dan watched me put a triangle around it. He gave me instructions on where we'd rendezvous, which I wrote onto my kneeboard pad.

Then from the squawk-box, "Pilots, man 'em up."

I ran my engine to 100-percent and looked over all my instruments. The sea ahead was flat. I gave a smart salute to the catapult officer, signaling I was ready. He faced into the wind, bent onto one knee, pointed at Oriskany's bow and then touched two fingers to the deck. This was his signal to the crewman who would fire the steam catapult. I braced my helmet into the headrest. The G-force slammed me back into my seat and two seconds later I was off the deck and flying. Gear up, flaps up, and I turned onto the course Dan had given me. I quickly caught up and settled my A-4 into a solid position on his left wing. I was airborne on my first combat mission.

We flew southwest until we arrived at the bay, where Dan began a turn west. It took me a few moments to understand we had arrived; the coastline looked different than what I expected from my chart. He continued the turn until we were right angle to the coastline. I slid back to my loose position and, keeping with him, felt the speed building. We were in a shallow dive. Dan made a transmission to Red Crown, the station that kept track of all aircraft over Vietnam—ours and also any Vietnamese MiG fighters in the air. He identified his aircraft, then announced, "Feet-dry with two."

My heart was thumping, I could feel it under my survival vest. We were over rice paddies, which meant that if I was shot down, no rescue. I'd be captured almost immediately by farmers in this densely populated part of Vietnam.

As I had been taught at the RAG, I jinked in three-second arcs as Dan led me to our target. We arrived in less than ten minutes. "Magic two, you have the target? Nine-o'clock," he said. "Tallyho," I transmitted.

He circled about half way around the little bridge, and then he called that he was "in hot." I saw his bombs hit, then felt them— thump, thump, thump, thump as their shock waves reached my airplane. "Magic Two is in hot, north to south," I transmitted. My logbook shows I dropped two MK-81 bombs and four MK-82s, a total load of one-and-a-quarter tons of ordnance. The bridge, Dan reported when he debriefed with the intelligence guys, was probably damaged. The level of adrenalin I had pumped into my system on my first time over the beach left me feeling both exhilarated to be alive and somewhat sick at my stomach.

My next mission, the following day—it was September 8—I flew on Skipper Engel's wing. He led us south, parallel to the coastline, staying a couple miles out. Over the radio the skipper sounded relaxed as he pointed out landmarks and checkpoints. I was tense, and wondered if I should feel more comfortable. It seemed like a long detour; we were well south of our target, and I grew even more tense until he finally reversed our heading.

We flew north, again parallel to the coast, until we came to a small bay with a thin, tan beach, and there we turned inland toward our target. I carried the same ordnance as the day before. In two days I had dropped two-and-a-half tons of bombs onto North Vietnam. A lot. Yet, somehow, I didn't feel as though I had made any difference. The next day we steamed for the Philippines. The line-period for Oriskany was over.

My indoctrination into WestPac culture, the ways of deployed squadrons in the Western Pacific, continued at Cubi Point. Barry Wood, the squadron's other ensign, told me to buy a barong tagalog as soon as I got ashore. I'd need to wear either that or a coat and tie to get into the dining room at the Cubi Point Officers Club. And the squadron was gathering there for dinner that evening.

The new white barong tagalog, formal wear in the Philippines, was of a fine fabric, beautifully embroidered down the chest panels. It featured a Nehru collar, and since it buttoned only partway, it was pulled over the head and not tucked in. What a comfortably sane garment for the tropics. I grew to love mine as it carried me through three WestPac cruises.

That afternoon I went with several of the guys up the hill to the Cubi Point Officers Club, the hangout for the fleet's aviators that gained such fame—infamy for some of the riotous escapades aviators pulled as they shook off their combat tension—that it would eventually be reconstructed as part of the National Naval Aviation Museum at Pensacola. The club was tucked into jungle and enjoyed an expansive view of the air station and Subic Bay beyond. Its walls were covered in plaques and memorabilia squadrons had installed. Hollywood, in all its excess, could not have invented a more aviator-centric dive. I fell in love with it.

It was a bright afternoon and I had already had a gin-and-tonic, when I spotted a lieutenant wearing a patch from VA-23.

"Hey, is Mike Confer around?" I asked.

"No. He's dead," he said. "Flew into the ground."

Like that, I learned of the fatal end of a buddy and fellow must-pump. The first loss of a guy I had trained with. Mike, the lieutenant explained, was killed on a night mission. He had launched rockets and didn't pull up, continuing in his dive until his A-4 smacked into a rice paddy. It happened up near The Hourglass, two rivers I'd come to know, and not far from the Red River. Probably he had taken rounds in the cockpit from anti-aircraft gunners, the lieutenant speculated.

Rockets at night are particularly dangerous. Their trails of fire point like yellow arrows back to the airplane that launched them. And for any accuracy with rockets, you must go low, down beneath your parachute flares. The silhouetted airplane makes a perfect target.

Vietnamese records released by Hanoi decades later confirm an aircraft was shot down at the location that night. Mike Confer was twenty-four, two months younger than I was at the time. I cannot recall what I did the rest of that afternoon. But I do remember the inner chill.

I wore my new barong tagalog to dinner that night. Our steaks were brought to the long table on iron skillets, sizzling. Bottles of Mateus wine were passed around. Skipper Engel stood to make a toast. It was lovely. But I couldn't get Mike out of my mind.

The three carriers assigned to Yankee Station each spent around thirty days flying combat sorties "on the line." They operated twelve hours a day, launching aircraft from noon to midnight, or midnight to noon, rotating that schedule in a sequence I never tried to understand. Noon to midnight was preferred. When one of the carriers went in to Cubi Point to replenish or for R&R to Hong Kong or Singapore, there would always still be two carriers on Yankee Station.

I flew two hops during the week we were in Cubi. Either the skipper or Dan Strong wanted the new ensign to have as much time in the cockpit as possible before going back on the line. On the way back to Yankee Station, we steamed through rain. A sprinkle, barely enough to wet down the flight-deck.

"Stand by, you're in for it," Louie warned me. I inspected the plastic sheeting over my rack, added more tape. Then I put the rain out of my mind. Several days later, however, I discovered water had soaked the foot of my mattress. For a couple days, I heard water sloshing, washing over the steel plates above me, searching for the one tiny crack in a weld. More rain found our ship. Through the remainder of my time on Yankee Station, I'd hear water gurgle overhead as the ship listed during turns, hear it coming for my mattress.

The anticipation became unease. Then, dread. Nearly every evening I'd readjust the plastic, yet always, some of the foul sauce would get through. Most, though, steadily dribbled to the deck below, where it gathered into a puddle an inch deep. As the ship moved, that pool would slosh in concert with the water I could hear above my head. Louie's flip-flops floated away.

I would not die because I would fly on Cmdr. Engel's wing; he had said that. And most of my sorties were with him. I sometimes did fly with others, several times with Leon "Bud" Edney. On one of those, Bud and I were assigned a portion of Highway 1A along which we were to conduct armed-reconnaissance, a term we shortened to road-recce. We were searching for targets of opportunity, namely trucks. As we cruised along at 3,000 feet, Bud and I spotted a "truck park," an amazing target to discover during daylight. To be more precise, what we had come across, from our perch more than a half mile above the road, appeared as a group of black dots tucked in the corner of a fenced field. We climbed to 9,000 feet and, taking turns, began to drop a single bomb at a time. Bud and I were both new at dive-bombing, so our skills were not where they would be later in the cruise. Which is to say, we missed.

After each bomb, the trucks rapidly moved to the other side of the field and they again parked haphazardly. A bomb missed; the trucks moved. After our third runs, Bud transmitted, "Hang on Magicstone Two. I want to take a look." He swept down well below our customary road-recce floor of 3,000 feet and flew over the trucks.

"Let's move on," he transmitted.

When we were back at the ship and in the ready-room I asked about it.

"Water buffalos," he answered.

"Good thing we were so shitty," I said.

"With us, they're safe."

Even today, we chuckle about that mission. But it was on-the-job-training, impressing on us the importance of keen observation—and also why we needed to work on our bombing skills.

I went to John Davis, our weapons officer, for tips. Much of what he told me I had heard back at the RAG, but now each detail, each step in the process, took on more importance.

"You want to be close, not over your target, but close for your roll-in," John said. "Ease your power back, I use eighty-five-percent, and pop your speed-brakes as you roll." I visualized flicking the switch on the throttle quadrant. He continued, stressing each step, each parameter to be met as the aircraft dove almost vertically toward the earth.

On my next mission, which was with Skipper Engel, I circled closer to the little bridge we were about to bomb. With my airplane banked steeply and with a little back-pressure on the stick, I brought the nose simultaneously down while turning 90-degrees toward the target, which now placed my A-4 on a north-to-south heading.

Yes, this was steeper, and the entry felt smooth and fluid. The earth below appeared to rotate, move up to fill my windscreen. The target, as John said it would, centered at the top of my bombsight glass. I was screaming down, building speed, hearing the change in roar around my canopy until—as John said it would—the airspeed stabilized at 450 kts. I hunched forward to squint into the bombsight glass mounted above my instrument panel, and I made fine adjustments with the control stick, "to walk the pipper," as John put it, smoothly up to the bridge. And, indeed, the glowing yellow inverted V on the bombsight's plate glass appeared to be moving along the green and brown patterns of the earth. I finessed the pipper's image toward the concrete bridge spanning a thin tributary of brown river while my A-4 sped fast toward the earth. Shifting my focus from bombsight to altimeter to airspeed and back, I watched my altitude unwind toward the bomb release number as the pipper crept toward the target. I tried to be smooth. No rudder; that throws the airplane out of balance, a recipe for a miss, John had warned. Scanning the airspeed dial, which was holding at 450, and the altimeter, as its dial came to my release-altitude, and, yes, the pipper, which at that moment reached the bridge, I "pickled" by squeezing the bomb release button jutting from the grip of the control stick.

A rapid series of bumps, which I felt in my butt, were the result of shotgun-shell-size explosive charges popping four bombs, one after another, free of my aircraft. And the bumps were my cue to honk back on the control stick, slamming Gs onto the airplane—five Gs, six, building toward seven, and as my aircraft's nose came up to the horizon.

I relaxed all Gs and pitched into a steep left turn, wings banked 90-degrees, and again pulled hard, slamming on four or five Gs—a jink to foil any gunner tracking me—and my jowls and oxygen mask once more pulled down heavily as the Gs worked on them, and I felt my face contort, my lower eyelids droop, while my G-suit's bladders inflated hard, squeezing my calves and thighs and belly, forcing the blood pooling in my lower extremities back toward my brain, forcing oxygen-rich blood where it was needed. Where it was required. To prevent a black-out.

In this steep turn, with the Gs on hard, I turned against the forces to look over my shoulder, back toward the little bridge. One-two-three-four. Orange flashes blossomed in rapid succession, each sending out an expanding concentric ring of concussion-cloud—brief, visible and enthralling—lasting a fraction of a second. Then from each blast center came a geyser of brown river water, lifted up and out, obscuring the little bridge.

Concussions from the string of 500-pound-bombs followed a second or so later, the way thunder trails a lightning flash, and they arrived under my airplane as a series of thumps—not bangs or explosions like sound-effects in every war-movie you've ever seen—but heavy thuds bumping the airplane.

"Good," the skipper said over the radio.

A few days later, I flew my first night sortie—again on Skipper Engel's wing. It was my ninth combat mission.

Like all to follow, my first night mission begins in red light. The passageways, the ready-room, the A.I. briefing room, even the heads, are all suffused in dim red light, and this is to protect our rhodopsin, the precious night-vision chemical building inside our eyes, the delicate molecules that in darkness slowly accumulate near our retinas and can be destroyed so rapidly by any white light. My flashlight and the tiny lamp on my kneeboard are both fitted with dark red lenses.

On the dimly-lit deck, I do a pre-flight inspection of my aircraft under red light from my flashlight. I man the airplane, start it, check the instruments in the dim cockpit light. And then a frightening catapult shot blasting my aircraft from standstill to 125 knots, some 144 miles per hour, into a black-velvet void. I find myself piloting an aircraft on instruments a scant sixty feet above the sea. A sea of destruction, if my airplane settles. No horizon, no visual up or down.

During these two seconds of violence, the instrument panel vibrates so viciously I can't read a thing, not even the largest gauges. And when the furious shaking ceases, I know I must trust the instruments, for with the least little slip-up, a second or two of distraction, that 60-foot margin between flying and the black sea will vanish.

I recognize the floating sensation. The immediate task is to establish a positive rate of climb, to scan between the gauge for airspeed—it must be increasing—and the vertical-speed-indicator—it must show I am climbing. Yes, good indications, and I am able to exhale, then flick handles to start the landing gear coming up, and the flaps. Once cleaned up and climbing, I have a chance to glance to a panel near my right knee. I turn a knob—click-click-click-click—to switch radio channels to the one the skipper will be on.

"Magic two airborne," I transmit. "Tick, tick," I hear in my earphones. It is the skipper clicking his transmission button twice to let me know he received my call. No extraneous radio chatter.

Within a few minutes I arrive at our pre-briefed spot in the sky using electronic navigation, the coordinates I'd written on my kneeboard pad during our briefing and which I don't need to consult, since the act of writing was enough to plug them into my memory. Now the challenge is to separate the dim lights of the skipper's circling airplane from a background of a billion stars that on this clear night all appear to be white airplane tail-lights.

A rendezvous is a tricky maneuver in daylight and much thornier at night. The concept is to fly a tighter arc inside the standard-rate circle that the skipper is flying. Done correctly, my path will intersect with his arc, and my aircraft will slip under his and fall into formation on his right wing. My airmanship is on display for my commanding officer. This circling, one airplane inside the locus of the other, can take time. I join up before the skipper makes a full circuit. Good.

My heartbeat doesn't settle much, because now we are flying in darkness toward the enemy's coastline, in this case a beach not far south of Than Hoa. Radar could come into play here. Properly adjusted—and if the radar was one that happened to work decently—a glowing green outline on my small screen would match the shape of coastline depicted on a scrap of a sectional chart clipped on my kneeboard. But on this night I don't mess with my radar at all, since the skipper is leading. I concentrate on flying smoothly on his wing.

Crossing the beach, Skipper Engel calls for us to douse our exterior lights. If left on, lights make attractive targets. Radar signals can also be tracked. He calls feet-dry to Red Crown, and I'm sure he shut down his radar. As wingman, I reduce speed enough to slide three miles directly behind. I'm flying in trail. "Magic two at base plus one," I transmit. I have confirmed I am flying 1,000 feet higher than his altitude.

This small separation—three miles and 1,000 feet higher—

vastly decreases our chance of a mid-air collision. I settle at our pre-briefed cruising airspeed. Using minimal radio transmissions, we fly through the darkness, matching turns, matching speeds.

As this blind follow-the-leader proceeds, we break our scans from instrument panels to squint outside into the blackness. The trick, I have been told, is to adjust the red glow of the instrument lights so dim that the gauges are barely visible, and this works if the canopy is clean and free of soot from Oriskany's oily stack gasses. Peering from our dim cockpits, the skipper and I have a chance to make out a few features on the ground. This night, as with all night road-recce missions, we search for trucks. Or a train, one with all its lights doused. But trucks and trains making a run for it are hard to detect, very hard.

Although the North Vietnamese were moving hundreds of thousands of tons of war materiel each night from ports in the North to support their war in the South, relatively few vehicles are destroyed. We rarely spot them, because, like our A-4s, they douse their lights. And they post lookouts, both in the beds of the lead trucks in convoys and along the route, to warn when jets are near. The lookouts hear us while we are miles away. And when we are heard, the trucks turn off the roads into camouflaged parking areas all along the route. They wait until we pass; we never delay them long, for we are covering some three miles every minute.

Every now and then, however, we are fortunate, we glimpse something, maybe a reflection, and we drop a flare, perhaps a string of two or three to keep us oriented in our bombing runs. The MK-24 parachute flare is an aluminum tube several feet long weighing almost thirty pounds. It free-falls ten seconds after it is released, and then a parachute deploys. Eight or ten seconds after this, the flare ignites. A compressed powder of magnesium and sodium flashes, then burns steadily with an incredibly intense white flame. Two-million candle-power of light, a bright cone, blooms. Thick brown smoke billows up from the flare to fill the parachute above it with hot gasses. Then something amazing: the darn thing appears to stop falling. It hangs there, suspended, swinging gently, buoyed by the rising gasses. Beneath it the shimmering bright cone dances over the packed red earth that the Vietnamese call a highway.

Not this night with the skipper, but on other nights, we do spot trucks, motionless, the drivers long gone to take cover in one of the millions of man-size foxholes peppering Vietnam. When we do have this luck, we circle, calling our positions to each other to ensure we don't collide as we climb to a roll-in altitude. At 9,000 or so feet, one of us will roll in, and in that inky blackness we hurtle toward earth. In the pitch black, this feels like a vertical dive. Any dive-bombing run is tricky, but at night it is particularly dangerous, for there is no horizon for reference. Only instruments tell you where your airplane is headed. There are no visual clues of your position above that hard earth. None.

But this is my first night mission, and the skipper and I take turns dropping flares at various spots along the road. We see nothing. We finish this road-recce search down the packed red earth of Highway 1A. At our alternate target, a road intersection, we take turns dropping our bombs under the light of our remaining flares. We crater the intersection. Which means that to fill in the swimming-pool size pits our bombs are blasting, the Vietnamese will have to assign workers.

They will swarm the task and toil through the night. By morning, the craters will be smoothed over. But we will have done something, some little thing to slow the transshipment of supplies to the Viet Minh forces fighting us in the South. We have blocked, for a few hours, an intersection. And we have caused them to assign hundreds of workers to the task.

We are done and the skipper calls Red Crown and declares us feet wet. I have almost completed a night combat mission. Almost. For me, the most stressful part of the flight is still ahead—a radar-guided approach to the ship and a night carrier landing.

The angle-of-attack indicator, a vital instrument, is on a readout placed above the glareshield on the A-4. I use it and all my previous training and I trap aboard on my first pass. I am pleased with my airmanship.

But the following day there came a demonstration of how, with great skill, a night carrier landing could be accomplished without that vital angle-of-attack indicator. Lt. Cmdr. Dick Perry had been on a twilight raid against a SAM site near the Than Hoa Bridge.

This was an extremely dangerous area. The Navy and Air Force had expended hundreds of tons of ordnance, along with way too many good pilots, trying to drop the Than Hoa Bridge. It therefore was extremely well defended; 37-, 57- and 85-mm guns as well as SAM sites ringed it. In a single six-month-period the previous year, nineteen pilots had been shot down around Than Hoa. The Vietnamese referred to the bridge as the Dragon's Jaw. We did too, and Tom Lemay also claimed it was the hinge-pin of the earth, saying that if we ever did drop the damn thing, the world would part right there at the Song Ma River—split wide open.

So the evening Dick Perry flew there, one of the 37-mm guns blasted away the nose of his aircraft and put shrapnel into his boot, injuring his foot. The hit wiped out all his navigation gear, and it also took away his radio and that angle-of-attack indicator. To make it worse, his airspeed gauge, a back-up to his angle-of-attack indicator, was unreliable.

Separated from his wingman, Dick Perry made his way to Yankee Station—a navigational feat—and he found Constellation. He brought his bird aboard in the manner the early carrier aviators did—by the seat of his pants, which is to say by simply *feeling* how fast his aircraft was flying.

When I briefed for my own hop that night, I knew only that Dick Perry was missing. Word had not reached Oriskany of his successful landing aboard another carrier. The next morning, I recall this vividly, Skipper Engel was ecstatic.

"You've got to know how much skill that takes," he said to me. "I am so proud of Dick."

Now I had a new goal. I'd strive to become an aviator with Dick's skills. There was work ahead.

# PART III

# VINH

La guerre n'est pas une aventure. La guerre est une maladie. Comme le typhus.

(War is not an adventure. It is a disease. It is like typhus.)"

—*Antoine de Saint Exupery*
*Flight to Arras*

The author shot this photo while awaiting his turn to refuel in the air. They are returning from a bombing mission near Vinh, the city in North Vietnam claiming Ho Chi Minh's birth.

## CHAPTER EIGHT

# *Mortality*

The ready-room was clearing after the evening movie, and Tom Lemay was headed for the back door. I caught up with him; I had a question. "I'm going to Phu Ly tomorrow, first strike," I said. Tom stopped and waited for me to go on. "In the morning," I added. I was stalling before getting to my question, a delicate one. He looked at me, waiting.

"Think we'll lose anyone?" I asked.

I was scheduled on the wing of Skipper Engel, who would be leading a force of over thirty airplanes to multiple targets at Phu Ly. It would be my first alpha strike (my squadron spelled it alfa in official documents—as in Alfa Romeo—while most other squadrons spelled it as alpha), my first raid to a major target on the wish-list of targets prepared by the Joint Chiefs of Staff. The targets at Phu Ly represented a strike okayed at the highest echelons in Washington, D.C

Lemay, a skillful lieutenant who by this time was nearing his hundredth combat mission—many of them alpha strikes—thought for a moment, and then without emotion he answered, "Maybe one.

Or two." Tom Lemay was not big on conversation. He turned and continued toward his stateroom.

In my moldy rack that night I had trouble falling asleep. I was trying to comprehend what it would mean if one, maybe two of us were shot down. I thought about how easily it could be me, a nugget must-pump.

I'd never devoted any serious consideration to death, my own death, until then. After all, I was, invincible, wasn't I?

What might the end be like? Would I, in a flash, find myself in heaven? Or, as the nuns had explained, first do a stint in purgatory to cool my heels for a time? Or would it be—poof—nothing. Nada. Nevermore?

The odor of my dank mattress seemed to intensify. I thought more about what might become of my soul if I were shot down over Phu Ly. Perhaps it is a quick trip from this world to a paradise, and that would be nice. But purgatory? I didn't buy the idea the first time it was pitched to me, in kindergarten of all places. And hell: what about that?

Hell: that got me working on what I could recall of the Fifth Commandment—Protestants call it the Sixth—the one about Shalt Not Kill. I tried to remember the lesson on that short commandment from my Catechism training, and I couldn't find any wiggle room, any interpretation that cut fine distinctions between methods of killing. Would there be a difference if I took a life with, say, a knife, or if I did it with a jagged bomb shard?

If I had visited a chaplain on the ship, or discussed this with Dick Hartman, one or the other might have clarified it for me. I know now that The King James Version translates the ancient texts loosely, using the word *kill* in the Commandment, instead of the original word *murder*.

"Well, you see," a chaplain or a rabbi might have explained for me, "you are only prohibited from *murdering*. While *killing*—such as in this war, my son—why, that's allowed. Semantics, you see, a small difference in translation of early Hebrew, between the words *harag* and *ratzah*: killing versus murder."

But I doubt that would have made me feel better as I tossed about in my rack that night before the Phu Ly strike. By then I was wavering on what the Catechism-nuns termed "true faith." But I did say a preemptive prayer. Whether the next day I committed either *harag* or *ratzah*—well, I'd covered my bases.

I can call up the odor of the moldering mattress and the clammy feel of my moist sheets, and the uneasiness of that night creeps back to grip me. All these decades later, it's still so close at hand.

I shifted positions, rolling from one side to another, and eventually I drifted off to a disturbed sleep, having come to no understanding whatsoever of death or hereafter. Which is where I remain today.

Along the Day River at the edge of Phu Ly, a town with a rail line, sidings and bridges, there is a string of buildings suspected to be transshipment warehouses. A square building with a metal roof is my assigned aim-point. I am number four in the division this morning, flying on John Davis's wing in this big strike force.

I fire off the port cat moments after John has shot off the starboard side. I catch him quickly on the climb-out, and our Magicstone division, four of us, rendezvous into a unit quickly, and then we climb higher and join the larger force circling above Oriskany. I have never been in formation with so many; it is thrilling to feel this power spread across the morning sky. We fly northwest from Yankee Station, settling into our slots, and then as we near the coastline we pick up speed. We cross the coastline south of The Hourglass, the easily distinguished feature formed by two large rivers meandering down the flat valley, and then we are near Nam Dinh, picking up light flak, all of it 37-mm. The flak abruptly disappears as we continue up a quiet green valley with karst ridges off our starboard wings. The flak has quit, but I don't breathe any easier. I feel my heart pounding, I work to control my breathing, and I am thankful I am not using my radio—knowing how dry my voice would sound.

Our strike force spreads further out as we turn and cross the karst ridge. Two divisions of VA-163 Old Salts break away and turn slightly more northward toward their target, a bridge. Flak is around us again—very heavy now, both 37- and the heavy, black popcorn shapes of 57-mm. Phu Ly is ahead. "Balloons," someone transmits.

And, yes, balloons—they appear to be repurposed weather balloons, big and dusty-blue—and they are tethered on long lines over the little city. Amazing. Balloons: a tactic with roots in air-defense reaching back to trench warfare, back to the First World War. No one has seen any in this war until this morning.

They float stable, their cables straight up and down and taut in the still morning air. They all seem to be at 3,000 feet, which happens to be the bottom of our pull-out altitude on a dive-bombing run. Are they tethered on steel cables, I wonder, intended to cut into the flesh of my airplane? Or are there little bomb packets tucked beneath each balloon, rigged to explode should I snag an anchoring line? Who knows? But it is a crystalline day with visibility of some seventy miles, so there will be no problem avoiding them; they accomplish nothing. The Vietnamese must agree, for guys on subsequent raids will not see dusty-blue balloons. We are nearing the target, and I feel well-prepared.

Before we manned aircraft this morning, John pulled me aside. "You'll be rolling in last," he said, "and you'll be steep. Pickle at 6,000." He handed me an eight-by-ten glossy reconnaissance photo, leaned over my shoulder and placed his finger under a little building fronting the river.

"That's your aim point," he said. "That building."

Now, an hour later with the balloons below and 37- and 57-mm shit blossoming around us, our targets along the Day River sit exactly as John showed me in the glossy. I pitch up for a little more separation, then roll in right behind him. The roof of the square building John fingered appears exactly as in the recon photo. Easy to pick out, and I acquire it in my bombsight and my dive indeed is steep, very steep, and the pipper makes its way to the building as the little hand on the altimeter touches the six and the big hand sweeps the zero—precisely at 6K—and I squeeze the pickle. Then I'm pulling up and off target, smashing Gs onto my aircraft, no balloons obscure my path and my g-suit is inflated hard as a football as the Gs pile on. My bird's nose comes through the horizon and I ease Gs, slam over into a steep left bank, which will take me back toward the karst, and then get Gs back on, turning hard to thwart any gunners tracking my path. Over my shoulder I crane to see the warehouses or storage sheds or whatever they are, disintegrate as our bombs rippled through the line of buildings. Excellent hits. Our division has done its job. Better than that, I hear no one calling that they have been hit. We lose no one.

In coming years, I'll think about those buildings, trusting they were empty that morning, hoping the workers heeded air-raid warnings and scurried to safe cover. I'll think about the little buildings along the river, hoping...hoping that I made it through the war without taking a life.

Hoping is one thing. Knowing is something else.

In December, a couple months after this strike, New York Times Journalist Harrison Salisbury—with the permission of our government and a visa from the North Vietnamese—visited North Vietnam. As part of his tour the Vietnamese took him to Phu Ly. It was very close to Christmas Day when he visited the town along the Day River. The Vietnamese, of course, played down any military significance of the bombed devastation he was shown. In Nam Dinh, for example, he was told the entire town was devoted to textile production, omitting information about the petroleum storage and rail yards that had been heavily bombed targets.

When they escorted Mr. Salisbury to Phu Ly, he was shown the remains of buildings along the river, the ones we obliterated. At Phu Ly, there had been forty fatalities, the Vietnamese claimed. Not long after that, another foreign journalist was taken to the site and was told that one of the buildings had been a button factory. I read that second story in one of the picture-news periodicals—Look Magazine, perhaps. I went over and over the piece, studying the accompanying photos.

A button factory.

There are topics we veterans don't visit much. The taking of lives: that's one I avoid.

## CHAPTER NINE

# *Blame Robert*

This must-pump thing was going to work out. I flew another dozen missions and began feeling more confident and part of the squadron. One morning Skipper Engel came into the ready-room—animated. In fact, in my month with the squadron, I'd never seen our squadron commander so excited. "Get up on deck. Belly got his MiG!"

A handful of us followed the skipper through passageways, as he walked briskly, taking long strides, and then we followed up the escalator (the only one on the ship; it carries pilots to the flight deck), taking two steps at a time. We gathered in a small group near the island.

Belly was Cmdr. Dick Bellinger, skipper of VF-162, one of Oriskany's two F-8 squadrons. Back in July, he had experienced a bad day, an abysmal one, on a raid not too far southeast of Hanoi. At the target, a MiG-17 got the better of Belly in a dogfight. Cannon fire had ripped into his Crusader's wing and tail. He lost both hydraulic systems, yet he managed to break off the fight and keep his airplane in the air. His Crusader shook violently. With no chance of bringing the ravaged bird aboard a carrier, he was vectored toward the nearest airfield, a Marine base not far south of the DMZ. With his hydraulics gone, he was unable to deploy his refueling probe, so he would have to make it with his remaining fuel.

He calculated there was enough, even after having burned so much in aerial combat with that MiG. But his battle-damaged airplane ate fuel at a rate greater than expected, and his fighter ran out sixteen miles short of Da Nang. "I'm going to jump," he radioed to his wingman. "See you later."

A rescue helicopter plucked him from the water. That he had been bagged by a MiG—one he lured into the fight—grated at Belly. He actively looked to even the score.

Now, on October 9, the score was settled. It's traditional for pilots, after a successful kill, to roar into the break and do a victory roll. So, we were on deck, a nice crowd of us, ready for the show. Belly and his wingman came streaking in from the stern, so low they were below the flight deck, and then they pulled up hard. As they passed the bow they climbed steeply in tight formation. Belly whipped his F-8 into his victory-roll. Nice. And once he was on deck and climbed down from his bird, his grin was infectious. I felt part of a special brotherhood.

I flew a mission that day, another the next, the tenth, and then a night-mission on the eleventh. On the twelfth the ship was operating on the noon to midnight schedule, and I was scheduled for two hops, a day-mission and another on the final night-launch. I flew the day mission with the skipper.

For the night go, I saw on the schedule that Frank Elkins was also flying. Four Ghostriders were to be in the air on the 2215-2345 go. I was to fly on the wing of Dick Hartman, my first time to team with him.

The other section was comprised of Chuck Nelson on Frank's wing. I may have briefly thought about asking to swap places with Chuck, so I could go up with the guy I considered the most shit-hot aviator in the squadron. But I understood that you didn't question the flight schedule, which was carefully put together. Especially if you were a very green ensign. So I said nothing.

The duty officer called. I was resting in the bunkroom and summoned to the one phone; I was to brief now. Early, I was to learn, because Robert McNamara, Secretary of Defense, and General Earle "Bus" Wheeler, Chairman of the Joint Chiefs of Staff, along with their entourage, were aboard. McNamara wanted to sit through an Air Wing briefing, but he also wanted to retire about the time it had been scheduled to begin. So we filed into the briefing space more than an hour ahead of time. A gaggle of television people from ABC News, along with McNamara, General Wheeler and several admirals were already in the room. Cameras, boom microphones, an array of klieg lights and the large assemblage of bigwigs, crowded the room. It was hot and excessively bright. I took a folding chair next to Frank.

Cameras rolled as we were briefed. We learned which portions of road each of the various sections of attack bombers was expected to patrol in the darkness, and following the target overview briefing, a meteorologist stepped onto the platform. I watched as Frank carefully drew a little mark on a prominent blank area of his kneeboard-pad, an arrow pointing southeast with a single tail-feather—the familiar symbol meteorologists use to indicate wind direction and strength.

Then rather abruptly we were dismissed. The klieg lights dimmed and cooled. McNamara huddled with the air-wing's intelligence guys for a few questions. The room emptied.

We four Ghostriders returned to our ready-room. A big intercom box, the 1-MC, was mounted above the duty officer's desk near the door. Frank used it to call air-wing intelligence.

"When do we get the rest of our brief?"

"That's it," a voice in the squawk-box said.

Frank shifted to a more aggressive tone.

"What are you saying? We don't get the order-of-battle?"

"Not tonight."

Now he was irritated. He wanted to know why.

This portion of the briefing, the voice explained, had been omitted because some of the information was classified. The television crew didn't have security clearances, the voice said. It couldn't be delivered with them in the room.

Frank asked if we would now go back to resume the briefing once the room cleared.

"No. That's it."

Frank was now pissed. "Why!"

The voice explained that Secretary McNamara might misinterpret a briefing without him. He might see it as an indication something had been held back.

I recall this exchange, because it was an important element in my education—my on-the-job training as a combat attack pilot. Until then, it hadn't occurred to me that the briefing had been cut. I was still so new that I hadn't missed the order-of-battle portion. Frank reminded me that order-of-battle—the part I hadn't even noticed was skipped—is where we learn about defenses. Where guns are located, where the Vietnamese have set up a new SAM site and how active all these defenses have been during the day.

Dick and I had been assigned a section of Route 1A, the primary Vietnamese highway running north to south. We'd be about five miles inland from the coast and some thirty miles north of the portion of this same highway assigned to Frank and Chuck. Dick and I finished our brief, so, with plenty of time before launch, I went to Frank. I wanted to know about that wind arrow.

"Winds-over-target, right?" Frank said. "He gave us winds at several altitudes, but I'm most interested in winds at six. You should be, too."

He waited for me to ask why.

"Six thousand is bomb-release altitude. That's the wind affecting bombing accuracy," he said. "This arrow points where the wind will want to drift my bombs."

He explained that with a glance at his instrument panel to confirm his roll-in heading and a peek at his kneeboard, he would visualize how the wind would drift his bombs after they left his aircraft. No mental math involved. The little tail feather indicated wind strength—how much aiming correction he should make.

I drew a symbol like Frank's onto my own kneeboard pad.

"The wind-arrow trick. All graphically displayed," Frank said.

From that night on, I began using wind-symbols instead of writing down the numbers—220-degrees at five knots and so forth. Within a few days I was placing bombs where I expected them to hit. The water-buffalos were fortunate I hadn't learned this earlier.

Dick and I were in the looking, not the bombing, portion of our road-recce along 1A. There was no moon and few stars. So far, we had seen nothing along the faint roadway below. Chuck Nelson came up on our frequency.

"Ah, Magic Three," he said to Dick, "have you heard from Magicstone One?"

"Negative," Dick answered.

Chuck explained he had lost contact with his leader. He would continue searching, he said, and he left our frequency.

Back at the ship we learned that as they crossed the beach not far above Cap Falaise, Frank had checked in. "Magic 411, feet dry with two."

They hadn't been over Vietnam very long when Frank called Chuck to warn of flak. Chuck didn't see any shooting, but he did see a SAM. And at that moment, Frank called again.

"That looks like a missile."

"Roger. It is. Missile away!" Chuck replied as he threw his aircraft into a hard, descending spiral.

The SAM appeared to be coming from around Vinh. It at first seemed to be tracking Chuck's airplane. But then it cut behind his seven-o'clock position, went down and exploded at low altitude. Chuck had spiraled from about 7,500 feet to 1,000 in his evasive maneuver. When he could not raise Frank, Chuck flew to a spot over the water where they were to rendezvous in the event either had a radio failure. He turned on his exterior lights and a strobe on his A-4. But Frank didn't join up, nor did he answer radio calls. Chuck flew back to where the missile had impacted. He searched but found no fire on the ground, no indication an aircraft had gone down.

Chuck Nelson navigated back to the ship alone, made his approach alone, walked alone in the blood-red illumination of the flight-deck to the island. He was alone making his way through the red to the A.I. spaces, where he debriefed and told the intelligence guys what he knew. Which of course was only that a SAM came out of the ink-black night and surprised Frank and him. The intelligence officers, of course, understood that it was fired from a site known to be there. It was a SAM-site Frank and Chuck would have learned about had our order-of-battle briefing not been cut.

The shoot-down of Frank C. Elkins is in some places recorded as 13 October, 1966, which isn't correct. We launched at 2215 the twelfth, and most missions were under two hours. He went down early in the mission, so it was still the twelfth when that missile lit up the blackness. A small fact, and it doesn't matter. One that does is that Frank's remains came home twenty-four years later. He is buried at the National Cemetery at Wilmington, NC, not far from where he grew up.

## CHAPTER TEN

# *Vinh*

Phu Ly was well defended, but Vinh was a place that—well, to say it frightened me isn't quite right. I respected it. In the way heavyweight boxers of the time regarded Muhammed Ali.

It's a small city, Vinh, tucked inland ten miles from the coast and 190 miles south of Hanoi. I didn't know at the time that Ho Chi Minh had been born in a hamlet near there, or that Vinh stretched the truth a tad to claim him as a native son. Every pilot had a personal ranking of scary places, and near the top of mine was Vinh. Hanoi and Hai Phong were at the pinnacle, as they were with almost everyone engaged in McNamara's bombing campaign. Than Hoa—more accurately a bridge spanning the Song Ma a few miles north of Than Hoa—was up near the very top. As were Cam Pha and Nam Dinh. But for me, later, after I had come close to being bagged there, Vinh would trigger a fluttering in my stomach—simply a mention of it.

It wasn't my first mission at Vinh that scared me. That one was a piece of cake. I was on Skipper Engel's wing—only him and me—not a big raid at all. He carefully briefed me that September morning, going over several eight-by-ten reconnaissance glossies covering a large rectangle of land, maybe ten or twenty acres, all rubble. It had been hit hard in the spring and summer. What I was looking at was formerly a large petroleum refinery with oil storage tanks. Ghostriders and Saints had flown alpha strike after alpha strike against the refinery, sending smoke and fireballs hundreds of feet into the air, eventually reducing it to this field of powdery white debris in the photos.

"We have intelligence there's a tank they're using. Still has fuel in it," Skipper Engel explained. He pointed to what looked like a portion of what once was an oil storage tank. A curved steel section, mostly buried. "They think this might be it. Let's go take it away from them this morning."

Only a single run each, he instructed, a few seconds apart and from different angles. We were to set up our intervalometers to drop our six bombs in a stick—that is a line of bombs spaced not far apart. He gave me the settings. Coming in at forty-five-degree angles, our lines of carefully spaced bombs would cross. In the center of an X, if we both dropped accurately, we'd obliterate this thing that might be a useable tank.

"Don't forget to jink. Going in and off target," he reminded me. "Vinh can be hot." And he would know, having been there on a number of those earlier strikes. But as it went, we picked up very little flak. In and out, and the mission was done.

I was disappointed, because as I looked back over my shoulder, I saw my stick march through the line of smoke from the skipper's bombs, forming a nice X of destruction. But no secondary explosions. We had rearranged the debris in that gray field, but we'd not found a vital storage tank of fuel.

I flew near Vinh a number of other times on road recce missions, but always gave it wide berth.

The mission that nearly got me came in late October. For an alpha-strike against Vinh's rebuilt railroad yards, I was scheduled on the wing of our air wing commander, CAG Rod Carter. The rail yards were a marshalling point for troops and supplies headed for the Mu Guia Pass—gateway to the Ho Chi Minh Trails. CAG Carter and I were assigned flak-suppression on a gun emplacement not far west of the yards. In reality, flak suppression amounts to a duel with gunners. CAG and I were to keep the anti-aircraft gunners distracted, keep their heads down and their guns silenced, while bombers in the strike force rolled in on the rail yards.

As briefed, CAG Carter and I moved out ahead of the strike-force as we crossed the coastline. From the air, the layout of our assigned gun emplacement—a classic ring of revetments, each encircling one of the anti-aircraft guns—looked precisely as in the photo he and I studied during our briefing. When we arrived, five or six guns were winking tiny white flashes, like Christmas lights seen from a great distance. CAG rolled in. I held off a second or two, as John Davis had coached me, to get closer for a steeper run.

I plunged down, and I could see deadly 37-mm projectiles—five or maybe more—coming up directly at me from the winking flashes. I had heard of this, that you can see projectiles coming head-on because there is no relative motion, but I'd never seen it until now. A cluster of tiny black dots, wavering in space, growing and widening, then flashing past. The gunners that day could not have aimed more perfectly. Firing clips of five-rounds each, one clip after another, the two men aiming the gun fired straight up my dive path. Only minuscule flexing of the barrels, little twitches induced by vibrations from previous shots, sent the perfectly aimed projectiles on slightly errant courses. If a single one had found my cockpit, guys would have said, "Flew into the ground." Just as Confer's squadron-mate had described Mike's death to me that afternoon in the Cubi O'Club.

Mike Mullane, on the next cruise, would memorably describe the phenomenon. He came into the ready-room one afternoon, flushed and excited, exclaiming he had been "the centerpiece in a bouquet of flak."

The vision, those black dots racing straight toward me, wouldn't leave. I kept seeing this moment, the explosive projectiles coming at me, as I'd try to drift off to sleep. And I would recognize the effect years later as I sat in the Seattle Cinerama Theater watching the first Star Wars movie. In the windscreen of the Millennium Falcon, as it made its hyperspeed jump to lightspeed, the big screen seemed to come at me like the lethal projectiles over Vinh. In the darkness, sitting with my wife and our little daughter, my heart-rate bumped up at the familiar effect.

CAG's bombs fell a little short of the ring of guns. The stick I dropped marched across its revetments, hushing them. When we debriefed back at the ship, he complimented my accuracy. Later, Skipper Engel told me CAG Carter had sought him out and praised my bombing. This was an example of leadership I'd carry into my business career: praise publicly, scold in private.

## CHAPTER ELEVEN

# *White Canvas Casing*

T hat flak-suppression mission on the alpha strike with CAG Carter was my thirty-third. I flew another that day. (McNamara, who micro-managed his air-war from Washington, D.C., had dictated pilots were to average one-and-a-half sorties per day. To accomplish this, we'd fly one mission, then the next day, two.)

The day following the mission with CAG, I was scheduled for one hop, a night road recce, which I flew with Skipper Engel. It went fine, too. The next morning, terrible monsoon weather blanketed North Vietnam and the Tonkin Gulf, curtailing flight operations.

We hadn't flown for three days, and now it was October 26, early morning. The weather was clearing.

I was suited up for a mission with Skipper Engel, waiting in the ready-room to head down the passageway for the 0730 brieing. At 0721, nine minutes short, the squawk-box came alive. Instead of a call to head to the briefing room, however, a young sailor said,

"This is a drill. Fire, fire, fire . . ." He stopped and began again with more urgency.

"This is no drill, this is NO drill. Fire, fire in the hangar bay."

I glanced around to the other guys in the room expecting action. No one moved. "Fires happen all the time," someone explained. "Generators overheat, bearings smoke when they lose lubrication, wires in electrical equipment short and burn. Shit like that."

A damage-control team would quickly have it under control, it was explained, and soon a call would come to say normal activities should resume. I continued sipping my coffee.

Smoke began filtering into the ready-room through a vent, and someone grabbed a chart and taped it over the grate. That worked for a few minutes, but then smoke began curling up from under the door. No one seemed alarmed, so I settled into my comfortable ready-room seat. The smoke intensified. Someone suggested we go up to the flight-deck, where the air would be clean, and this seemed a good idea. When the ready-room door was opened, though, we confronted a solid wall of churning brown smoke. The door was slammed shut.

Dick Perry said he knew a quick route out the back door of the ready-room that would take us up to a sponson. But the back door also opened onto a wall of smoke, and smoke now gushed into the ready-room. We began to cough.

"Get in a line. Everyone grab the belt of the guy ahead," Dick commanded.

He opened the door again and headed into the thick brown smoke. I was about two thirds back in a line of a dozen or so guys. The smoke was heavy; visibility was a foot or two, no more. I could see only the back of the guy ahead of me. We all stooped lower, where there was marginally less smoke. I held my breath. We moved along swiftly, hunched over and hanging on to the belt ahead. Then we stopped.

"The hatch. Dogged down!" Dick yelled.

The guy ahead of me turned around and turned me. The line had reversed. I grabbed a new belt, and we rapidly backtracked—

which took us aft, down a long passageway. Knee-knockers were encountered at the expected intervals, and no one tripped over one. Someone began coughing, and I, too, could no longer hold my breath. "Get down. Near deck. Air's better," a voice commanded through coughs. I crouched very low, duck-walking.

A deep gulp of oily smoke set me coughing and gasping. I felt vulnerable, suddenly aware this might be a way to die. We were all coughing now, but our duck-walking conga-line kept going. The air cleared the further aft we went. Until we could see again, then breathe again.

We stood, relaxed our grips on the belts ahead. Then we were up a ladder, onto the flight-deck, taking in good air. But Dick wasn't with us. Dick Perry had fallen away from our line.

We organized into a search party and headed toward the bow, which was crisscrossed with firehoses. We were looking for a source of OBA's, the oxygen-breathing-apparatus we'd need to go back to rescue Dick. And then, close to the bow, we found another group organizing a search for missing men. Heading up this group was Dick Perry.

He explained that he called out that the hatch was dogged by way of giving us information, and then he simply un-dogged it. He stepped into fresh air on the sponson, only to discover he was alone. He imagined that the dozen men he had been leading had all succumbed to the smoke. Our two groups huddled and briefly talked about what we had been through.

We understood now that this was a serious fire. From the port side of Oriskany, a column of sooty brown smoke billowed hundreds of feet into the sky. The ship was dead in the water and listing. Alongside, a destroyer had come in close. Her crew, manning fire-hoses, was shooting high-pressure streams of water into our hangar-deck. Oriskany's damage-control crews charged forward, dragging fire-hoses, which all led down to the hangar-deck.

Four sailors on the corners of a stretcher came onto the flight deck and laid an officer down near the island. The man on the stretcher was partially dressed, wearing his khaki trousers and an unbuttoned blouse. He had no shoes or socks. He lay lifeless, with a very red face staring blankly at the sky. A corpsman put a stethoscope to his chest, then began doing CPR. A sailor came over and leaned in with a camera, snapping a photo. A chief petty officer was immediately on the sailor and snatched the camera, then flung it over the side. I began walking away as the chief lit into the kid. The corpsman behind them continued heavily pumping with both hands, his arms stiff, on the man's chest.

The scene was surreal, and I felt helpless.

A few yards away three men, young officers who obviously had escaped the inferno up forward, lay side-by-side on the rough surface of the flight-deck. I spoke with one, who delivered the first details of the explosions and fire raging up forward. I asked if he was hurt, and he answered, yes, pointing to his feet. Like the lifeless man, he had no shoes, and his soles were blistered and red. A corpsman spoke with him. The man came to a sitting position. The corpsman gave him an injection in the thigh, then cut open the officer's t-shirt. With a felt-tipped marker the corpsman, a kid maybe eighteen years old, wrote onto the man's pale chest the dosage of morphine he had injected, along with the time he injected it. The corpsman then moved on to administer aid to the other two.

I spoke with others on the flight deck, and we exchanged what little we had learned of the fire. It had started near the forward elevator and had burned a helicopter and an A-4, maybe more airplanes. Fuel had spilled and spread the blaze. And it was still burning. The ship was now listing heavily to starboard.

I had been through fire-fighting training in boot camp, and again while in pre-flight training eighteen months later. Maybe I could be useful. I wandered the deck looking for an OBA unit, asking sailors who had come up from the hangar deck if they knew where one could be found. A sailor handed me one, but it was fully expended and inoperative. I continued the search. Three enlisted men manned the corners of a stretcher. I asked if they needed a fourth. They did, and they had an extra OBA. This one worked. We went down to Hangar Bay One, which appeared as if it had burned a long time earlier, as if this were some ancient war scene. An A-4, partially burned, dripped water and foam. The canopy was shattered. Heat had fired the ejection seat's rocket-charge. The nose was partially burned away.

On the starboard side, near the forward elevator pit, the skeletal remains of a Kaman helicopter dripped water. Sloshing through an inch or two of water were sailors in pairs and small groups. Some were manning hoses, but most were wheeling bombs to the portals. Bombs, still so hot they steamed, water played on them until it was their turn, and then they were heaved over the side. Other sailors were pushing aircraft back to the Number Two Elevator to clear them from the hangar deck. Tangles of fire-hoses, rock-hard with water pressure, had been dragged into the two passageways leading to officers' country.

The fire started, I'd learn later, when an untrained sailor tossed a hissing flare into a locker stacked with flares. After ten seconds, its parachute popped free and then the flare ignited, converting the flare-locker into a bomb.

The inferno sent fireballs hurtling through the forward part of the ship. Heat had cooked off the burned A-4's 20-mm cannon, and rounds had ricocheted around the hangar deck. Fire and smoke raced up both sides of the ship and into living spaces for officers— which included my bunkroom.

At the passageway on the port side of the Number One Elevator pit, the four of us, with our stretcher at an alarming angle, climbed steep stairs into dark officers' country.

We began feeling our way down the black passageway; I could hear my heavy breathing in the OBA. Electric power to this section of the ship had been cut; there were no lights, no ambient light. The further in we went, the blacker it became.

In total darkness we came upon a group of sailors carrying a stretcher going the other way. We exchanged our empty litter for theirs, which was weighted with an unconscious man, and we began working our way back toward light. As we negotiated the dark ladder, we tried to keep the stretcher level, but the man's weight shifted. His foot, which dangled over a corner, pressed against my wrist. It was wet, oozing from his burns. When we emerged onto the dim light of the hangar deck, we were directed to carry him aft toward the middle of hangar-bay two. He was wearing only his skivvy shorts. I recognized him: Pinky. I knew him only by his nickname. And I saw then that some of his skin had sloughed from his foot onto my hand.

We carried Pinky to the officers' mess, the spacious wardroom was now serving as a triage station for sick bay. It was well lit and mercifully clear of smoke. Chuck Nelson was there, and he began administering mouth-to-mouth to Pinky. Chuck would tell me later that when he grasped Pinky's hand, the skin slid off. Pinky could not be saved.

It took more than three hours to extinguish the last of Oriskany's fires, and far longer to locate and rescue some of the survivors. Minutes after the fire started, John Davis realized this was serious, and he left his stateroom. His roomie, Bill Johnson, was behind him, but turned back to finish dressing. Those few seconds cost Bill his life. John had felt his way through the dense smoke. He thought he knew a route out—a left, a few steps, a right, a few more steps...but he got lost. Then, at the moment the reality struck him he might not make it, a hand reached out.

"In here," a voice said. John was pulled into a stateroom.

It was the admiral. They hunkered down in that somewhat protected space, sealing off vents and the crack under the door to keep the smoke at bay as the fire raged. The admiral's telephone still worked, and they let damage-control folks know they were alive. Yet it would be hours before a rescue team could reach them.

Barry Wood and some of the other guys I lived with in the bunkroom had escaped by running forward and out through a space I didn't know existed, a place where the ship's anchor chains came into the ship, a chain locker in the forecastle. Those who went aft and attempted to go down ladders on either side of the Number One Elevator—the only way I knew—were found dead in bunches where they had been felled by the heat and smoke.

Hangar Bay One had been ravaged, the catapults were both ruined, warped by buckling plates, and the Number One Elevator was inoperable. Officers' country up forward was destroyed. As we steamed back to the Philippines, crews cleaned up much of the debris, tossing it into the South China Sea. They tore away burned insulation hanging in ragged shreds from the overhead. They hosed away soot. The hulk of the Kaman chopper, like bones, went over the side.

We docked at Subic Bay the morning of October 28, two days after the fire. Oriskany's colors were lowered to half-mast. A Marine Guard, rifles at present-arms, honored the flag-draped caskets as they were carried down onto the dock. Two chaplains, the Catholic wearing vestments, stood side by side as the bodies were brought down in their metal boxes. I stood on the flight-deck that morning surveying the perfectly aligned rows on the wharf, an American flag covering each, the corners folded military-perfect.

Beneath four of those flags rested the bodies of fellow Ghostriders: Clyde R. Welch, our executive officer, a nice man known as a smooth and competent pilot; Dan Strong, our operations officer; Jim Brewer, a young lieutenant j.g. with an infectious smile; and Bill Johnson, who had bounced his tailhook off the water flying with Frank Elkins.

That first mission with Dan Strong seemed so recent. I had known him less than two months—from that first week of September, when we went after a small bridge, until October 26. His death, two weeks after Frank Elkins disappeared, hit me hard. Because his stateroom was adjacent to the flare locker, where the fire ignited, Dan was the first of the forty-four to perish in the unspeakable fire.

He had been asleep when his room spontaneously erupted in flames, ignited by the intense heat of hundreds of burning magnesium-packed flares roaring next to him. In seconds, his room transformed into a retort, like a steel crematorium oven. His ashes were found in a position that suggested he had felt the heat, sat up, and managed to swing his legs over the edge of his bunk before he succumbed. That quickly, death had come. Nothing remained intact in his stateroom except his wedding band and the cloisonné portion of one of his medals.

Under another of the flags rested the remains of Rod Carter, our air-wing commander—CAG—the good leader. Under other flags were the remains of guys I lived with in the junior-officers bunkroom. I felt detached, gazing down on the rows of flag-draped aluminum boxes. There were forty-three.

There was one other who had perished in the fire, but he was not under a flag on the wharf. The remains of Lt. Cmdr. Omar R. "Whitey" Ford remained aboard Oriskany. He would travel part way back to the States with us, for he had requested burial at sea.

This ancient mariner's ritual took place the fifth of November, a clear and bright day. We were in the Pacific, riding on deep, glassy water. Oriskany and her destroyer escorts slowed to steerage-way. Most of the ship's company and the entire air-wing, wearing service dress whites, were formed into ranks on the deck near the island.

Whitey's remains rested on a small platform on the number-two aircraft elevator opposite the island. He had been stitched into a white canvas shroud, over which was draped an American flag.

We were called to attention. A chaplain spoke. Marines fired a twenty-one-gun salute. Then, taps, the mournful twenty-four notes from a bugle that calls up tears. Always, for me, calls up tears. After that, six of Whitey's mates tilted the wooden platform. Lt. Cmdr. Omar R. "Whitey" Ford, inside that canvas, glided from beneath the flag, silently dropping to the deep and glass-blue water burbling alongside our ship, the one with call-sign Childplay. I did not hear the splash.

A vision of that ageless rite, the chaplain speaking, the slim white canvas casing quietly tilted off a platform...it is one of the most heartrending memories I carry.

CHAPTER TWELVE

# *Dick Hartman*

We returned to Lemoore, and the squadron was reconstituted with pilots to replace Frank Elkins and the four killed in the fire. The guys who had finished tours with our squadron departed, and their replacements arrived.

A new skipper joined us—Cmdr. Doug Mow—who in a few weeks would replace Cmdr. Engel. Our new operations officer arrived: Cmdr. Robert Arnold, a rare senior officer who was still unmarried.

The hail-and-farewell party for the guys leaving and the new arrivals was held at the Officers Club. We wore dress uniforms, because this was a traditionally rather formal affair. Nevertheless, Deny Weichman arrived with a buzzer in his right hand, and he zapped his fellow officers when they met his handshake. Corny, but that was Deny.

Skipper Engel made a short speech and welcomed his replacement and the other new officers to the squadron. And then Cmdr. Mow had a few words to say. After that it was all conviviality—a few drinks, followed by a nice dinner. A string quartet played softly while we dined.

I liked all the new junior officers. Mike Mullane and Larry Cunningham earned their commissions after completing college, so they now held the Lt. j.g. rank. They were new guys, but nevertheless senior to me. Same with the new intelligence officer, Jim Waldron, a guy with horn-rimmed glasses who appeared so young he was immediately nicknamed Young Dumb Kid—often shortened to YDK. Don Purdy and Roger Duter, both ensigns, were NAVCADs, which meant they were junior to Barry Wood and me. Barry immediately handed off the onerous task titled Coffee Mess Officer to Duter, which entailed collecting dues from fellow officers—all of whom felt they were far too busy to pay dues to the pesky ensign nailing them for three or four bucks.

Not long after he took over operations officer duties, Bob Arnold called me aside. "I've selected you to fly in my division," he said, and he told me I'd be on Dick Hartman's wing, while Barry Wood was to fly on his. "We're four bachelors. I'm calling us Hoser Flight."

I thought about this for a moment. I'd be Hoser Four. With Skipper Engel, I had been Magic Two. Sounded better.

Having flown on Dick's wing several times on the previous cruise, I knew him to be a smooth and competent aviator. But unlike Bud Edney, another lieutenant commander, a guy who would joke around with us, Dick was quiet and subdued. He was a man who stood quietly at the fringe of a gathering, speaking up only to answer a direct question or interject something profound, something maybe obvious but overlooked. For this, Dick Hartman was appreciated and welcomed in every group. He was the attentive listener, the guy with the quick mind who would rescue the discussion when the bull started slinging. When Dick spoke during a conversation, it quieted. Folks paid attention; he was that bright.

After we'd flown more at Lemoore, I knew Dick and I would gel into a competent section. Not flashy, but solid and good. Richard Danner Hartman was so steady and dependable that he'd been accepted—or perhaps recruited—into NASA's astronaut program. I once asked him why he didn't do it.

"I need this first," he answered.

By "need this," Dick meant combat. It was understood that battle-tested career officers—those who racked up their 200 missions, earned battle decorations and demonstrated leadership in stressful conditions—would move into the highest ranks. Dick intended to make the Navy his life's work.

Dick had moved steadily up the ladder and not missed any promotions. His career was on track, more than on track. After combat duty he'd reapply for the space-program, he told me. And certainly he looked the part with his salt-and-pepper crewcut hair, crystalline blue eyes and lithe, athletic frame. At five-nine he was not too tall; he'd fit comfortably into one of those tight space-capsules.

Dick's education pretty much assured he'd make a fine astronaut. He, along with Bud Edney, was a 1957 graduate of the Naval Academy. And a few months before joining our squadron, Dick had received a masters degree in aeronautical engineering from the Naval Postgraduate School at its beautiful Monterey campus.

The Navy preaches integrity and honor, insisting (or at least hoping) its officers incorporate these traits. The guy I am flying with is a model of those qualities. His influence begins to rub off.

My new section leader is a member of the Officers Christian Fellowship, he doesn't swear or go in for the heavy drinking some of us love so much. He likes sports cars, and he loves to fly near the edge of an airplane's performance envelope. He once gave me a ride in his Ford Thunderbird, a pea-green '57 with a porthole on either side of its removable top. On the padded dashboard he had mounted a silver Saint Christopher medal about the size of a quarter. I knew he wasn't a Roman Catholic, and I thought St. Christopher was reserved for the religion I'd drifted away from, but he liked it there.

Later I'd learn he carried one when he flew. There's a little pocket on the shoulder of our flight-suits mostly used by smokers for their cigarettes; it's also perfect for a religious medal.

By June of 1967, Dick Hartman has been my section leader for almost seven months. We keep tight and stable formations, communicate easily with hand-signals or the nod of a helmet. I am a steady wingman—working hard at that—so I enjoy flying with Dick. I trust him, trust my life to him.

I have also been selected to become our squadron's next Landing Safety Officer—our LSO. I am to train during the next cruise under Tom Lemay, our current LSO. And to prepare me for my apprenticeship, I've been sent to NAS Miramar at San Diego for a week of classroom training.

Then in mid-June, when we return aboard Oriskany, I'll join Tom at the aft end of the carrier—the LSO platform. From our little perch near the fantail, I'll learn from Tom and the other LSOs—always at least two, sometimes more—as they monitor each landing. From them I'll discover the right moment to deliver a simple command, for instance a call for "a little power," how a few words at the right moment can convert a dangerous one-wire landing into a safe three-wire trap. It will take hundreds of hours on the platform before I qualify as an LSO. But I'm proud, because this new duty signifies that I'm considered to be a skilled carrier pilot—or at least one with the ability to mature into one.

On a training flight, Dick and I flew from Lemoore to the bombing range at Fallon, Nevada. We checked in and circled the target, and in turn we each dropped eight practice bombs, toy-like twenty-five-pounders painted blue and armed with a shotgun shell. With puffs of smoke they marked our hits. An observer in a tower called each impact over the radio. I don't recall our scores that day, but I keenly remember the flight home.

Extraordinary. Dick veered from the direct southwest course to Lemoore and instead took us due west toward the Sierras. We hugged the terrain as it rose to become the east slope, and then we crested a ridge a little north of the Heavenly Valley Ski Area. Dick kept low coming down the west slope, making small adjustments to ensure he didn't overfly developed areas. Ahead lay the broad flat shield of Lake Tahoe. I slipped into a loose formation behind Dick and followed him down lower and lower until he was skimming feet above the cobalt-blue surface. Then, before we arrived at the western shore, he snapped up into a steep climb. Water sprayed like a race-boat's rooster-tail, a white streak on the lake where his A-4's exhaust blasted the water. Spectacular.

I followed, leaving a second white streak on the blue lake.

The remainder of the flight home that afternoon was equally glorious. It was the kind of aviation we envisioned when we began flying—low, at times the width of a wing above the trees, flat-hatting and fast. We dropped into canyons, rolling into steep banks to follow terrain. It was the winged magic that Saint-Exupery promised. We are solid together in the air.

Yet on the ground Dick and I go our separate ways. I to the bars and clubs, and Dick...I don't know. At a party, Bud Edney—we called him Budney—would hoist a few beers with junior officers, laugh with us over stupid jokes and at an appropriate moment propose a toast. Dick, though, would be nearby, enjoying the camaraderie, quietly.

That is Dick: educated, religious, competent. An aviator's aviator. I on the other hand am still somewhat untamed.

Dick had a career plan, a design for his life. I was not so sure. As a college dropout I could see only two paths. Fly a lot and make it to lieutenant commander—a career of twenty years—and that might be okay. A monthly retirement-check at age forty would be nice. And I could find another thing to do afterward.

Or the other choice would be airlines—to leave the Navy and sign on with, say, Pan Am. But the regimen of an airline company, coupled with thoughts of operating an airplane as part of a committee, left me lukewarm.

I carried an unsettledness that Dick and Budney and Skipper Engel probably never felt.

They knew where they were going, they enjoyed sharply focused goals. I was a NAVCAD, a rather typical NAVCAD, one with limited possibilities and a fuzzy vision of the future.

## CHAPTER THIRTEEN

# *Iwo Jima*

I'm still not senior enough to qualify for a berth in a stateroom. Once more, I'm in the J.O. Bunkroom, though I now merit a lower rack away from the door to the head. Don Purdy and Roger Duter—NAVCADS, of course—join me there.

Customarily, ships on the way to the Western Pacific—Westpac—enjoy a week in Hawaii as the carrier replenishes and the air wing does more training. But Oriskany's fire-damage repairs have forced her behind the Navy's schedule, so now to make up time, we'll have only twenty-four hours at Pearl Harbor. With only one day of liberty, five of us—Roger Duter, Jim Waldron, Don Purdy, Larry Cunningham and I—have vowed to make the most of each minute.

We snagged a taxi shortly after Oriskany tied up—it was well before noon—and headed for Honolulu. One of us saw a bar, it was open, so we dismissed the taxi, and inside, pitchers of beer were ordered. "Keep 'em coming, barkeep," Cunningham said, as the first two plunked onto our table.

Don Purdy knew a drinking game, and because Jim—Young Dumb Kid—had attended Catholic schools, Don said he'd help him become a cardinal. "It's easy, a few ritual steps," Don told YDK. Whenever he made an error in the ritual, however, Jim was obliged to down his glass and pour a fresh one. The more mistakes he made, the more beer he consumed, and the more often the mistakes piled up. Soon it was clear he was too tipsy to ever get it right. Great fun, we all thought, but now we had to take care of YDK.


In town, Cunningham rented a pink Jeep. We piled in and drove up the spine of Oahu, laughing. The little Jeep was overloaded with four and a drunk. It rained. It was beautiful.

We arrived back in Waikiki mid-afternoon. The bars fronting the beach were filled with pilots and sailors drinking and laughing. Somehow, by early evening, our group had dispersed, and I found myself carousing with a cluster of F-8 drivers. And they had found school teachers from Denver, young women enjoying a summer in Hawaii. The fighter jocks had been dancing with them, buying fancy cocktails. I danced with one, a cute girl who taught home economics. Then it was late. The F-8 drivers and I were walking the teachers to their apartment, when a pink Jeep came roaring down the street, only Cunningham in it. He threw it into a tight left turn and the Jeep went up onto two wheels, skidding toward a curb. Somehow, he caught it before it flipped. We all laughed.

In their apartment, tall bottles of beer appeared, 78-rpm records were stacked on a turntable, we danced some more. In the early morning hours, the girl from Denver and I nestled onto a couch, where we dozed until daylight seeped into the apartment. One of the fighter pilots was speaking. Loudly. Waking everyone.

"We're in deep shit," he barked. "Deep shit. Call a taxi."

And he was correct. Oriskany's lines were to be cast off at 0700, and it was at Pearl Harbor while we were in Honolulu—somewhere in Honolulu—we weren't sure where. "Missed ship's movement:" that's the offense, and it's a court martial for sure—not at all a good way to go off to war.

It seemed to take forever for the taxi to come. The Denver teacher and I exchanged mailing addresses. We promised to write. The F-8 drivers and I piled into the taxi, begging the driver to be fast, promising a huge tip. At Pearl Harbor we begged him to drive right out onto the pier. We threw money, big bills, into his lap. We ran.

The officer's brow had already been lifted; we couldn't go aboard there. Along the pier sailors were standing at the bollards, readying Oriskany's lines to be cast free. We ran aft, to the enlisted men's brow, which was about to be lifted. We were the last to board the ship.

While we were still in range of Hawaii, a supply plane came aboard with mail. In a letter from his wife, Don learned she was pregnant. "What have I done?" he kept saying. "I could die, and the world will have one more fatherless child."

Don had married not long after they began dating and not too many months before we left for Westpac. Like warriors before and since, he'd rushed into it.

"We'll make it; you're gonna make it," I assured him. Don wasn't so sure.

He came up with a couple of Nordic names for the baby. He put them in a letter to his wife, so she'd have them on hand in the event he didn't come back. If it is a boy, he will be Eric, he wrote, and if a daughter, she will be Kristine. In the ready-room he tested the names. Later in the cruise, when survival was a gamble, guys would tease him by referring to "Little Orphan Eric." Torturing one another: a splendid way to ease tension.

As we sailed west, Oriskany's captain wanted the air-wing exercised. Catapult launches, landing operations and the intricate, choreographed dance of men in colored jerseys on the flight-deck were the focus. Many of the enlisted guys in colored jerseys were still in their teens.

The colors signify the jobs the sailors and their officers have trained to do: ordnance men wear red; airplane handlers, blue;

green jerseys for catapult crewmen; fueling crew wear purple. Those in yellow are airplane directors, men whose hand signals we pilots must follow while taxiing. They all have important duties to hone. What we did in the air with the hour-and-a-half between launch and recovery was up to our division leaders. Sometimes we practiced bombing smoke flares on the water, or we strafed them. And sometimes we loitered around the ship, maybe looking for an unsuspecting F-8 to jump and lure into a mock dog-fight. Hassling, we called it.

One evening in the ready-room, Bob Arnold gathered Hoser Flight: his wingie Barry Wood, Dick and me. He was excited. The next morning, he told us, Oriskany would pass within 180 nautical miles of Iwo Jima. He calculated that from when we launched, it would be a little over a half-hour's flying time to the island. Time enough, he said, to make it there and back, with none to spare.

For such a tiny spot on earth, Iwo Jima carries a heavy legacy. History buffs know Iwo Jima was site of one of the bloodiest battles of World War II. Nearly 30,000 lives were sacrificed in thirty-six days of murderous fighting. Almost 7,000 were American Marines, while three times that number of Japanese fighters perished. Bob said he planned to ask the little airfield's tower to clear us for a single high-speed pass down the runway.

"We'll form a diamond. Tight, like the Blues," he said, referring to the minimum-clearance formations the Blue Angels maintained at air shows.

"Duthie, you're slot."

I had never flown slot—or any other position in a diamond formation, for that matter. Yet as number four, flying slot was my proper place.

"Tuck in directly behind me." He instructed. "Keep just aft of my tailpipe."

He glanced up to look at me.

"Don't get in my jet-wash. Touch it. Feel it with your vertical stabilizer."

As we finished, he said to me. "Don't get low." He smiled. "You'll know if you do." That last was a hint at how very low he planned to skim down the tiny island's runway.

The next day broke clear. We rendezvoused as we climbed to 34,000 feet. Far beneath us a scattering of puffy afternoon clouds left dark shadows on the ocean's metallic sheen. Soon the carrier was out of sight. We flew in a comfortable, loose formation. It allowed sightseeing, superb that afternoon. In every direction, nothing but silvery sea and tiny clouds, like scattered popcorn, far below. About halfway to the island, Bob reduced power and started a long, fuel-conserving descent.

Nearing Iwo Jima, Bob called us to pull in tight. As we descended through 3,000 feet, with the tiny island on our nose, Bob transmitted two words: "Diamond now." Barry and Dick nestled, overlapping Bob's wings with theirs to form a V, and I slipped under Bob's airplane. Gingerly, I eased forward and up until I, too, was in tight. We were picking up speed. In close formation you instinctively add or subtract power in concert with the lead. I felt the speed build. Bob steepened our dive toward the island—which I could not see. My view was restricted to almost straight up.

We crossed from water to land, where rising bubbles of heated tropical air, turbulence, pitched us around. It required powerful concentration to maintain position. And then in my peripheral vision, green foliage flashed past. Damn, we were scary low.

The runway was short and the end came up quickly. The Gs came on as Bob pulled his diamond up steeply. Then he rolled a full 360-degrees; Bob rolled the formation!

From the control tower, a young man's voice: "Thank you! One more pass, sir?"

Bob answered with a single word: "Sure."

We loosened up as he entered a gentle climbing turn to the left. I slid back to Dick's wing and got my first look at the island. So small: a tiny exclamation-point-shaped lump of green, with Mt. Suribachi, more a hill than a mountain, providing the dot. We climbed to 2,500 feet.

Bob called our attention to dark shapes visible under the clear water not too far off the long beach: sunken machinery.

This stretch of sand off our wing was the bloody landing beach, scene of the beginning of the huge battle that began February 19, 1945, more than twenty-two years before.

It took more than a month of fighting for the United States to wrest this island from the Japanese. By nightfall of the first day of battle, 2,250 Marines had been either killed or wounded. And the first to die never made it to the island. They were aboard blown-up and sinking landing craft, these dark shapes I saw beneath the surface of the clear water below us.

As we rounded the south end of the island, Bob gave the command, and we re-formed into a diamond. Again we roared down the runway for the entertainment of a few young men in the tower. Again Bob rolled the formation.

After the flight, we relaxed in the ready-room. It wasn't so much a debriefing as four guys savoring the details of an adventure. Other divisions also would make the round-trip to Iwo Jima that day, but Hoser Flight's four bachelors remained convinced ours had been the best.

Unlike the lumpy 1945 voyage for the Marines crammed aboard transport ships traveling toward Iwo Jima, our trip to combat was an easy one. Yes, we, too, were headed into battle, but we lounged in the ready-room on a ship that didn't roll or pitch very much, we watched recordings of stateside television shows and we dressed for evening meal, enjoying good food in a quiet wardroom.

Inconceivable that two weeks from that beautiful flight, Bob's Hoser Divison would be reduced to only him. And how could anyone guess that thirty-three years in the future, Captain Bob Arnold would perform my daughter's wedding. Or that for his eightieth birthday, I'd send a letter to thank him for my memory of our splendid journey to Iwo Jima.

# PART IV

# CO TRAI

"I feel better! I feel! I feel!" until he quit that too and said quietly, looking at the familiar wall, the familiar twin door through which he was about to pass, with tragic and passive clairvoyance: "Something is going to happen to me."

*—William Faulkner, Pylon* 1935

Dick Hartman was the author's section leader in Hoser Flight, a four-plane division of bachelors. Dick had turned down astronaut training for combat-flying, which he considered essential for a solid Navy career.

CHAPTER FOURTEEN

# *Portent*

Oriskany arrived at Cubi Point in time for a quiet July Fourth celebration. I spent most of that day at the swimming pool with squadron mates, downing gin and tonics. Over the next few days, several of us made after-dinner excursions across a bridge from Subic Bay Naval Base into Olongapo City. This was a Filipino liberty-town that outdid most Asian ports in the sin-city category. We'd head to one of the notoriously scandalous bars, The East End Club or New Pauline's.

"You buy me drink, one drink," girls would demand, fluttering their eyes as they took seats at our tables. For ourselves we'd order San Miguel beers at a dollar, while the drinks delivered to the girls—ginger-ale bubbling in chilled martini glasses—cost $2.50. The girls sipped at their drinks at a pace ensuring they would finish at precisely the same moment the first of us emptied his beer.

"You want San Miguel? You buy me nudda drink, I like you berry much." They earned a portion of each high-profit fake cocktail we bought for them, not for what we consumed. "You buy me one. I need a drink," they would say.

There were curfews at the bridge connecting Olongapo and the Navy Base, and Marine guards at the gate ensured they were enforced to the minute. For officers it was 0100—1:00 a.m. We'd get up to leave the clubs with time to make it. The bar girls understood how the curfews worked.

"You don't worry about the gate," they would whisper in our ears. "You come home with me. I love you tonight."

Oriskany headed for Yankee Station—to war—the morning of the eleventh, and once more, the captain wanted the air wing to hone skills. The weather was bad, at times improving to marginal, but we flew. The next day, one of VA-163's aircraft was to launch into the crud, but it dribbled off the bow. There had been an error calculating the steam-charge for the catapult shot. The pilot ejected safely and was recovered. Flight ops were called off after that, and I assume the catapult officer was called to the bridge.

Our first day of combat, July 14, Dick and I flew the first launch, an unremarkable and easy mission: no flak whatsoever. I came into the ready-room, having finished debriefing, grabbed coffee and was headed out for the LSO platform, where I was scheduled to train with Tom Lemay. At the front of the ready-room, I spotted Cunningham. Here was an opportunity to needle a fellow junior officer.

C-10, a reference to the number of letters in Cunningham's long last name, was scheduled for the third launch on the wing of Deny Weichman. Good. They had trained together as a section, and they were both strong pilots.

"Where you going?" I asked C-10. He showed me a circled spot on his chart. "Ooo! Really hot there," I said. Deny, king of practical jokes, smiled. I left them and continued to the platform.

I recalled the churning anxiety I felt ten months earlier when I briefed for my first trip over the beach with Dan Strong. It would be normal for C-10 to have butterflies tickling his belly even before my mischief.

The target C-10 showed me was a railway and highway bridge near a place called La Khe Thanh. This was down in the southern area, well clear of the hot places like Vinh and Than Hoa, and it should have been a piece of cake. Customarily, the targets an air wing selects for the first couple days are lightly defended. And the rookie was flying with a leader who knew how to avoid trouble, for Deny Weichman was our most combat-seasoned pilot.

Those two words—combat-seasoned—fall far short. Deny had flown some 300 missions in previous deployments, and two thirds of them had been in 1964. In secret work with the CIA, he'd worn civilian clothes and carried a fabricated civilian identity. He showed me his fake ID card once: under his photo, the name Charles Charles. "Funny name," I remarked. "Easy to remember," he said. "Charlie Charles." And the irony wasn't lost; Charlie was the moniker for Viet Cong.

Mostly in '64, Deny piloted T-28s, ostensibly training South Vietnamese pilots. But other missions—exceedingly dangerous assignments—took place flying C-123 twin-engine transport aircraft. Piloting those, he was ferrying South Vietnamese mercenary paratroopers across the demilitarized zone, a border that since 1954 separated the North from the South. He would return for any surviving mercenaries a week or so later, landing the little transport at night on unlit abandoned fields in North Vietnam. On one mission, Deny's C-123 took several mortar hits while on the ground. He was wounded, his co-pilot was killed, along with everyone in the back of the airplane. Yet he was able to get airborne that night, and he managed to bring the C-123 back to South Vietnam, flying as it burned fiercely. He lifted his shirt once to show me a jagged red scar running from his back around to his navel. Plainly, Deny Weichman was the most experienced combat aviator on the ship.

Deny and C-10—Wuff One and Wuff Two—crossed the coastline between Ha Tinh and Vinh. Their objective, the bridge, was not far from the Laotian border. A rather long flight to get there, but so far, no shooting. Deny rolled in. His hits were good. He called Cunningham. "On my smoke," he transmitted, telling the rookie where to aim.

"Wuff Two in," C-10 transmitted.

Amid the earth and spray thrown up by Deny's bombs, C-10 focused on where he thought the bridge had been, and when he reached his drop altitude, he pickled. Then, as in training, he pulled on the Gs.

BLAM, he was hit. His aircraft had met one of the many 37-mm rounds a gunner had thrown into the sky, and the force of the blast knocked him about, so he didn't see his aircraft's nose rip away in the 450-knot slipstream. He didn't see the debris flash past his canopy to be sucked into the big air intakes for his engine. But he did hear the turbine begin shredding. He certainly did feel the dreadful change in his aircraft—how it no longer wanted to fly.

His engine instruments confirmed this, underscoring the severity, as they flickered for an instant and then began to fall below the green arcs on their dial faces, winding down the wrong way.

To make his situation worse, the radio and other electronic gear housed in his A-4's nose had all been gobbled by his engine. Most of the sensors for his flight instruments had likewise disappeared into the turbine's spinning compressor. He was left with an altimeter, an engine exhaust-gas-temperature gauge and a back-up compass. He focused on that EGT gauge, adjusting power to keep the needle somewhere below the red arc that indicated the engine was close to melt-down. And he used that compass, a little magnetic affair no more sophisticated than what you'd find on an ancient Piper Cub. It became crucial, his chief means of survival.

Deny did not see his wingie's airplane begin to shred. Nor was he able to raise his wingman on the radio. Deny surmised C-10 may have headed toward Laos if he had been hit. So Deny searched there.

Without a radio, the rookie pilot, flying his first mission on the first day of Oriskany's '67 combat cruise, headed for the coast, silenced and without electronic navigation assistance.

To find Oriskany on the South China Sea, Cunningham, like Dick Perry the previous year, needed to accomplish a marvel of airmanship. Like Dick, he would rely on dead-reckoning—DR it is called, the same crude navigation technique Charles Lindbergh relied on to cross the Atlantic in 1927, the same archaic course-plotting Christopher Columbus employed to return home from the

New World after his great discovery.

Cunningham could not summon enough power to maintain level flight and was forced to descend until he was at 800 feet, dangerously in range of small-arms, when he flew over a village near the coast. Yet he felt he would make it, believed he would get back to his ship.

With his airplane burning and explosions from his engine increasing whenever he inched up the power, with his few engine instruments reminding him of the deep shit he was in, Larry Cunningham—C-10—concentrated on navigation. As the coast of Vietnam slipped behind his airplane, he found himself skimming above the waves, and this low altitude deprived him of the advantage height lends to a visual search. Far above he could see other aircraft heading the same direction. They, too, were returning from their missions and headed for the carriers on Yankee Station. They confirmed his heading. He continued on, adding power whenever he drifted too low, too slow, then decreasing it when the explosions became dreadfully intense. He spotted USS Constellation, but continued on, to somehow find Oriskany, a tiny dot on the water. He had dead-reckoned some 150 nautical miles from where he had taken that hit.

I was at the back of the flight-deck, learning my new LSO duties, when Cunningham's airplane unexpectedly appeared in the landing pattern. The A-4 trailed flames twice its length. With his engine shuddering and banging and that long tail of fire streaming behind, he was about to attempt a carrier landing.

Crazy.

The air boss called the platform: "Don't let that plane aboard."

Tom Lemay hit the button for the red wave-off lights. They began flashing as Cunningham turned into final lineup, the groove. The wave-off lights didn't matter, for at that moment, less than a quarter mile aft of Oriskany, Cunningham lost control. The nose pitched down, and he ejected. He swung once under his parachute before splashing into the ship's wake.

The ship's plane-guard helicopter, a little Kaman HU-2, was

quickly overhead, descending into a hover above Cunningham. A rescue swimmer dropped into the water to assist the young pilot. Within a minute or two the little HU-2 landed on the aft flight-deck. Cunningham, dripping wet, stepped out. He was a few yards from our LSO platform. I called out to him.

"See, I told you it was hot there."

But Cunningham, with his fine sense of humor, wasn't smiling. Decades later, whenever he talks about it, he says he was lucky to find the ship. There was a small measure of luck involved, yes, but mostly it was great headwork.

C-10 should have received a distinguished flying cross—but he didn't. He'd have to wait until later in the cruise and a mission to Hanoi to earn that medal.

The following day, one of the Lockets, Robin Cassel, became the first fatality of the cruise. His A-1 Skyraider had been attacking a boat—a water-borne-logistic-craft, in the jargon—strafing it. He was hit, and not far beyond his target, Cassel's aircraft splashed into the sea. He didn't get out.

The day after that, an F-8 Crusader flown by Butch Verich evaded two SAMs. He spiraled down, evading them, when a third SAM found him. He ejected. During efforts to rescue him, another Crusader was hit, arriving back aboard with a hunk of its tail shot away.

Butch spent the night in a cave on a karst ridge near Phu Ly, still a highly defended area. This was his second shoot-down; he had been bagged the previous August on the '66 cruise.

Rescue efforts were finally called off that evening, but at first light the next morning, one of the Saints, Marv Reynolds, led a bold new effort. Defenses were softened by attacks from A-4s, F-8s and Locket A-1s before Big Mother, piloted by Lt. Neil Sparks, was escorted across the beach near Hon Ma Island. The huge SH-3A Sea King chopper attracted no flak there, though that was normally a very hot spot. Sparks picked his way around gun sites until he arrived at the karst ridge. After a bit of searching, Butch was spotted. Vietnamese defense forces had likewise spotted the big helicopter, and now it began taking hits. Systems were lost, radios were shot away, and yet Sparks remained in a hover long enough to snatch Verich from the ridge. It was a daring rescue plan, audacious and dangerous. Yet the enormous risk paid off. Butch Verich was back. The admiral on Yankee Station took great pride in this.

The next day, the seventeenth, we lost no one.

CHAPTER FIFTEEN

# *A Quiet Breakfast*

B efore we take up our utensils, Dick bows his head. He prays silently. With his head lowered this way, I notice his hair, his crewcut, peppered with gray. Thirty-two, and he is an old man to me. Then, for a moment or two, I lower my own head.

This breakfast together is a first. Dick suggested it last night, set the time. So at 0530 we are in the officers wardroom seated across from each other, at one of the long tables. Its smooth tablecloth is, even at this hour, topped with white linen napkins and weighty silverware. It is always quiet in this big space. Especially this morning, because the wardroom is nearly empty. So early.

Where is Bud Edney? He's not with us at breakfast, yet he and Dick share a two-man stateroom. They are not only roomies, but good friends. At the Naval Academy, although he and Dick were assigned to different companies during their four years, they knew each other well.

So, yes, where's Budney? He's assigned to this mission, the

first alpha-strike of the day. It would make sense for the two room-mates to eat breakfast together. Surely the two awakened at the same time, and both must have donned their flight gear about the same time in their tiny room. I have a mental picture of them sitting on the edges of their bunks, facing each other as they lace up their brown flying boots before leaving the room. So, Dick must have wanted to have breakfast one-on-one, with me only, his wingie. A bonding thing. It's effective; I won't forget any details of this break-fast with Dick Hartman.

It is July 18th, three days before my twenty-fifth birthday. In the previous four days, I've flown five missions. And during this short period, Air Wing Sixteen has lost four airplanes with one of their pilots KIA. Yet this morning, Dick and I show no particular anxiety.

We leave the wardroom and head for the briefing space. We don't talk, because with tight spaces and ladders throughout the ship, it's best to walk single file. As we stride down the passageway, it is as if we are merely hurrying off to work—which in fact we are.

As we walk, I try to visualize how this mission will play out. We'll see flak this morning, certainly we will. Dick and I understand this. But we understand unmistakably that we'll come back over-head Oriskany an hour and a half after we launch. We'll deliver our bombs at our target, jink madly back to the water, and a few miles off the coast we'll re-join in formation to visually inspect each other's aircraft for battle-damage. Dick will check in with Red Crown and report we are two Magicstones, feet wet, safe. Then we'll cruise toward Yankee Station, conserving our fuel. Along the way, Dick will use his hand to pantomime drinking, as if he has lifted an invisible bottle to his oxygen mask. This hand-signal asks how much fuel I have. With 1,600 pounds still in my main tank, I'll answer with fingers—index finger up, then fist closed, then index finger out horizontal—a one and a six.

He'll hand-signal a change of radio channels and on this fre-quency he will check us in with Childplay, reporting our fuel-state, using the lowest of the two of us. In return Childplay will acknowledge and issue us our "charlie," a time, to the minute, when we are expected to cross the ramp and land. When we arrive overhead, we'll see the tiny shapes of Oriskany and her plane-guard destroyer, their wakes thin, indicating they are loitering. We'll drop our hooks early —because this is one less thing to remember in the landing pattern. Then we'll loiter until nearly our charlie time, when we'll fly down to parallel Oriskany's wake, passing abeam her one minute before our charlie, noting the heading, which will be 180-degrees from our downwind heading, and as we pass the bow, Dick will use another swift hand-signal, this one as if he is kissing his fingertips, and in the same instant he tosses that bye-bye kiss my way, he'll slam his airplane into a 90-degree bank. Two seconds later—a-thousand-one, a-thousand-two—in one fast series of operations, I'll pull throttle to idle, pop out my speedbrakes and slam into a 90-degree hard bank, mirroring what Dick has done. My airspeed will dissipate under the hard-G-load until I have slowed enough to drop landing-gear and flaps.

Our two-second separation will stretch as we both slow and complete our turns downwind. Dick will trap aboard precisely at our assigned charlie time, and my landing will be thirty seconds after his. I'll catch the three-wire, if I have flown a precise and smooth pass. Or maybe the two or the four, if I haven't.

The deceleration when I catch the arresting-cable will throw me hard into my shoulder straps, and when my A-4 has stopped, I'll lift the hook and turn to taxi fast, clearing the deck for the next aircraft in the groove. A director, a young man wearing a yellow jersey, will guide me as I go forward. Young men in blue jerseys will push my bird into a space that will place my wingtips six inches from the next aircraft. While the plane-captain in his brown jersey will chain my aircraft to the deck, I'll open my canopy, sigh and take in fresh air coming over the bow, and with the strong shot of adrenaline pumping through my veins, I'll feel so very alive.

I'll look for Dick and together we'll cross the flight-deck to the island, our helmets and kneeboards in nylon bags once again swinging at our sides. We'll make our way down to the A.I. spaces, where we will debrief with Jim Waldron, YDK—so youthful with his thick glasses and long hair. We'll tell him where we think our bombs impacted, assessing the results, often using the word "possibly," which we suspect will be changed to "probable" as the report is moved up the chain-of-command. And we'll move along to tell another A.I. about defenses, about the 37-, 57- or 85-mm we saw. And of any SAMs that came up for us.

From there, we'll head to the ready-room to debrief together over coffee, mentally reliving the flight. We'll go over details, what we did right and wrong (though for pilots, wrong is hard to admit). We may discuss how we can become even tighter, even more effective as a section. Neither Dick nor I smoke, but most of the others do, and the ready-room's air will be blue. There will be laughter; adrenaline fuels laughter.

At some point the LSO will come into Ready Four to read us our landing grades, one-on-one, scolding gently if an ugly pass has bothered him, or worse, frightened him. As he speaks, he will refer to coded symbols written by an assistant into a small black notebook. This is the duty I perform when I am on the platform—encoding the LSO's verbal assessment after each pass.

The LSO's debrief will take maybe fifteen seconds, less time if we have flown a steady glide-slope on airspeed and then picked up the three. The best grade, the one we strive for, is an *OK*, a perfect, textbook pass. For a slightly ragged but safe pass, the grade will be *Fair*. A *No Grade* is bad, and the debrief will be longer; the LSO will use it as a teaching opportunity. The worst grade, the equivalent of an F, is a *Cut Pass*. You do not want to receive a Cut, ever. Fly several—well, that will cost a pilot his wings.

After this, Dick and I will settle into our deeply cushioned ready-room chairs. We will drink coffee from mugs and continue dissecting our flight, talking fast, moving our hands through the air, palms flat, illustrating maneuvers we put our craft through dodging missiles and flak. It's always animated, these minutes after we shed our flight gear and gather. There is always that adrenaline-fueled laughter. We unwind, we're smiling. But this will come after.

Right now Dick and I enter the briefing room. All the metal folding chairs will fill quickly this morning, all of them because this is an alpha-strike briefing and there will be so many pilots. The CAG will be here, even though he is not flying, because he'll want to know everything, as will the skippers who are not on this flight, but have pilots who are. Dick and I are early enough to find chairs side-by-side in the middle of the room. I strap my kneeboard to my left leg, where I'll take notes on blank 4x6 cards.

An electric buzz of anticipation floods the briefing space, an energy you feel acutely before these big raids. Probably because this is early in the cruise, the keenness and excitement seem magnified today. Some guys, latecomers, are standing along the bulkheads. Heightened anticipation, yes, but there is no fear, none on display. What does show is the bravado of the young. We're up for this and anxious to "press on," as Skipper Engel said over and over last year.

Most people don't realize we are all volunteers. Any pilot can call it quits, hand his wings to his commanding officer and be done; the next day he'll be on his way to a desk job back in the States. No questions, other than this: "You're sure?" Yet of all the hundreds of pilots I get to know during my nearly seven years in the Navy, I'll see only two guys do it, relinquish their wings. Undeniably, we believe we're invincible. And there's that honor thing, as well.

At the front, a young lieutenant in khakis steps onto a low platform. He glances at his watch, waits a few seconds and then begins speaking precisely on time. It is 0600. Timing will be to the second for the rest of the day's operations. In his hand is a long wooden pointer, and with practiced élan he uses it to tap a spot on the huge chart behind him.

"Your target this morning," he tells us without drama, "is the Co Trai Bridge." Everyone in the room knows this, and knows, too, that the target is a pair of bridges, side-by-side.

The lieutenant is part of the small cadre of air intelligence officers assigned to the air-wing. Each squadron is assigned an A.I.—YDK is ours—but once aboard he becomes part of an air-wing pool. I don't know which squadron supplied this guy, but he is experienced and comfortable when speaking. His remarks, very brief, include the strategic justification for wiping it out. He passes out black-and-white glossy photos. Dick holds one, and I lean over to take a first glimpse of the bridges. What I see is a short and narrow concrete structure substantial enough only for small trucks, and next to it, a single-span rail bridge, something that may have been built by the French in the late nineteenth century. The waterway they cross is without a name on my chart.

The lieutenant then calls on a pudgy chief petty officer and hands him the pointer. The chief rolls a weather chart into position. He tells us the sky is clear with unlimited visibility, CAVU. It will be clear over the target and clear at the ship. Excellent news. I visualize the day outside.

Since yesterday evening, I've remained inside Oriskany's vast hull. I've seen only a maze of haze-gray steel bulkheads, all bathed in harsh fluorescent lighting, day and night. In darkness this morning I had that one glimpse of dark water burbling past the Number Two Elevator.

CAVU will make my rendezvous with Dick, and after that our join-up with the flight group, straightforward. Easier to find the target, as well. And clear air affords a chance to see any SAMs early; you can't outmaneuver what you can't see. Very good news from the chief.

He gives us winds-over-target information, and I draw a large wind-symbol, as Frank Elkins taught me, onto my kneeboard pad.

Following the chief, another A.I. delivers the order of battle—everything known about defenses. We pay close attention.

"You may encounter triple-A shortly after crossing the beach here," he says. His delivery is matter-of-fact. He taps a swarm of yellow dots on the chart near the coastline. Everyone in the room understands this. Whenever we go feet-dry this far north of the DMZ they shoot. We will coast-in not far from The Hourglass. Cassel died near there. Three days ago.

"Expect 37-, 57-, possibly 85- around here and here," the lieutenant says, touching the pointer to colored push-pins that indicate gun emplacements near Dinh Binh and Ninh Binh. He's good with that stick, making perfect little circles around threats. Avoid these, he tells us. We might enjoy relative quiet as we navigate the forty or so additional miles up the valley, but as we pass abeam Phu Ly and begin our turn toward the bridge, he warns, anticipate escalating ground defenses. Including SAMs.

At our turn-in point, we will fly into range of SA-2s, the SAM sites Russia has supplied (and some say, operate) that are arrayed around Hanoi. With the tip of his pointer, the lieutenant taps colored pins fifteen to twenty miles north of our target, the half dozen or so SAM sites defending the southern edge of North Vietnam's capitol. Yes, we'll easily be within the twenty-eight-mile lethal range of those. He runs through a short list of recent firings from each site.

SA-2s are huge, big as telephone-poles, and they come fast, accelerating to Mach 3, five times faster than we will be flying. Their boosters separate four or five seconds after launch, often unseen. From an A-4's cockpit, what you see coming for you with such malice is the second stage, a bright pink spot of fire writhing like an angry snake, homing, seeking only you.

Even a nearby detonation—a miss—will take your aircraft down. This SA-2 missile is a radar-guided instrument of death. Doing its cobra dance, it burns for twenty-two seconds after separating from the booster. And it runs on common kerosene—kerosene mixing with exotic fuming nitric acid. Only twenty-two seconds.

But twenty-two seconds is forever if it's tracking you.

This year they have a new tactic, the A.I. with the stick reminds us. The North Vietnamese have solved their supply issues, so they have a comfortable inventory, plenty of missiles. They use them freely. SAMs are being launched in volleys of two, sometimes even three. I take this in. We might outmaneuver one, even two, but it was the third that took out Butch Verich two days ago. Three. The A.I. also reminds us we may enjoy less warning from our ALQ gear. The Vietnamese are better operators these days; they now acquire a target with their Fan Song search-radars, and in a flash switch to their guidance-mode. They skip a step or two. Expect less time between the low-warbles in your earphones and when they launch it.

That's the way with wars: ever escalating. As our side polishes defense tactics and adds better weapons—such as our new radar-seeking Shrikes—the other side answers with tactical innovation. In this case, skilled radar operators and trains of missiles flying through the air. Two. God forbid, three.

## CHAPTER SIXTEEN

# Man 'em Up

Magnolia waves off the pointer as he steps onto the stage. "Magnolia" is the affectionate nickname of Cmdr. Bryan Compton, skipper of VA-163, the Saints. He'll lead the strike this morning.

"Right here, we demolish two bridges," he says, touching a spot on the chart.

Among the gaggle of very colorful aviators aboard Oriskany, Bryan Compton is foremost. Magnolia has made a name for himself in the air wing for the sweat-crystals on his dirty flight-suits. He's too smart to be oblivious; he graduated very near the top of the Naval Academy's Class of 1951. So, it's certain he takes pleasure projecting this ragged edge. Proud of his Southern roots, too. Ask where he calls home, and he'll smile. "Demopolis, Alabama," and after a pause, he'll add, "at the confluence of the Tombigbee and Black Warrior Rivers."

Approachable, sure, yet he demands you know your stuff. Only a fool would attempt a bluff. "You're sure of this? Check it for me." He will not smile as he says this.

He's not only one of the sharpest intellects on the ship, he's one of the bravest, too. No one disputes this. Magnolia absolutely doesn't need that pointed stick.

Touching the chart, he indicates our target. It's a small symbol crossing a faint blue line some cartographer drew using an especially fine pen-nib. This matches the thin line meandering down the folded chart I'm holding.

Magnolia goes on to outline the composition of our strike-force. With a red dry-marker he draws on a blank whiteboard, sketching little triangles to indicate positions various divisions of airplanes will maintain. Navy nomenclature is confusing at times. In the air, his squadron's call-sign is Old Salt, but otherwise they are VA-163, the Saints. Similarly, our squadron's call-sign is Magicstone, but when we aren't airborne, we're the Ghostriders of VA-164. Just as Oriskany is CVA-34, but when hailed from the air is Childplay.

He continues the sketching. Magicstones here, Old Salts here and here. His own four-plane division is at the apex of the twenty-eight aircraft he will lead into combat. The strike-bombers this morning will be six Magicstones and six Old Salts, each loaded with 3,500 pounds of bombs. If we all drop accurately, over forty tons of ordnance should effectively destroy the two bridges.

With a sweep of his hand, he indicates the place on the chart where he'll bring us feet-dry, giving the heading he'll fly once we cross the coast. I write this number on my pad below the wind arrow.

"Up this valley," he says. He's now moving his hand along our route, and then he arcs it from a northwest heading to northeast. "I'll turn in here," he says. We'll be wheeling like Rockettes at Rockefeller Center. "Y'all on the outside get some power on. Keep up." The turn will come not far north of Phu Ly.

"You Iron-hands, get yourselves pointin' at the threat." He's talking to the pair of Magicstones assigned to protect the force with A-4s armed with Shrike anti-radar weapons, missiles far smaller than Soviet-built SAMs. Yet a well-placed Shrike will disable an entire SAM site.

He is back at the whiteboard. Rounding out our force, he says, will be two Tarcaps, F-8s tasked with protecting everyone from MiGs. Tarcap pilots are hunters, the only ones among us hoping a couple of foolish MiG drivers venture our way. He doesn't need to tell us how they will fly wide S-figure paths above us, flying considerably faster to keep their kinetic energy high.

"We'll rendezvous overhead at 7,000," Magnolia says. "Two circuits around the ship, then I'll head out on course." He adds, "Stragglers, catch up."

Twice last cruise, Dick and I flew this route to the violent Red River Valley, and both times we flew up this same karst valley to get there. There will be no element of surprise; the Vietnamese know this route and what comes next.

Magnolia delivers more information—the radio channel the strike-group will use and a few other details—and then he's done. He looks over his pilots, this gathering of young men who for once are unsmiling and focused and serious-minded. "Questions?" There are none.

He steps from the little stage. "Let's go get 'em."

With the briefing over, Dick leans toward me and gives me a location and altitude to use if we get separated after we pull off target. It is a spot over water, three miles off Vietnam's coast.

Back at VA-164's ready-room, near the front, he and I join the other guys flying on this raid. It's a stand-up briefing, and we gather around Skipper Mow. Not one for theatrics, the skipper speaks quietly. He tells us where his division will rendezvous before we join the strike force, and he gives us a few other details, including how he wants us to maneuver should any SAMs come our way. It is here that Dick and I learn we will not operate as a separate section; we'll be appended to Skipper Mow's four-plane division. Naval Aviation tactics are designed around elements comprised of either two-plane sections or four-plane divisions. But six? I've never flown into combat as part of a super-sized division such as this.

Dick doesn't make much of it. We'll handle it, seems to be his attitude.

My roommate Don Purdy is in this huddle. Today will be his first alpha-strike. He'll fly on the skipper's wing. Roger Duter, another bunkroom mate, will fly number-four on the wing of Rock Hodges, a lieutenant. In this formation, Dick and I will become Magicstones Five and Six. Only two of us—Dick and I—have ever flown on an alpha-strike before. But the experience will not be entirely unfamiliar for Roger, Don and Rock, because our air-wing practiced these big formations before leaving the States. (On one, we nearly bombed a farmer in a pickup truck with live ordnance when a navigating error by the flight leader put us off the bombing range.)

The others of Hoser Flight, Bob Arnold and Barry Wood, will not be with us. I would prefer they were, and later I'll wonder if the day might have gone differently had Dick and I been flying in the division with which we had trained at Lemoore.

The Navy and Air Force have a bomb shortage; newspapers in the States have reported this. But the services and the White House vigorously deny it. This morning, Skipper Mow, in his measured tones, informs us our aircraft will carry an odd mix of ordnance, a load that includes two ancient bombs. Our squadron's ordnance crew is right now loading two M117s—750-pound fat bombs, they're surplus from WWII—onto our aircraft. The only way to explain this is that we are indeed running short of MK-82s. Mixing these old bombs in with MK-82s, the 500-pound streamlined bombs we are experienced at dropping, will cause an aiming problem. Air friction—drag—on the fat bombs will cause them to fall short of the MK-82s. How will we set up our intervalometers to release all eight bombs, sequenced one after another, to create a line of bombs—a stick, we call it—across the target? The bombsight settings are different. What do we do, average the settings? No. After a discussion we agree to set our bombsight mil-leads for the MK-82s. Fuck the fat bombs. They'll have to drop short. I hope they hit harmlessly.

Errant bombs—and these M117s are destined to be errant—sometimes fall onto civilian homes, schools and occasionally even churches. Collateral damage. It accounts for some of the destruction the Vietnamese showed that reporter Harrison Salisbury. Wild bomb-hits furnish evidence for the Vietnamese to use when they call us air-pirates.

I know that one well-placed MK-82, striking a weak spot, will destroy the motor-vehicle span, the target for our division. The M117s, these fat, thin-skinned things, are said to do no more than go splat, make a lot of noise and paint a big smudge on hard concrete. The MK-82s, on the other hand, are tough. With the proper time-delayed fuse they penetrate deep into concrete before detonating.

I've been handed an updated list of bombsight mil-settings printed on a sheet that I clip onto my kneeboard. This new sheet includes settings for M117s should I want to drop them separately. I don't study it. I'm going with the MK-82 setting, and that's that.

Standing with us at the front of the room are Gus Jones and John Davis, both with experience from the '66 cruise. Today they'll fly Iron-hand protection. After Skipper Mow finishes, Gus and John work out fine points with each other, then head off to fighter-pilot ready-rooms to coordinate with their escorts. As Iron-hands, their assignment is a form of dueling, shoot-outs similar to the Wild West. They'll launch air-to-ground Shrikes against Soviet-built surface-to-air guidance-radars when they light up. The advantage, in theory, will tilt slightly in the Iron-hands' favor, since they can fire Shrikes as soon as electronic gear in their A-4s alerts them that a Vietnamese fire-control-radar has commenced transmitting. This gives our guys a few seconds lead, while the SAM-site operators work to lock onto a single aircraft and then switch to their more accurate Fan Song guidance-radar. That's the theory. The equalizing factors, however, are that the Vietnamese operators are becoming faster and that their SA-2 has almost twice the lethal range of a Shrike.

Also defending the strike-force will be Pouncers—flak-suppression. Today Deny Weichman, along with an experienced VA-163 pilot, will take on this especially dangerous task. I don't see Deny, he must be off briefing with his Old Salt counterpart.

The stand-up-briefing has taken maybe three minutes. Time to suit-up. Our flight gear—helmets, g-suits, torso harnesses, survival vests and personal sidearms—are all stored in a small locker-room aft of the ready-room. We move quickly. Once suited up, we indeed look like warriors. Our g-suits have medieval overtones with their crisscross lacing on the outside of each leg. We need this. Compressed air will inflate the g-suit's internal bladders as the Gs come on. Such a flimsy looking garment until you get it zipped into place; then it transforms a pilot's lower body into a sleek and athletic form.

The torso harness does the same for the upper body. This garment is interlaced with hefty, industrial-looking nylon straps, which are a component of the aircraft's parachute system. Heavy steel clips at the waist and shoulders buckle a pilot to the ejection seat at four points.

Strapped in this way, we are not tossed about the cockpit as we throw the aircraft through brutal maneuvers. Worn below and in front of the torso harness is an inflatable vest to keep us afloat should we go into the drink. Above that we don a survival vest. The two garments—survival vest and water-wings—bulk up our upper torso so that from a distance we appear barrel-chested, warrior-like.

The survival vest is merely a pair of zippered nylon pouches containing dried food, a medical kit, a silk map of Vietnam, matches in a waterproof canister, a signal mirror and anything else we think might be useful should we be shot down. Some guys carry drinking water. I don't. Later I'll wonder why.

In a separate pouch positioned over our heart is the most important piece of gear: a UHF survival radio. There is another survival radio in the seat-pan, the hard cushion we sit on. It comes with us if we eject.

We each carry either a 9-mm Browning Automatic or a .38 Smith & Wesson in a holster on our chest. I've chosen a little five-shot snub-nose .38 Smith & Wesson, not because it has any firepower, but because of its ultra-light titanium construction. Our shoulder holsters and bandoliers of ammunition make us look fearsome in photos. We carry knives, too. We were issued dull, rather useless, K-bar survival knives, but like most other pilots, I've ditched the K-bar and purchased an expensive Buck knife with a six-inch blade. I keep it honed sharp. I've heard about guys bobbing around in life rafts who have had their knives slip out of their hands to be lost in the depths of the sea, so I've tethered the Buck knife to its leather sheath with a length of nylon parachute shroud-line, tensile strength 250 pounds. The sheath is stitched to my G-suit, low, on the calf. I have another in a pouch inside my survival vest, a folding knife.

As we emerge from the locker room, our maintenance chief, hands me a clipboard. On it a yellow-sheet describes the condition of the aircraft I'm assigned. Since each bird has its own personality, I look at notes from other guys who have flown this bird. And while I have it, I write the precise weight of the bird onto my kneeboard. I then do a bit of arithmetic, adding that weight to the 7,800 pounds of fuel I'll carry, and then combine that sum to the weight of the bombs and the bomb-racks. I come up with a total gross weight for the airplane I am assigned—which this morning is AH-415. I hand the clipboard back, and O.C. tells me where to find 415 when I go on deck.

Geared up for flight, I step back into the ready-room. There may be time for a coffee. I see smokers lighting up. If I'm to get nervous, this is the time, so I keep any jitters at bay with mindless chat. We all do. If there is fear in this ready-room, it doesn't show.

After a few minutes, the 1-MC comes alive. "Man 'em up," a disembodied voice from pri-fly orders. It's not a rush, but then we don't dally, either. The passageway is alive with pilots, and I arrive at the base of the escalator to see the line of pilots being lifted steeply up to the flight deck, and it's a magnificent sight. All these guys going on one raid. Dick is ahead, and he and I step off the escalator and walk through the base of the island to the flight deck. High above, up there in pri-fly, sits the air-boss. It's on his say that our aircraft will be started, launched and, later, recovered back aboard.

We walk with the casual swagger of the first-string, champions of the ship, for Oriskany, this 872-foot-long vessel with her 3,000 sailors, has a single purpose: get the attack birds into the air. Attack aircraft are what it's all about. The fighters offer us protection, as do the other birds designed to assist our mission. That letter "A" in Oriskany's designation—CVA-34—stands for attack. We're not full of ourselves, but close, and we carry it in our stride as we walk to our birds.

The morning light is lovely. But because the ship is loitering, black smoke from the stack swims down the island to swirl across the deck. The stack-gasses mix with exhaust vapors from a helicopter that has been started, and the fumes assault—thick and choking. Our gaits pick up, and the pilots streaming from the island fan out and head toward aircraft lining both sides of the deck. At a casual glance the airplanes might appear a jumble, yet they've been positioned wing-tip to wing-tip along each side in a considered order. Our maintenance chief has told Dick and me precisely where to find our birds.

Pure energy abounds, all about us, as deck crews in their colored jerseys hustle. I'm alert. Golf-cart-size vehicles, low-slung and without windshields, are buzzing about. Step in front of one of those yellow carts, and it's a quick ticket to sick bay.

Dick's bird, AH-404, is parked aft of mine. Both are on the port side, pushed so far to the deck's edge that their main wheels are almost in the scuppers and their tails hang out over the Tonkin Gulf. I stop at AH-415 and Dick parts without a gesture, continuing toward 404.

My bird's plane captain is at the foot of the ladder leading to the cockpit. Hearing-protectors protrude through cut-outs in his brown cloth skull-hugging cap. We greet one another by name—some of the plane captains mix-up Roger Duter and me, so either of us might be greeted as Mr. Duther. But this earnest young man has my name right, and he takes my helmet bag, then turns and clambers up the eight-foot ladder to place it in the cockpit.

It's a coincidence that today I'm flying the aircraft with my name stenciled beneath its canopy. This business of putting names on the sides of the aircraft is somewhat contrived, because we have twenty-two pilots in our squadron and only fourteen airplanes, so obviously some names must share a bird. As with everything, it's a seniority thing. I've moved up the list enough that on 415 my name appears on the favored port side. As with horses, we mount from the left side of the airplane, so it's my name I see when climbing the ladder. Don Purdy's is on the other side.

This personalization harkens back to earlier wars, when each pilot was assigned his own craft, and he flew it and only it. Now it is more efficient to assign a pilot to whatever airplane is fueled, loaded with ordnance and on deck. It's random fortune that I'm assigned AH-415. This feels lucky.

I continue my inspection. From the fantail of the ship, I hear Lockets idling, warming the oil in their enormous 2,800-horse-power engines. These are straight-wing birds, massive throwback flying machines that, with their wings folded, look like bank robbers under arrest, hands above their heads. Very mean bank robbers. When they approach the catapult and are given the signal to unfurl those wings—fifty feet, tip to tip—Locket Spads transform into beastly fierceness.

Although the A-4 and the A-1 were designed by Heinemann, they are as different as ballerinas and wrestlers. Whereas the A-4 is svelte and sleek, the Spad is angular and thuggish. It was introduced ten years before the A-4, and plainly it is meant for an earlier war, not this modern conflict. Nonetheless, although slow, Spads can remain aloft five or six hours, carrying staggering loads of ordnance. A Cadillac can be strapped under each wing and the bird still has lifting capacity, or so the Spad-drivers like to brag.

On combat-search-and-rescue missions, you want a well-armed airplane that can stay on scene long periods. The Lockets carry pods of rockets and up to eight 250-lb. bombs, while jutting from their wings are four 20-mm guns, each supplied with belts of lethal firepower. Each round is almost an inch in diameter—meaning, yes, a Locket can wipe out a truck or barge or halt enemy troops. Because they are slow, A-1s are effective near the ground; Spad drivers have time to see, and at slower speeds, their airplanes are maneuverable. That also creates vulnerability. A year ago, Spads from Oriskany flew hundreds of sorties over North Vietnam. But loss rates were high. Unacceptably high.

So on this cruise, the Lockets are to cross into Vietnam only in the event of a shoot-down. They will then take on dangerous duty escorting a rescue chopper inland. Four of the Lockets warming their engines now will cross the beach this morning.

I rise from under 415's nose and continue my pre-flight inspection. With a grease-pencil I mark that gross-weight figure I calculated in the ready-room onto the nose-gear door. Moving along to the starboard wing, I test the slat and I tug on each bomb to see it has been properly snugged down; you don't want one flopping loose on a catapult shot. I also inspect each one to ensure it is correctly fused. Then I sight down the wing to ensure it isn't damaged. Such a graceful wing.

Beneath the slat is the blunt nose of that ugly M117 bomb, the fat fucker. I pause for a moment—a second or two—and flash on that photo-story in the magazine, recalling that allegation from the Vietnamese about civilian deaths last year at Phu Ly. I make sure the fuse is correctly rigged and give it another firm tug. The other bombs under this wing, the ordnance that will hit the bridges, the MK-82s, are armed with time-delay fuses set so they will smash down into the concrete of the bridge before they blow. I check the settings.

I ensure safety pins with their red streamers are affixed to each bomb. You want these in place; a bomb detonating onboard a carrier is recipe for disaster. (Eleven days from now, ordnance without safety pins will cause a deadly fire aboard USS Forrestal. A young pilot named John McCain will escape his burning A-4 by seconds in this disaster, and in the airplane next to his, a lieutenant junior-grade named Dave Dollarhide will not be so lucky.) The ordnance guys must have had extra time. They've scrawled messages for the enemy in chalk onto some of the bombs:

"Fuck you Uncle Ho."

"Take this, MFs!"

"Hello Goodbye from Catoosa County."

I shift my attention to the several antennas sticking out from the fuselage, plastic things the size and shape of ice-cream cones. These delicate cones are crucial to the ALQ, electronic gear that will alert me of a SAM about to launch.

I try to hurry along, because the stack-gas fumes have found me. Part of the airplane cannot be inspected anyway, because it hangs past the edge of the flight-deck. Nothing is leaking back there, and the aft ALQ antennas look okay. There's no way to look closer, because six stories of open air separate the rear of my aircraft and water. With its main wheels almost at the edge of the ship, 415 appears precarious. But no worry, the bird is chained securely to the deck.

CHAPTER SEVENTEEN

# *Flying Through Water*

**B**ut then Bill Searfus had tie-down chains when he manned his aircraft. Yes, but someone on his carrier, Coral Sea, removed those chains early. Maybe to save time, or maybe a hand-signal was mis-interpreted. I never heard why. But his chains were off, and then jet-blast from a turning aircraft swept up under Bill's A-4, lifting his nose until the front wheel came up. His bird tipped back. So far back that it continued over the side. Six stories.

It is possible, a hydrodynamic possibility, that as his airplane was sinking, slipping down into the jade-green waters of the South China Sea, it began flying. Gliding. They say an airplane will sail through water just as through air, because both air and water are fluids: Bernoulli's Theorem.

I think of Bill Searfus often, remembering how he so joyfully danced with his shoes off to Little Richard's music in his living room. And then my mind goes to the tie-downs, how in a moment a fine officer was simply blown into the sea. I wasn't there, but I play it often through my mind's little theater. I see his airplane parked with the aft fuselage hanging out in space, like 415 is parked this morning, and I see the jet-blast swooshing under his nose, lifting it slowly up until the airplane's center of gravity has rotated out over water, sixty feet from the deck to the water, and I see the slow-motion flip backward in my memory as if I witnessed it. He hits upside-down. He's pinned in his cockpit. The Coral Sea's huge wake tossed his A-4 around, and I see that. When an airplane falls onto the water, it will at first flutter side to side like a coin flipped into a fountain, and then—I see this every time I think about it—his A-4 settles nose-down to begin that glide. Stabilizing, sailing through the warm green shallows, then down and down to the cold black depths.

Bill Searfus, father and husband, skipper of VA 155—he had already survived ferocious raids against Phuc Yen Airfield, a place massively defended with triple-A, with radar-guided anti-aircraft guns and SAMs. He had survived the savagery of the defenses arrayed so thickly around that MiG-base near Hanoi, and he had dodged SAMs swarming up like wasps, to, in the end, be trapped in a cockpit, strapped into twelve tons of aluminum and steel gliding through the dark waters of the South China Sea.

Many years later, I'll find myself weeping in the warm water of my morning shower. Trance-like, I'll see Bill Searfus flying through green seawater.

I continue my pre-flight inspection. With the heel of my hand I bang each chain, hard. There are three this morning. In heavy weather there would be more.

The plane captain follows me, ready to answer questions. I move forward along the port side of the fuselage and continue the pre-flight, and I find everything is as it should be, so I climb the ladder and step over onto the wing, open a servicing hatch—good. The hydraulic-fluid and oil-reservoirs are firmly capped. No stray tools have been left inside the bird or the intake. We're good to go.

Like a valet, the plane captain helps me strap in, locating each shoulder strap from behind and placing it onto my shoulder. Plane captains are kids, most eighteen or nineteen, but for this job they are selected for maturity. They take responsibility for a single air-plane, and they mother it through servicing and light maintenance. We get to know them, and when there is time we chat. Today we don't have this luxury. I click the shoulder straps into steel Koch fittings on my torso harness, then locate the seatbelt straps and do the same. I am now firmly affixed to the seat pan and the ejection seat. I cinch the straps tightly. If they aren't so snug they pinch, first time I pull negative Gs or do violent maneuvers, I'll bang my helmet on the canopy. Clunk-clunk. I've done it.

Now I plug in my oxygen mask, clip it onto my helmet, flick a switch and—ah, sweet, pure oxygen flows into my mask.

I run through a quick check in the cockpit. Start an airplane with the gear-lever in the up position, and you might drop the craft onto the deck, though I've never heard of this happening. I check the gear handle and see that bomb- and gun-switches are in safe positions.

The ladder is pulled away, the air-boss calls for the jets to start, and soon enough, two low-slung tractor carts driven by young sailors speed across the deck to my aircraft. One, the huffer, a yellow vehicle about the size of a golf cart, whines like a jet, be-cause in fact it has a small jet turbine engine aboard that will create compressed air to spin up my engine. The other, also yellow and slightly smaller, is the power cart. A cable from it will supply elec-tricity until my airplane's engine begins generating its own.

The plane captain darts under 415 with a flexible hose from the huffer. He steps back into my field of vision, and I flash another hand signal. Then with a slow rumble that builds to a whine, my engine spins, and when it spins up to enough rpms, I move the throttle. Ignitors light off the turbine.

Okay. Good start. The yellow vehicles dart away.

Exhaust gasses from running jets thicken the air. Up and down the line pilots are pulling canopies shut. We might be wise to leave our canopies open, because to go over the side with one closed means water-pressure will lock it in place. Yet, those hot fumes—I follow the example of the others and pull mine shut.

161

I adjust the air conditioning to full cold, and tiny balls of ice spit from the vent nozzles on either side of the instrument panel to bounce off my helmet.

This oxygen comes to me from far back in my fuselage, where a frosty green bottle the size of a soccer ball is tucked into a compartment. An hour from now that green bottle, source of this sweet oxygen, will nourish a fire that will kill AH-415, and Bureau Number 151986 will join 362 other A-4s to be destroyed fighting in Vietnam. Now, though, the oxygen is refreshingly crisp. It clears away the taste of kerosene and stack gas in my mouth and throat.

With another hand-signal from me, the plane captain again darts under 415 to emerge holding up three pins with long red streamers that he's pulled from the landing gear. I turn on my radio and other electronics, then check in with Dick.

"Magicstone Six up."

"Six, roger. Go to launch."

In five words, Dick has confirmed that we have both successfully started our aircraft, that our radios are working, and that it is time to switch to the carrier's launch frequency.

## CHAPTER EIGHTEEN

# *That Rattlesnake Sound*

Magnolia brings us to the coastline, with the Hourglass coming into view at my one-o'clock. Waters from the two rivers flush into the Tonkin Gulf in a muddy bloom and stain the sea the color of mocha.

I recheck my bomb switches and flip on the master-arm. The formation has settled in a V, like geese fly, with each division staggered back 25- to 30-degrees. And we are spread out. You don't want to be close enough for a single SAM to knock down two airplanes with one detonation. Later, this distance will be quantified at 700 feet, greater than our separation this morning. The guideline will not come soon enough for a pair of Old Salts who will get bagged with a single missile forty-four days from today.

I take a moment to ensure the proper mil-setting is cranked into the bombsight perched before me on the glare-shield as the coastline slips beneath my aircraft. Magnolia has pushed the power up, and he's in a shallow descent. We're accelerating. He calls the picket ship.

"Red Crown, Old Salt One, goin' feet dry with twenty-eight."

The voice of a young sailor responds: "Roger. Old Salt One with twenty-eight."

My breathing quickens, and a new surge of adrenaline comes like surf. The tan beach is now beneath me. Then another of Magnolia's transmissions: "Masta switchus."

Mine is on, but I recheck; no sense enduring this risk, flying all this way to pull off target with my bombs still with me. Yes, the red cover is up and the master switch is, yes, in the ON position.

My headset has come alive with the voop-voop of low-frequency search-radar, and now the sounds of acquisition-radar mix in. One of the Old Salts is jinking wildly, energetic little turns back and forth, but it won't help him here. Big sweeping course changes—three seconds or more—are required for an effective jink. Must be a new guy.

Magnolia presses ahead. I maintain my position off Dick's starboard wing. He flies a steady course, smooth as always.

We are over land now with the Hourglass directly off my right wing. To my left and a little behind, the pale tan beach runs south in a thin streak. From this altitude the surf appears as nothing more than a fine white line.

The strike force continues in a shallow descent, and our speed builds incrementally. We're over farmland now. Square and rectangular rice paddies defined by berms running in straight lines slip beneath us. I am on my way to dump almost two tons of high explosives onto Vietnam, onto this partitioned country's bridges at Co Trai.

If there are farmers walking along the dikes below, we can't make them out. And at this altitude, rounds from their rifles—everyone in the North carries a weapon—cannot reach us. But I can visualize these farmers. At our high-school, we Clods gazed over a parapet along a breezeway as we prattled about nothing, and we'd watch a family work a small rice paddy. It looked so hard, all of it, but especially the planting. Mud to their ankles, a man and his wife shoved plant after plant into the paddy, both of them stooped over, working without letup. We marveled at how they kept the rows straight and the young plants so evenly spaced. The memory comes to me as I look down, but only fleetingly. I have other, more vital, thoughts flashing through my head,

Nam Dinh is ahead, a few miles off to our right. Always flak around Nam Dinh. Expected. And today the black puffs appear—suddenly, yet below us, and not a threat. Magnolia presses ahead. More guys are trying to jink, bobbing around at a fast pace. Dick follows Skipper Mow's example and flies steadily on. Rock Hodges is on the skipper's starboard wing, with Duter on his, and they remain steady. Duter is in good hands, for Rock, a former Air Force Strategic Air Command pilot, is an expert on SAM threats. Dick and I are flying formation on Rock and Duter. Purdy, over there on the skipper's port wing, is solid. Our six-plane division, as if charging along a steel track, drives purposefully toward the bridges.

We begin taking flak close aboard—37-mm at first. Seconds later, heavier stuff, 57-mm, is added to the mix. So far, none of the lethal 85-. When that comes up, it is almost always radar-directed, so it appears close-by as sudden black blooms with balls of fire flashing in the centers. Popcorn-shaped puffs streak past.

Ahead, a denser layer of 37-mm. It's barrage, which means they're throwing up a curtain of shit. Not aiming at anyone in particular. But it is also quite close to our altitude—and menacing. Magnolia drives on, and after thirty seconds or so we are clear. Still nothing directed by their radars. If so, we'd hear the buzz of the fire-control in our headsets.

The guys trying to jink within our formation have become more energetic, bobbing and weaving, yet now some of the birds are spread out enough to effectively make the larger S-turns. But most of us drone steadily ahead.

My skin feels prickly, like tiny needles, the effect of all the adrenaline. I need to settle down, so I concentrate on regular breathing. And for a few moments, I try to appreciate the beauty below.

Later in the summer the rice paddies and tea-groves down

there will be mostly yellow or brown, but the patchwork this morning is all variegated hues of green. Karst ridges slide along to our right. Lush green foliage covers these ancient features jutting up at severe angles from the flat valley floor. Peeking out from the green vegetation are the faces of steep cliffs, patches of white limestone where vegetation can't take hold.

We fly the planned course and keep the karst ridges between us and Phu Ly. It's about 30-degrees off our nose now: one-o'clock. Seeing it doesn't help my breathing; Phu Ly makes me anxious.

Our F-8s weaving overhead are anxious, too. They've trained and trained for aerial combat, but like so many fighter pilots, they may serve a full cruise and never engage an enemy fighter. We attack pilots, on the other hand, do our thing every mission.

I glance inside my cockpit to check engine instruments, then return my scan outside. We should get plenty of warning from our ALQ gear, but seeing the SAM is the true defense. This year there's additional warning, a rectangular red warning light in my instrument panel that will flash SAM-SAM-SAM should a site's guidance radar lock onto my particular aircraft. The warning light, this enhancement, will also be accompanied by a rattlesnake sound in the headphones—a noise intended to send a bolt of adrenaline straight to the heart.

We press on.

Until now our flight up the quiet valley could have been pleasant, with our gentle turns, easy transitions to changing altitudes, and our views of exotic scenery below: the mélange of phthalo-green of tea plantations on hillsides and Crayola's meadow-green of rice paddies laid out flat in their quilt-patchwork pattern on the valley floor.

Erase the hyper-alertness, the flak we've already seen—and the flak we know is ahead—and this would rival some of the finest flying I've enjoyed. But it is not that, and we are coming abeam Phu Ly. And my helmet is filled with new sounds generated in my ALQ gear.

"Got a low warbler," someone announces.

"Rajah," Magnolia answers. He's acknowledged a SAM site's acquisition-radar is sweeping someone's aircraft. By now, most of us also are hearing ugly songs in our headsets.

Old Salt One takes us into our final turn toward the target, where defenses will be heavy and where we expect SAMs. Those push-pins, the ones on the chart during our order-of-battle brief representing SAM sites—I can see these places now, not far to the north.

"High warbler," the unidentified pilot announces. This means a higher-pitched warning has entered his headset, telling him that acquisition radar from a SAM site has narrowed down to a target—which could be his airplane.

"Rajah," Magnolia says, his voice calm as a gentleman sipping a julep on the veranda. I increase my vigilance; no more peeks at engine-gauges in the cockpit. *Keep your head on a swivel*: that's the mantra.

We aren't far from Hanoi now; the outskirts of the city come into clear view. Dick and I are inside of the turn. We're slowing, we begin to wallow.

Dick slides out of our division's formation, and slips in behind. He and I form a separate section now, two planes in trail behind Skipper Mow's division. We open some more distance, and we're able to hold more speed here; our controls no longer feel like mush. Magnolia's strike force is not only turning, but also picking up more speed. We're descending to the briefed roll-in altitude of 10,000 feet, and ...

"Missile. Ten-o'clock," someone transmits.

"Two, there's two," another voice says.

I look, but don't see them. Old Salts on the inside of the turn roll past vertical into an evasive maneuver. This sets off a chain. Skipper Mow, now more maneuverable with four planes, has rolled his division steeply left into a descending spiral.

Much of the strike-force is evading this first salvo of SA-2 missiles, and the formation begins to fall apart. Dick rolls us hard to the left, too. Which is toward the missiles. Which I don't see.

My antsiness disappears. I focus on this challenging maneu-vering, matching Dick's bank angle—he's nearly upside down—and we shed altitude rapidly, going down like...deep breath...we're pointed almost straight down toward the earth. It is good we are no longer connected to the skipper's division, Dick and I. We're now a far more maneuverable section, but right now we are flying steeply down. Finally, Dick rolls his wings level and starts a pullout. To stay with him, I'm pulling heavy Gs. I never see the SAM—or SAMs, plural.

Dick begins to level, then turns left until we are on a reverse course, and we are climbing. This carries us back across the karst ridge. We are once again over the more peaceful valley, where we complete a full circle as we regain altitude.

Meanwhile, much of the strike-force has resumed a course to-ward the target. A second missile launch sends the four planes in the skipper's division and a few others into another altitude-eating evasive maneuver.

Four Old Salts converge on the target, but they are too low to make effective bombing runs. Skipper Mow's six-plane division is now reduced to him and Purdy—a two-plane section. They reach the pair of bridges and more or less toss their bombs at it. But they are too low. Later, post-strike reconnaissance photos will show everyone missed.

Dick, meanwhile, completes the 360-degree circuit and once more lines us up for a run to the target. The heavy drag from those M117 pigs keeps us from climbing well, but as we pass through about 7,000 feet we are on a steady 070-degree course toward the target, which is now no more than five miles ahead. It's obscured by smoke and dust from bombs already dropped.

A number of A-4s are coming off the target on a reverse course. Cleaned of the drag from their bomb-loads, they fly fast and low, jinking hard, streaking back toward the karst ridge that sepa-rates the perilous Red River Valley from the more peaceful one where Dick and I circled. Their airplanes look better, sleeker with-out all that clutter beneath their wings. They're hauling ass.

Dick and I are straight and level now at around 8,000 feet, pushing toward the target. I'm off his right wing in a loose formation and ... shit! I watch a SA-2 lift on its booster in a great cloud of red dust. It launches from a SAM site on Hanoi's outskirts. And another. I call them, trying to keep my voice under control.

In his professional-aviator's tone Dick responds evenly. "Magic Six, I've got 'em."

I pick up a high-warbler and right after that, the rattlesnake enters my helmet. Dick presses on. In quick succession, one after the other, the missiles drop their first-stage booster rockets. The damn things are accelerating incredibly fast. I'm fixated. They arc up rapidly on a trajectory bringing them to our altitude. So fast.

I'd expected thirty-five-foot flying telephone poles—a description I have heard guys use—but what I'm seeing are two pink-orange dots of light, one a second behind the other, leaving trails of pale smoke. The first is now level at our altitude, then the second. They are coming directly at us. The lead dot of light remains fixed in the same spot on my canopy, an indication I am quite surely on a collision course.

"Magic Five, they're tracking. Nine-o-clock."

Dick answers, his voice still professionally even. "I've got them."

It seems like forever, like we'll be demolished. They are tracking, these pink dots of fire—and then, finally, Dick's airplane rolls hard over. In the same way we practiced back in the States, he flips past vertical, nearly onto his back and begins turning hard into the approaching SAMs. I'm matching his bank angle, and we are pulling Gs, downward, losing altitude at an astonishing rate, our noses once again aimed at the valley floor.

We're plummeting toward the earth, and I lose sight of the SAMs because I am trying to fly this wild maneuver and at the same time remain with Dick. And we are heavy...shouldn't we be starting a pull-out about now? Dick's airplane begins to arc back toward level flight and I follow. Now we're pulling heavy Gs to keep from flying into the ground and—holy shit!—the two missiles, one, two, streak past me, right behind my aircraft. I glance over my shoulder to see their impacts, one after another, near the base of a karst ridge not far away. They throw up yellow-brown dust clouds with their silent explosions. In a fleeting glimpse, I take all this in. Dick stays low—we're maybe fifty, far less than a hundred, feet off the deck—and he swings back toward our valley, the calm place where we regained our altitude after the first SAM evasion.

I know what he's doing. He's determined to gain enough altitude in that quieter place for another go. We're not done.

We have enough fuel for another run at it, and Dick is resolute; we will accomplish an accurate dive-bombing run on the Co Trai Bridges. We'll go back, climb once again over the calm place, a do-over. He's carrying a lot of power, and I have my throttle full ahead.

## CHAPTER NINETEEN

# On the Karst

The nose of Dick's bird lifts enough to clear the karst ridge ahead, to skim over it as we did in our flat-hatting in the Sierras, and I see his airplane zoom-climb to about 800-feet. The ridge passes beneath him. I'm several hundred yards behind, in trail, when...it's Dick's voice, no longer calm.

"Four-one-five I'm hit!"

Is he saying that I am hit? I'm in 415. No, he's calling me, using my aircraft number instead of Magic-Six.

Ahead his aircraft blooms into a swelling orange orb.

Then his bird stops, comes to a halt in the air. I close swiftly. When I reach him—which is a matter of seconds—two roiling fireballs begin their tumble toward the earth. Neither is flying; both fall.

I'm nearly alongside, when Dick's ejection seat flies clear of one falling ball of fire. He shoots out parallel to the karst ridge below, and when he is barely clear of the fiery orange ball, his parachute snaps open. Vital, because he is less than 100-feet above the ridge. Had he punched out a half-second later, he would have been too low to survive.

Dick gets two quick swings under the canopy, then slams into the rocky ground atop the ridge.

Where his Skyhawk exploded, the air is filled with thousands of fluttering little squares and rectangles. A flickering layer, as if most of his A-4 has been reduced to confetti the size of business cards. White smoke spreads in the clear morning air.

I turn hard left to fly along the ridge, and over my shoulder I watch Dick stand up. He's dealing with his collapsing parachute canopy. I switch to Guard-frequency on my radio, while I begin a turn back to the right, which will take me out over the safe part of the valley. I wait a few moments until Dick has had time to get his handheld emergency radio turned on, then I transmit, using his Magic Five call-sign.

He responds. His voice is once again professional; he has recovered his aviator cool.

"I'm okay."

"You're not burned?"

"No."

I tell him we'll get him out. Then on the strike frequency I announce I am switching to channel-19, a frequency reserved for rescue operations. I make a transmission, and wait. No reply. Nothing.

Dick finishes gathering his parachute. I watch this a second or two, then look forward to see where the heck I'm going. Not at all far ahead, two streams of pink tracers are crossing at my altitude. Flaming balls stream up to make an X. This crap spews up from the valley floor—our supposedly safe valley. Astonishing. How can it be here? The streams of flak—this is tracking flak, not barrage, for it moves with my aircraft and at my speed—remain harmlessly out in front. (Later, when I have time to reflect, I'll realize the gunners peering through their sights were using a lead-factor they had been trained to give A-4s. Fortunately they were not compensating for my slow climbing speed, encumbered as it was with M-117 fat bombs. A slow aircraft requires less sighting-lead.)

Then the flak disappears. I have flown out of range—or perhaps the gunners have adjusted their aiming and are still shooting, but now behind me. Near the base of the karst, movement. It is a sight that will amaze me the rest of my life. Below Dick's position, dozens and dozens of troops run out onto a skinny laterite road. A whole platoon forms up in lines, smartly, in the same way we formed up as Class 24-64 outside our cadet barracks in Pensacola. I'm transfixed. In all my flying over the North, I have never seen such a display. A Jeep-like vehicle races out from camouflage cover onto the road and speeds toward the troops.

Things happen swiftly. I'm in this climbing right turn, and I focus my attention in the cockpit flipping through plastic-protected pages on my kneeboard, searching for that new chart, the one with the M-117 bomb-sight settings, and...here it is. I need this new bombsight-setting for the fat bombs. I intend to drop them one at a time to protect Dick. The intervalometer is tucked low in the cockpit, and I lean forward to reset it for one-at-a-time bombing runs, working the switches Frank Elkins quizzed me on last year. I continue turning 415 as I reset all switches to off except for one controlling a fat bomb on station three. I've circled back over the ridge and nearing the place I saw all the tracers.

Whack!

It is as if someone hits my airplane with a metal baseball bat. Hard. The sound of impact comes from behind me, somewhere aft in the airframe. My fire-warning light illuminates immediately, and almost at the same instant, two yellow lights in the center of my instrument panel flick on and off and now both come on to inform me that pressures in my airplane's two hydraulic systems, in quick succession, are unwinding toward zero. Time to go feet wet. I reverse my turn to southeast—which will retrace our ingress route.

Clean off the airplane. Yes, I should do that, so I pull the yellow T-handle that jettisons everything under my aircraft. My centerline fuel tank, now empty, and the bomb racks with all my ordnance fall away as one. I feel the thump as they blow free. Climb. The book says to climb when you are on fire.

I'm too occupied with emergency procedures to feel heightening emotion and all the fresh adrenaline pumping madly into my bloodstream.

Smoke flows into my cockpit. Then my oxygen, the crisp clean O2, goes away, and I unsnap one side of my mask so I can continue breathing. This is extremely bad, for it tells me that green tank of liquid oxygen back in the fuselage is burning—liquid O2 is feeding a fire and producing the heat of a cutting-torch. But so far the smoke is not that bad, nothing close to burning-Oriskany smoke. I can still breathe it.

I don't want to admit to myself that my airplane is deteriorating rapidly. I adjust my course toward a karst ridge on the other side of this valley. I reach the new heading, and the control stick pulls free of my hand, smacking full forward against the instrument panel. Although the stick is positioned for a steep dive, the airplane continues to climb, which is more bad news, for it tells me that backup control-cables, which I could use to fly this thing, have been cut by the torch back there.

I have now lost all control. Yet the sturdy little A-4 continues. It levels, it feels stable. I reach forward for the trim button on the stick. I'm strapped in so tightly that it's a stretch, but I get my index finger to the button. It moves up and down, left and right as it should, and—nice surprise—I find it provides me some control. I'm still the pilot of AH-415.

Flying with only my index finger, I continue toward that karst. The dense foliage on the little hill might afford me a hiding place, a chance for rescue. If I have to eject. But I won't, will I?

I'm nearly to the karst when the trim fails. The marginal command I had from the trim button has disappeared. I have guided my burning A-4 almost twenty miles from where I was hit to this point—which is short of a patch of karst not far from Nam Dinh. Now I'm riding a projectile; I have no influence.

It is here that 415 eases over into a right bank, a gentle roll. There is no possibility of making it to the coast, to the safety of the warm waters of the Tonkin Gulf now, and maybe no chance of reaching this hill not far ahead.

I key the mic and transmit that I'm about to eject, giving my position relative to where Dick went down. This is nowhere close to a precise location; I've pegged my potential rescue relative to Dick's ejection site. Rescuers will have to know where that was to find me.

The gentle roll continues and the nose of my burning airplane dips below the horizon. I'm entering a dive. Gus Jones, apparently the only pilot in the strike group to have switched to channel-19, answers in that gravelly voice of his.

"Okay, Magic Six. We'll get you out." His voice is calm. He tells me this as evenly as if he is suggesting we go to the wardroom for a midnight hamburger.

The roll-rate increases, and the nose falls through well below the horizon, and it continues until I'm going inverted. The dive steepens further, and the view filling the windscreen is Vietnam's green earth. Time to go.

## CHAPTER TWENTY

# *A Hillside*

I have ejected from my burning airplane, and I'm hanging from my 'chute with fresh air blowing up from my boots, and there off to my right something has caught my eye at the base of the karst formation I hope to land upon. It takes a moment to register. Then I understand it's the crashed remains of my A-4E Skyhawk—burning. It is in this moment that I realize I was knocked unconscious during the ejection. Had to be. I went out at 500 knots, almost Mach 0.8.

This explains my confusion when I came to, why I thought I had gone blind when my helmet was down over my face, and why I hadn't seen my bird impact. It's burning there on the ground; the fire well along. I can't see the airplane itself because it is engulfed in billowing smoke, white smoke, like Dick's airplane. What's with this white smoke? In every film I have seen of crashes, the smoke is an oily, charcoal black.

I return to my boots, gazing straight down to gauge my drift. Serious trouble, for I'm drifting backward. Out toward the valley.

Away from the safety of the karst hill. To parachute onto farmland means capture. Within minutes. But make it into jungle foliage, such as covers this hill, the one I'm drifting away from right now, and … well, there's a chance, a sliver of opportunity to evade long enough for a rescue.

I remember something important.

During our training we were told that our 'chutes can be guided forward by pulling down on the front risers. I reach over-head and grab them and pull hard, straining up into a chin-up. Yet this backward drift, away from safety, continues. My muscles labor, my arms begin to quiver.

My airplane's wreckage continues to burn, white smoke curls straight up, which indicates there is no wind near the ground. I'm trembling now and relax my strain on the forward risers to catch my breath. I glance down at my boots once more. I've passed through a wind shear, and now a faint breeze at this lower altitude is enough to reverse my drift. It's gently pushing me toward the hill. The green karst—where there is a chance.

The sensation of being suspended in the sky disappears as I near the ground. The trees come up rapidly. I'm over jungle now, about a third of the way up the hill. This is good, but now another fear: trees. A parachute-landing in trees is dangerous. I revert to my training, and lower my helmet visor and tighten the knob, lock-ing it in place. Then I snap my oxygen mask back on. My face is pro-tected. I press my boots together tightly to keep my legs from straddling a branch (but I don't cross them at the ankles. Our train-ers warned that a branch can lever a crossed leg to a breaking point). I cross my arms over my chest, elbows tucked in tightly, hands cupped protectively under my armpits to protect vulnerable soft skin and blood vessels from branch punctures.

And here comes the tree.

I hear the tearing and crunching, but feel no contact. Then— why, it's as if I've been on an amusement-park ride. I've stopped falling, I haven't banged down onto hard karst, and yet I'm not trapped high up in a tree. Instead I find myself suspended a few inches above the ground. I release the risers and step onto a hill in

North Vietnam, a nation I have been fiercely bombing for five days now.

I've endured fear, I've been blinded, experienced the strange sensation of wind blowing up from my feet, felt the cold dread that I might fall onto rice paddies instead of this jungle-covered hill. I've survived all that, and now more luck; it is my 'chute, and not me, hanging up there in a high branch of this tree. My seat-pan swings before me, suspended on risers running up to that white nylon canopy. Then it hits me—my 'chute may as well be a dazzling-white flag advertising: *Here! Look under this tree!*

At one corner of the seat pan, I locate a zipper. But the parachute riggers have stitched down the little pull-tab to prevent the zipper from working open in flight. To make quick work of it, I reach for my Buck knife. Missing. Torn away by the violent 500-knot ejection. The frayed end of the snapped nylon lanyard blooms like a weed flower. I fumble for my other knife inside my survival vest. Here, too, I find only snapped line. So, standing before the seat-pan with my hands trembling, I attempt to untie the thread securing the zipper's tab. But first I must gain control of my shaking hands, must slow my panicky breathing in order to pick away at the tiny knot.

It takes a while. What I find inside is a spare survival radio, and some dried food. I need these. I also find a solar still, an inflatable device that can turn seawater into drinking water. And there is also a life raft, along with shark repellant and dye-marker, powder to color the water around your raft a brilliant yellow-green to aid search-planes as you bob alone in a vast sea. There are smoke flares for daytime signaling and bright night flares. There also should be a tin of fresh water, which is what I want right now—about a pint, and attached on the bottom should be a key to open it, like a sardine can.

I toss the raft aside, pitch the shark-repellant, the dye-marker, solar stills and other stuff of no use. I turn on the homing beeper of that second radio and stuff it, along with packets of dried food, into my survival vest. And here it is, that tin of water. Just seeing it

179

makes me realize how terribly thirsty I am. Parched. Thirst is a consequence of all the adrenaline I'm burning. But that little key—the fucker is missing. What else can go wrong?

I have no knife, and I certainly can't bite the damn tin open. I unholster my toy-size .38 Smith & Wesson, and for a brief moment contemplate aiming the pistol at the edge of the can, meaning to blow it open—like some cowboy stunt you'd see in the movies. It is a pitiful little weapon that doesn't fit my hand, yet I go so far as to aim it at the can's rim. Fortunately, in a flash of clarity, I realize I'll certainly hurt myself with this foolishness. Far worse, a gunshot will alert anyone in the area to my whereabouts. I slip the little pistol back into the holster, and stuff the tin into my vest with the second radio.

Otherwise, it's a glorious morning. The sun is warm, but not yet hot. The air is fresh. I inhale a couple deep breaths and take in my setting. I'm in a room-size clearing next to the tall tree that snatched my parachute and cushioned my fall. And right over there, maybe ten yards down the hill, is a cave. Its mouth is about three feet high, and the shape is like—well, like a gaping frown. I could slide into it and—if it goes back far enough—slip completely out of sight.

Dumb idea. This handy sanctuary is within sight of my parachute, the bright white pointer to guide searchers directly to this location. May as well erect a billboard: *Yankee Air Pirate Here!*

I'll go up the hill, put some distance between me and my parachute. Okay, I've got everything I need from the seat pan. Not going to loiter any longer, I'm outta here, up the hill.

I fall.

I'm up again, taking this hill and...and I fall again.

Up, come on, let's make some time here.

I fall a third time in less than fifty feet. This time, while I'm lying on the ground I glance at my leg, my right leg, which splays incongruously out from my knee. And at this moment, this instant of recognition, pain shoots from my knee to my brain. Until I have seen the grotesque angle my lower leg makes, I have felt nothing. Now raw pain.

I struggle to my feet. With care I center my weight squarely over that knee. I take a step. Okay. Another. Good. If I don't introduce any twisting, the damn thing works. And the pain is endurable; it has to be. Moving is all about centering my weight, about equilibrium. And I must move up this hill, must put some distance between that parachute and me.

I take a couple deep breaths and forge ahead. Carefully planning each step, getting my weight just so, I move up the crumbly karst. This works. I'm climbing again.

I have left the clearing and am under the canopy of trees in deep mauve shade. The jungle floor is surprisingly clear; it is not the tangle of foliage I expected. I'm terrified, and my mind races, but I pause for a moment to take in this scene. Trees evenly distributed, their trunks smooth, soar up a hundred feet or more, and their top branches spread like umbrellas to form a purple-green canopy. I've seen the other side from the air, and from that vantage it flows under my aircraft like a lumpy green carpet. But from beneath, it appears high and dark, like the interior of a gothic cathedral. It is speckled with dots of daylight and blue sky peeping through tiny openings.

I climb with care, but continue to fall from time to time. And I'm exhausted. I fall again, and this time I remain where I've hit the ground. I must catch my breath. I'm in good physical condition; it isn't this. It's the pain. It sucks away strength.

Down the hill, through an opening in the trees, I see my 'chute. Damn it. I've climbed and climbed, and yet, here I am only a few hundred yards from my parachute. I've gained maybe seventy-five feet of elevation, which places me about eye level with the white nylon. I pull out my survival radio and work a switch that toggles between beeper-mode and two-way communication. In the communication mode, I listen. Nothing. I switch back to beeper; search aircraft will home on the beeper's signal to find me. That's the most important thing right now. I push myself up onto my feet and resume my trudge up the hill. It is slow going, and I'm exhausted, but I know my life may depend on this climb. I go, fall, go, fall and I press on.

There is a big rotting log where I have fallen yet again, a good place to hide and rest for a short while. I stretch out along the log and take a handful of soil to dirty my white hands and face. We had been taught escape and evasion skills in a jungle-survival school near San Diego, training we hated. But it is this training I'm using now. Near me is an elephant-ear plant. I pluck a big leaf, shove the stem under the front of my shirt so it covers my pale neck and face. This is the evasion part, this camouflage effort with a dirtied face and a leaf.

CHAPTER TWENTY-ONE

# *Barking Like Dogs*

From below, voices. People are climbing the karst hill, and they're imitating dogs—dogs barking with a Vietnamese accent. There is some laughing mixed in. People are coming up this little mountain to find me, and for them it is a celebration, a caper.

We've been told there is a nice reward paid to farmers who capture a yankee air pirate. But right now I don't feel like an air pirate, not even like an experienced warrior. It has been ten months since I finished my transition into A-4s and flew my first combat sortie. This I never envisioned, yet here come the barking dogs with accents. I have waited here, motionless beside my log, and now they're closer. I adjust the leaf over my face. The fake barks have devolved to a form of laughter. Yes, a caper. They're closing in, talking among themselves—softly. It's hard to figure out how many there may be. Three or four? Five? A dozen, maybe?

They arrive at my 'chute. An outburst of chatter; they're gleeful. I picture them finding the raft, the solar stills, the shark repellant, the dye-marker and all the other stuff scattered about. They are near. I snuggle in closer to my log and try to silence my breathing. This was the secret to hide-and-seek games when I was a kid: you become still as death. I wait.

Someone is walking this way, crunching up through the karst gravel.

I slip my sidearm, the tiny .38, from its holster. It's like a toy, but I clutch it in my right hand, slide up my left hand and place it on top of the right.

I'm ready. I imagine coming rapidly up into a kneeling position with the pistol at eye-level, my arms extended stiffly, the left hand steadying the right. My fingers entwined. It will be like holding a putter, like—like what? I try to picture myself shooting a man in the back, surprising him.

Posed as if laid out by an undertaker, I'm quiet as death. Except it's a small gun, not a rosary, in my grip.

The steps are close now. Motionless. I'm not breathing. They are so close, within a yard, no more than two. The footsteps crunch past.

Now! This is the time to come up on my knees and shoot my pursuer. In the back!

But I don't. I find I'm not a shoot-in-the-back type warrior. Driving this Boggs-like clarity, this decision, is my pitiful marksmanship. I recall the disgust of the Marine at that handgun range near Fallon, remembering how he held the unscathed paper silhouette, the target that had been only six feet away from this same pistol.

So, I forgo a shootout with someone carrying a military rifle. I remain still as a cadaver. The sound of the crunching feet diminishes. He continues up the hill. Good for now. But soon enough I'll be captured; I'm convinced of this. They are all so close.

Oddly, when I feel certain I'll soon be captured and am almost consumed by anguish and fear, that in this brief moment the Denver home-economics teacher comes to mind, a girl I have never had an in-depth conversation with and kissed maybe twice. In this moment of despair, it comes to me how, after I'm taken prisoner, I'll never see her again. I listen to the voices down the hill. The laughter. They, too, believe I'll soon be taken. There are no atheists in foxholes: an old bromide, but probably true. I recover hope. And I rediscover religion. I'm praying silently to God as I hide motionless next to the log. But what I ask is shameful. I ask that I be spared, which is natural enough, but then go further. I bargain with the Heavenly Father. If someone must be captured, I pray, let it be Dick. Dick has the faith for it. Dick will be better at captivity than me.

I'm on the ground in North Vietnam, deep in the territory of the enemy, and instead of pure and faithful reverence, instead of a simple plea, I am suggesting a deal—a dishonorable deal—with God. I propose something terrible, something Faustian involving this fine man I respect so much. This is an act time will never soften on my conscience.

Though I'll accomplish brave and honorable undertakings in years ahead, I will at times dwell on this quick prayer and feel all the good I accomplish is negated. When I am forty-two and confronting a midlife crisis, I'll sit in a soft chair in a small office. I'll confess this sin to Lance, the psychologist, and he'll ask, "Have you cried about this?" Then he'll tell me I must allow myself to forgive myself, to grieve, to cry and to talk about that day and those years in Vietnam. And I do. And it helps. But all this will be in the future.

As if God has answered, I hear the sound of a prop-driven aircraft. It's a Spad, the sweet baritone of an A-1 Skyraider.

Spads don't dance through the air—none of this ballerina stuff—they charge ahead like NFL linemen. And one is over me right now. My radio has been transmitting on beacon mode, but now I switch to voice communication. I call. The Spad-driver identifies himself as Sandy One.

"Been trying to raise you, Magicstone Six," he says.

I quickly tell him there are enemy nearby.

"Strafe my 'chute," I tell him.

He asks for my location.

"A little way up the hill," I transmit on the handheld.

185

"I hear them at my 'chute," I add.

He wants to pinpoint my position before doing any shooting, so he brings his Spad around for another pass.

"Tell me when I'm overhead," he transmits.

When Sandy One is feet above the trees, almost to pass above me, I call. He rolls his wings 90-degrees, which done this close to the ground requires great skill—a little top rudder to keep from losing altitude, but not too much. I see him through his canopy; he's looking down through the trees, and for an instant our eyes meet. He passes over me, and right after, a huge noise shatters the air with the shrieking scream of a 7.62-mm Minigun firing 6,000 rounds per minute.

In concert with the fierce noise, the tree canopy overhead parts, it rips open, as if a huge mower instantly cut a swath through it. It's about now I realize there are at least two Spads working the hill. Not long after this—but from my spot on the hill I cannot tell precisely when—four of Oriskany's Locket A-1s arrive to join the race-track pattern.

They space themselves so there is precious little letup between firing runs. The Lockets introduce more cacophony with their thumping 20-mm cannons and thunderous booming of Zuni rocket fire.

As each airplane pulls off from a run, I hear tinkling sounds, shell casings ejected from the guns, hundreds of pieces of brass falling through the new gash in the jungle, bouncing off branches and each other as they rain down to the jungle floor.

Spads make run after run. I'm astonished by how enormous and concussive the sounds of war are when you witness it from the ground. Pounding waves of blasts and booms.

Whenever a Spad-driver fires a rocket, the impact is as deafening as a nearby thunder clap. In quiet intervals I hear nothing from the celebrants down near my 'chute. I know, however, that my pursuers have not departed.

The strafing and rocket firing go on, and after a time it shifts down the mountain. I remain still, stretched out alongside my log.

It is after some time, perhaps an hour, when Sandy One—Maj. Theodore Bronczyk—tells me a chopper is inbound. He instructs me to light off a smoke-flare.

Until now I've been motionless, but I stand, I fish a smoke flare from my survival vest and hold it above my head like the Statue of Liberty. Bright red smoke billows from it, rises no more than a foot, and then it falls down my arm, down my body and onto the jungle floor, where a faint breeze catches the thinning red cloud and carries it slowly uphill. I hold the flare aloft until it burns out, and about then I hear the whump-whump-whump of an approaching chopper.

By its sound, it's coming into a hover uphill from me, which is where the crew of Big Mother 67, a large SH-3 Navy helicopter, sight a pink mist emerging into a small clearing. Rather than try to direct the rescue bird down to me, I scramble—as much scramble as I can manage, placing each step carefully—and I make my way up the karst hill toward the pounding noise.

With my bum knee, it's agonizingly slow. But Big Mother 67 isn't far, a few dozen yards from my log. I come into the clearing, and hovering right in the center, is the huge gray bird. With my loping limp I hustle the final few yards to stand under it. I'm directly below it, looking straight up at its huge boat-shaped belly, yet the jungle-penetrator does not drop.

I yank my radio out of its pouch and call. "Lower the sling. I'm right under you."

But instead, the chopper noses over, moves forward, gains a little speed and rises. Leaving. He's leaving me!

Sandy One comes up on the radio.

"Magic Six, that bird had to go. We've got another. Hang on a little while."

Across the clearing, opposite where I have come into it, movement catches my eye. Pale smoke drifts slowly from the jungle—the telltale white puffs of rifle shots. The white cloud is nudged by a hint of a breeze, and lazily it spreads along the edge of the clearing not far from me. Someone there has been shooting. So close. Right there. Firing a rifle.

The shooter doesn't want to step out into that clearing to become an easy target any more than I want to stay here in the open. I limp back into the jungle, opposite the white smoke. I sit down and prepare for my capture by pulling my dog-tags from under my t-shirt. I look at them and study my name, rank, service number and date of birth. This is all the information—indeed the only information—I am to give up during interrogation.

A numbing fear grips me now. Without doubt, the shooter spotted me. I was standing in the clearing under the chopper, waving my arms over my head, getting out a radio and talking. Certainly the shooter saw. He will be here in a moment.

Sandy One calls. "Magicstone Six, we have to leave. We have another helicopter coming for ya."

One of the Lockets, Hank Miller, has also departed. He's escorting Big Mother 67, but the other three—Jim Harmon, Boo Langlinais and Jack Baker—continue to work the hill with their A-1s, eradicating gun emplacements and slowing the stream of Vietnamese headed up toward me.

This is the fog of war. With the Sandys gone and the Lockets at work elsewhere, around me the hill becomes freaky silent. There is no chatter or laughter from down near my 'chute. And the guy uphill from me—he's somewhere near—makes no noise. Neither does he call out, ordering me to surrender, nor does he fire a shot my way. Silence.

I sit on the ground, switch my radio back to beacon mode, and wait. How long, I can't say. Time seems to stop. I'm dreadfully thirsty, my knee is throbbing, there is a pursuer not far from me who has a rifle, the rescue chopper has left without me and I'm listening on the radio to no one. I sit here trying to figure out what to do next. I can't go further up the hill; I'll run into the rifleman (and probably there are more than just him).

I shouldn't remain here, because at least one guy knows I'm here. But on the other hand, maybe I should stay put. Sandy One said another helicopter is on its way. The truth is, I'm on a hillside in North Vietnam without a plan. And time has stopped.

I discover I'm still clutching the big leaf I employed as camouflage over my face, and instead of dropping it, I carefully fold it and stuff it into my survival vest. And I pick up a pebble as another souvenir. Hope has not totally vanished.

I wait. I'm not back into the deep, cathedral-like, jungle, but I am out of the clearing and hidden.

The silence fractures with the whoomp-whoomp of a chopper. And it's near. Coming toward the clearing. I ensure my radio is in voice-mode and call, and I begin to hobble back toward the clearing's edge.

The chopper overflies my position, then turns around. It drifts slightly and its blades tear off the top of a tree. Branches and leaves fly and—oh God, the bird's going to crash!

But it doesn't. The hover is stable. It's slightly downhill from where I have come back into the clearing, and I limp toward it. Downhill is tough on my knee, but I manage to keep from falling. The jungle-penetrator on the end of a cable drops down to ground level, I'm almost to it, and I have been trained for this.

There are three metal arms that fold out like flower petals from the plumb-bob base, and I am to fold down any two to make a seat, which I am now doing. Then I am to unzip a nylon pouch at the top of the penetrator, extract a safety strap, wrap that around my torso and snap the free end into a steel fitting. When ready, I am to give a couple stout tugs on the line, at which time I will be reeled up. Except this is not what happens.

I'm on the two steel seat-petals, and I begin unzipping the pouch, and ... what the hell, I'm swinging out in the air. I'm above trees. The chopper accelerates. We're moving out fast, and I'm hanging from a cable in the slipstream. The tops of trees are below me, and then I'm at the door. We've climbed to maybe three hundred feet and we're hauling ass. A tall crewman operating the winch pulls me into the bird.

This has not at all gone like the training. But I have been rescued. Rescued!

## CHAPTER TWENTY-TWO

# *Jolly Green 37*

It's an HH-3E Jolly Green that I've been pulled into, a Sikorsky weighing almost six tons, an Air Force bird specially modified for rescue operations. Armor-plates protect its vital components, and to increase its range for long-distance rescues, drop tanks from F-100 aircraft were fitted on either side, but that fuel has been used and the tanks were jettisoned when the helicopter dived to make a final rush to me. This rescue will call for every pound of that additional fuel, for Jolly 37 has already flown across the wide part of Vietnam from a base in Laos that is secretly operated by the CIA—and now it must retrace the long route back.

The crewman who pulled me aboard has gone forward for water from a tall, galvanized steel Igloo jug. It's near the cockpit, some distance from where I'm sitting near the tail of this huge bird. He returns with a tiny Dixie Cup, a little paper cone holding maybe two swallows. The accommodating crewman goes back for more. Here we are skimming over jungle canopy in one of the most dangerous places on earth for an American helicopter to be flying, and this kind young man is serving me water in a dainty Dixie Cup. Minutes ago, people were shooting at us, trying to kill us all. But I am parched, and he is making trip after trip to the water jug.

The other crewman, a shorter guy, interrupts. He comes from the cockpit carrying a helmet, a chart, and a ballpoint pen. He motions me to don the helmet, and then plugs it into the intercom system. The voice of the co-pilot asks me to draw a circle on the chart exactly where Dick landed in his 'chute. It's a Sectional Chart, 1:500,000 scale, which is what I had on my kneeboard a few hours ago. It takes me a few moments to get oriented, then I pinpoint the ridge where Dick ejected. I mark his position.

I'm holding an empty Dixie Cup and about to ask for more water, when the shorter crewman hands me an M-16 rifle. We're going in to get Dick, he informs me. He motions me to an open window on the port side. "Shoot anyone shooting at us," he yells in my ear. He demonstrates how to switch between automatic and single-shot mode.

"Which will I want? Automatic or single?" I yell.

He shrugs. "You'll know."

We fly down the ridge, a spine of karst that may be the one with all the crisscrossing tracers this morning. We're low, coming in fast. I'm vigilant with my weapon jutting from the open window. But Dick doesn't come up on his radio. We hear nothing.

The big Jolly Green banks tightly, and we backtrack northwest along the karst. I hand the rifle back to the crewman. The co-pilot and pilot are discussing fuel. They don't use terms like "bingo" or "RTB," which in Air Force terminology means return-to-base. We slipped beyond that point when we burned fuel on the detour searching for Dick, and likely this aircraft was at RTB fuel-state even before it came in for me. There is no elevation in tone, but from what I overhear, we may not have enough fuel.

We're over remote jungle, clear of the development around Hanoi and clear of the populated farming areas, too. We fly on. I watch featureless jungle pass beneath us, an undulating sea of green tree-crowns, so different from the deep shade that lies beneath—shade where not many minutes ago I hid. The green stretches to the horizon in every direction. I rest. My knee hurts, and I think about it, and it hurts more.

We're climbing, now, and flying above a layer of clouds. The two turbojets powering us gain efficiency at higher altitudes (the reason airliners fly so high). This HH-3E is without oxygen or a pressurized cabin, so we'll level off at 12,000 feet.

The tall crewman comes to me carrying a parachute. He helps me into it.

"We may have to jump."

He explains we may run out of fuel and flame-out. "If we do, we jump," he says. He doesn't appear worried. He heads back toward the cockpit.

There's a secondary reason we are wearing parachutes now. The pilot has been warned that Bandits—code-word for Vietnamese MiGs—are headed our way. I'll learn after we land that the MiGs did cross our path. But they flew their radar-guided intercept at low altitude, below the cloud layer where helicopters normally operate. So, while we were at altitude conserving fuel, the two North Vietnamese fighters searched underneath the thin layer of clouds concealing us. Our serious fuel circumstance, forcing us to fly at 12,000 feet, saved us from being shot down.

Even with the critical fuel situation, my fear and anxiety wash away. A photo is taken of me sitting with the tall crewman. I'll discover it decades from now, on the Internet, and in this photograph I appear relaxed. I'm smiling. You'd never guess I am in pain.

The noise inside this chopper is massive. I lean in close to the ear of the tall crewman and ask him to write the names of the crew. I hand him my empty Dixie Cup (which I still have). He folds it flat, and with a ballpoint pen writes:

Maj. Glen York, pilot;

1st Lt. Billy Privette, co-pilot;

Staff Sgt. Ted Zerbe;

Airman 2nd Class Randy McComb.

The tall crewmember is Ted Zerbe. He asks if I'm hungry, then brings me a box lunch. Decades from now, Ted and I will talk at Glen York's funeral, and I'll learn it was his own lunch he handed me; he went through the rest of the day without a midday meal. I eat most of the lunch, and then Zerbe shows me to a stretcher suspended from the port side of the Jolly. My knee throbs less when I recline. My helmet is still connected to the intercom, and I notice there is scant communication between the two men in the cockpit. Major York is not one for idle chatter. Years later Billy Privette will tell me he and Glen York mostly communicated with shrugs or raised eyebrows, even when flak became intense. I rest on the stretcher.

As we close in on Laos, the cloud-layers thicken and knit into a broad gray expanse. The intercom comes alive. I hear York and Privette in discussion, and it appears only the distance measuring equipment—the DME—is functioning. York asks Privette to calculate a heading to our destination. When Privette gives him the number, which is corrected for wind-drift, York adds five degrees to it and says they'll fly that. Puzzling. We are deliberately flying five degrees north of the wind-corrected dead-reckoning heading to the tiny Lima field we are hoping to find. Why not fly the heading as calculated?

I know that DR relies on assumptions, so it is almost inevitable you'll miss your mark by a little. Once you have flown your calculated time, conventional practice is to set up an expanding-box-search to find the destination, which is what Amelia Earhart vainly flew out there in the Pacific on her final flight. She was searching for Howland Island, a tiny dot, after her long dead-reckoning. But such a pattern eats fuel, and she ran out before finding the island. I know, too, that this Jolly Green doesn't have enough to even begin a box-search.

After we landed, I asked Glen York why he added that five-degree factor to the calculated heading. He answered that he wanted to ensure that if they missed he could be certain they were north of the field. He said he'd watch the DME mileage unwind to a halt, and if it didn't stop at zero, he'd know they were to the north by whatever miles the DME showed. No need to set up an expanding search pattern. They'd execute a 90-degree left turn, to the south, and the DME would begin falling once more as they flew directly to Lima 36. It was a brilliant navigation trick that I'd never heard about.

But as it turns out, a circling airplane will guide us directly to Lima 36. Visual navigation over the featureless cover of clouds has been challenging, and York and Privette have seen no rivers, no peaks or ridges—no visual markers whatsoever—to confirm our position and update navigation. We've been flying on pure dead reckoning for over an hour, when I hear Privette make a transmission. He requests that a pilot flying single-engine Air America aircraft orbit the dirt airstrip at Lima 36, our destination. The pilot agrees, then keys his mic. Maj. York homes on that signal using ADF electronic gear in the Jolly.

As we close on the field, a solid cloud-layer shrouds the terrain. York and Privette, following a needle pointing at an orbiting airplane, begin a descent. We are low when we break out from the clouds. The dirt strip angles ahead of us, but we don't have enough fuel to fly a normal pattern. York lands as soon as we reach the approach end of the strip. Our bird settles awkwardly with its huge rotor blades sweeping close to the packed red earth as the engines unwind.

The Jolly Green burns about 1,200 pounds of fuel per hour, but in our tanks only seventy pounds of fuel, a bit over ten gallons, remain when the engines are shut down—meaning we've come within about four minutes of flaming out and falling from the sky. In fact, there is not enough fuel to lift into a hover or taxi down to the fueling area. Close.

We are safe at Lima 36, a scruffy, CIA-supported Air America base tucked into a remote northeastern corner of Laos. Very secret. Secret from the American public, at least, for our politicians have assured war-weary Americans that this war has not expanded into Laos.

## CHAPTER TWENTY-THREE

# The Shack at Lima 36

It is afternoon. I was on Vietnamese soil almost four hours, and now we've flown more than another hour to arrive here. Ted Zerbe helps me step down from the Jolly Green. I'd like to do that kiss-the-sweet-earth thing, but I can't stoop down. I realize my back is tweaked, as well as the knee. I shake hands with Privette, Zerbe and McComb, but York is not here. He has clambered seventeen feet up the outside of the huge Jolly Green and is atop the fuselage inspecting rotor blades. He pulls each around to him, then runs his hand out toward the end of the blade, feeling for damage from that tree-trimming exercise in North Vietnam.

Several indigenous men, Hmong fighters wearing military fatigue uniforms, have gathered around our little group. After York has climbed down, he speaks with them. Two men head down toward the fueling area. York hands a third Hmong man a camera. We pose. The Jolly Green in the background sits awkwardly on its partially collapsed nose gear. In this photo I'm standing there between Privette and York, smiling. Privette smiles, too. Glen appears satisfied, with a hint of a smile. The two crewmen stare into the camera, however, revealing the true expression of men who have been through heavy combat and endured hours of stress. In this photograph, I've shifted most of my weight onto my good left leg, and I've masked my pain to present the image of a happy young aviator, a survivor so glad to be alive—overflowing with the gratitude of a man saved from years of torture and confinement. That's truly how I felt at the moment. Later, though, the authentic emotions crewmembers Ted Zerbe and Randy McComb display in the photo will visit me. And they'll stay awhile.

Not much time passes before the two Hmong men return to the chopper in a pickup truck loaded with fuel barrels. These guys, I learn, are mountain tribesmen who hate the Pathet Lao and their Communist North Vietnamese allies. The Hmong fighters serve under General Vang Pao, a CIA ally, with headquarters at another CIA site, Lima 20A.

While I watch refueling begin on the Jolly Green, a single-engine airplane lands on the sloping red-clay runway. The CIA has purchased a number of Helio Couriers, exotic single-engine airplanes for use in this secret war. No one takes much notice, and the little craft pulls clear of the dirt strip well down the hill from us. Probably this is the aircraft that circled the field with a keyed-mic to assist us.

Refueling the chopper is strenuous. Some 6,800 pounds of fuel—around 1,000 gallons—must be transferred from fifty-five-gallon drums into the chopper's internal tanks. There are no spare F-100 external drop tanks at this little dirt strip to replace the pair York jettisoned before coming in to pick me up, so the internal tank capacity will be all the fuel this chopper will carry until it returns tonight to its base at Udorn, Thailand. Ted Zerbe's title is aircraft flight engineer, which puts him in charge of the fueling—and today that means he's doing most of the work, grinding away at a hand pump. I watch.

Billy Privette leads me into a nearby shack. It's surrounded by weeds, a ratty looking place maybe eight by sixteen feet that's been thrown together with plywood sheets and rough-cut wood studs.

A corrugated tin roof and splintering plywood floor complete the place. An excellent collection of *Playboy* nude pinups warms the shack. The lovely airbrushed centerfolds are tacked onto the bare plywood. There's a military bunk-bed along one wall, but no mattress. For a table, an ammunition crate has been turned on end. Two smaller crates on either side serve as stools. A single-burner stove, for brewing coffee, sits next to a disproportionately large upright propane tank.

Billy explains that this shack has exchanged hands several times, most recently in February. Here and there light streams through splintered holes—the results of past firefights. The Pathet Lao who occupied it for a period carried away everything of value. Except the pinups.

"They like them," Billy says, "and leave 'em alone."

After the last battle, Billy tells me, enemy dead were buried nearby. He points to a shallow ashtray resting on the ammo-crate table. It's small and grubby with butts and ashes overflowing onto the wooden crate top. It's clear this thing disgusts him. "That's the top of somebody's skull," he tells me. "I don't know who put it here." I understand immediately why it overflows; no one wants to touch it to toss the butts out the door.

Pain in my knee is building. I ask if I can lie down. The lattice of steel straps suspended from small springs around the perimeter of the pipe-frame bed is familiar. I have a history with a rack like this. It feels better to relieve my leg of weight, and reclining also eases the pain in my lower back. The refueling continues.

After a while Glen York comes into the shack. He's been to a CIA base at the top of a nearby hill, and he's carrying a single-sideband radio, a portable transceiver about the size of a twelve-pack of beer. He sets it near the rack so I can hear it.

"We're going back for your buddy," he says. "If we don't get him today, he's not coming out." He shows me the controls on the radio. "You can listen to us on this." He also tells me that another helicopter will come, later in the afternoon, to pick me up. Then he and his crew man the Jolly for another dangerous mission into North Vietnam.

Three decades later, after he has retired from the Air Force and he and I connect again, Glen York says that I asked to accompany them when they were preparing for another attempt to rescue Dick. He claims I insisted. And decades later, when I speak with Billy, he tells me the same thing. I don't recall this, and it doesn't make a lot of sense. Perhaps I thought I could be useful manning that port-side window with the M-16. But how stupid it would have been to burden them with an injured guy who in reality was a terrible marksman. Yet they say I made the gesture, and I'm as proud of that as I am ashamed of the deal I proposed to God earlier in the day. Perhaps shame drove me to volunteer. Maybe I meant to show God I wasn't serious about the other thing.

The Jolly Green comes to life. Red dust lifts and swirls around the shack. I'm in the doorway. York adds power and the huge blades, the ones he carefully inspected, bite into the air, smashing it in whomp-whomp-whomps as the six-ton aircraft lifts. I watch its crippled nose gear fold into the fuselage as the Jolly tips forward and gains speed down the runway. Jolly 37 turns east toward a rendezvous point where it will meet up with escorting Sandy A-1s from Udorn and then it will press on toward Dick.

I return to the rack and listen to the single-sideband. It is quiet for long periods, and then—I cannot believe this—after the Jolly has requested permission to enter Route Package Four, the Navy's area of combat where Dick is stranded, the voice of an admiral, who identifies himself by his title, comes through.

"Negative, negative," the admiral says. "The Navy takes care of its own."

What should have been a perfunctory request has been denied. The Navy will not allow Jolly Green 37, these competent and courageous Air Force rescuers, to re-enter its area. I sink back onto the steel slats. From time to time, Hmong soldiers stick their heads into the shack and smile, but they say nothing, and then disappear. My knee is throbbing. I lay there the rest of the afternoon thinking of what York told me about Dick's chances if he isn't pulled out today. Every hour passing lessens his chances.

I hear the whomp of a helicopter. Did I sleep? I don't know. But it's late afternoon, and deep shadows have moved way up the valley, up to the concertina wire surrounding the CIA base atop the hill.

It's another Jolly Green, and it rolls out on the runway, then turns and taxies back up the slope toward the shack. I'm hobbling by now, heavily favoring that bum knee. I hand one of the crewmen the single-sideband radio, and then I'm helped into the chopper. We head out. I don't have a helmet, so I can't hear the radio or intercom chatter. I settle back. It's a surprisingly long flight from Lima 36 to Udorn in Thailand. It's dark when we land at the sprawling Air Force Base.

It will be dark on Dick's ridge, too. I think about how he'll be hiding, knowing there won't be another rescue effort until morning.

At about this same time, aboard USS Constellation, four men are inspecting the battle-damage inflicted on Big Mother 67 when it hovered over me. They are not the same crew who flew it out to attempt my rescue, but at first light tomorrow this is the crew that will go to rescue Dick. Pilot-in-command is Dennis Peterson, a lieutenant; co-pilot is Don Frye, an ensign; and the crewmen are AX2 Don McGrane and AX2 Bill Jackson.

Maintenance personnel are at work repairing Big Mother's battle damage. They've counted twenty-eight bullet holes in the bird, but Patterson and the other three crewmembers looking it over are assured nothing vital or irreplaceable has been ruined. Big Mother 67 will be an up-bird when before daylight they board the chopper to fly it to Dick. The maintenance guys will work through the night, they say, if that's what it takes.

At Udorn, I'm taken to the medical center, where an Air Force doctor examines me. My knee is swollen fat, and I tell him my lower back hurts a lot. Sandy One's pilot, Ted Bronczyk, comes into the room while the doctor is looking me over.

"After you finish here, come down to the O'Club." He tells me they're celebrating my rescue and their successes. "We got jumped by MiGs," he adds. He says his bird took a number of hits. But he's happy, having had a beer or two already.

I'd like to join them, to thank them, but I'm feeling so rotten, and the doc advises against it. I'm led to a barracks, where I'm to share a room with a young first lieutenant whose roomie was shot down a week ago.

The first lieutenant loans me a pair of his skivvies and a t-shirt, because mine reek. I shuffle off toward the shower. This day, this long, hard, terrifying day is finally over.

And it started so well...with a breakfast in the quiet of a ward-room.

# PART V

## SAIGON REDUX

The most glorious moments in your life are not the so-called days of success, but rather those days when out of dejection and despair you feel rise in you a challenge to life, and the promise of future accomplishments.

*—Gustave Flaubert*

Minutes after landing in Laos, with Jolly 37 in the background, are the author's rescuers. (L to R) Ted Zerbe, Randy McComb, Glen York, Duthie (favoring his injured leg) and Billy Privette. York earned the Air Force Cross and the other three crewmembers, Silver Stars for their bravery that day.

## CHAPTER TWENTY-FOUR

# *It's Not Water*

I wake early after a fitful night of appalling dreams. I couldn't know then that dreams last night would be the first of a long string of dreadful nightmares ahead. All involving Dick Hartman and Vietnam and fire and me. The events of July eighteenth altered the sweep of my life.

The seismic shearing during waking hours that day—and days to come—were at first subtle. Tiny temblors of doubt. Slight reservations about the price we were paying, fleeting questions slipping nimbly along fissures in my thinking. Over time the temblors intensified, shredding my simplistic understanding of life, ripping away facile certainty. I can't pinpoint when the comfortable simplicity of black-and-white transmuted to a complex gray. But it did.

I sometimes miss that certainty, the quick and easy answers, and at times I covet the guileless solutions and facile answers that glib guy at end of the bar is so quick to deliver. Oh, to have the easy answers again—life was so much simpler that way. But the stark and simple solutions I enjoyed before I discovered my mortality, they fell away that July day.

My temporary roomie, the first-lieutenant, tells me my fatigues are too sweat-fouled for the meeting I'm to attend. It's with an Admiral in Saigon, he informs me. I accept one of his clean flight-suits, and we both understand there is no way I can return it. A car whisks me out to the flight line where a Navy executive jet, a shiny blue and white T-39 Saberliner, is waiting. I find I am the only passenger. It's as if I am high-ranking brass.

Our destination is Tan Son Nhut. We land, and I'm amazed. It has been transformed into a fast-paced American Air Force base. The sleepy facility with the character of a rural French aéroport that I departed six years ago in an ancient DC-3 airliner, has become the busiest airport in the world.

Once again, a car is waiting. The driver, a young enlisted man, navigates dense morning traffic, and after a few minutes he stops at a military office complex. It's a single-story building, unmistakably temporary. I make my way, each step planned and deliberate, down a long passageway with a highly waxed floor, to the office of the admiral.

Scattered about the admiral's desk are photos taken shortly after Dick's shoot-down. I admire the photo-reconnaissance jocks. To make these photographs, a daring RF-8 driver streaked along ridges close to where 37-mm nailed Dick's airplane and then mine. From the angles, it's clear he flew perilously low.

Together we look over the glossy black-and-whites. The admiral lifts one from the table and hands it to me. He wants to know precisely where Dick parachuted onto that ridge. I point to a spot. "He won't be there now," I say. He agrees. Dick certainly will have put some distance between where he was yesterday morning and now. The admiral asks a few more questions, then this. "What does he need?"

"Water. I really needed water once I was on the ground."

"He has water."

The admiral points to a series of white fissures down the face of the karst. The streaks in this black-and-white reconnaissance photo do resemble waterfalls.

"Sir, that's karst. It's white like that."

"Water. All he'll need." This the admiral states with a tone of finality.

Unstated, but understood, is that I am a young officer, one many ranks junior to the knowledgeable flag-rank officer. This is not up for discussion. He easily could have cast one of those dark, mind-your-place stares my way, but he doesn't bother. Doesn't even glance up.

I'm dismissed, but told to hang around. Someone from the ship is flying in from Yankee Station. "You'll want to talk with him," the admiral says.

I sit on a couch in a waiting area in the flimsy building with the highly buffed floors. There are copies of Naval Aviation News, one of the slick magazines the military publishes. The most popular feature in each issue of NA News is a safety-oriented column called "Grampaw Pettibone," in which an incident or accident is described and then analyzed by Grampaw. He highlights headwork errors with crusty comments along the lines of, "Holy Mackerel, what was this lad thinking? He's already got a bag of snakes in that cockpit, and he introduces another one by not shutting down the autopilot. We coulda lost an aircraft in this fiasco!" Fun reading, and always instructive.

Hours pass. Once or twice, I gingerly make my way down the passageway to the head. If I walk deliberately straight ahead, my knee supports me with surprisingly little pain. It takes concentration. Make a small, absentminded detour from the rhumb-line, and the leg splays off at an angle and a stab of pain snatches my breath.

The significant events of that morning I recall as crisp as an Ansel Adams print. The admiral's insistence that Dick had flowing water close at hand is one. But the curious thing is that toward the end of that day, my memories become normal: fuzzy and disjointed, like recollections from childhood. Without the juice of adrenaline, we retain only glimpses, little three-second pictures with connecting details jumbled or reimagined. This must be the nature of a mind moving on, getting on with life, this business of jettisoning the connecting elements, sometimes dumping entire days and weeks.

A final strong memory, sharp as the blade on my missing Buck knife, is the arrival of the promised pilot from Yankee Station. It's Bud Edney. He's still wearing his flight-suit, and I recognize him immediately as he strides briskly down the burnished passageway. He's yards away when I gather from his determined pace and expression that he's troubled. He greets me, then checks in with the yeoman inside the admiral's office. He's to wait. We stand close together so we can speak in low voices. He begins.

Dick is still on the ridge. An attempt to rescue him yesterday failed when Clementine, a Kaman HU-2 helicopter escorted by two A-1 Barn Owls, was shot up badly as it closed in on Dick's position. The bird, shaking violently, made it back to its destroyer's deck. The rescue this morning failed, too, Bud tells me. Worse than failed.

Bud goes through the ugly scene. Big Mother 67 and her four-man crew was again escorted by Lockets as it flew a circuitous route carefully planned the night before by Lt. Peterson. The course required additional time over enemy territory, stomach-churning time, but it carried Big Mother and the escorting Locket A-1s clear of every gun-site the intelligence guys had pinpointed on their big charts.

Following his plan, Peterson's route took the rescue chopper across the beach well south, and once feet-dry he skirted along karst ridges, working northward, to eventually dash across a small valley of remote rice farmland near Dick. Peterson's hours of planning paid off. Big Mother encountered no flak on that long flight toward that ridge where Dick spent the night.

After all that, Big Mother was almost to Dick, almost over him.

Bud's face takes on an agonized expression. "I called on Dick to light off a smoke-flare," Bud tells me. "I had Dick in sight, but they didn't. Big Mother overflew him." Bud takes a deep breath, glances at the door to the admiral's office. His pause lengthens. He looks so weary.

I thought I understood why. He'd flown to Saigon from the ship, some 900 miles, and such a flight isn't easy. He'd done it in one long leg, much of it over water, concentrating on fuel-management and navigation. And this after he'd led the grisly mission in stressful combat. Heavy combat.

But it wasn't fatigue. It was his roommate.

Although Dick and Bud shared a stateroom on Oriskany and were classmates at the Naval Academy, these aren't the reasons Bud was selected to lead the rescue effort. Simply, Bud Edney was absolutely the correct choice. He knew where Dick landed and he had a mental picture of the ridge. The effort required someone with combat experience, and Bud gained plenty on the '66 cruise. Furthermore, and perhaps the best reason to call on Bud Edney, was that he is known to be ice-vein-brave.

Once tapped for the job—and he was anxious to do what he could for his roomie—Bud threw himself into the preparations. He stayed up much of the night planning the dash to Dick's ridge at first light. The mission was complicated, however, by expectations of the Task Force 77 Commander, the admiral in charge of operations on Yankee Station. He had been awed by the rescue of Butch Verich two days earlier, when the Oriskany F-8 pilot had spent the night on a ridge near Phu Ly and was then snatched off it in a surprise dawn rescue. The admiral—yes, that same Navy-takes-care-of-its-own admiral—loved it, and he allowed himself to be satisfied all such efforts would go as well.

I remain convinced that this admiral's hubris the day before was his reason to deny Glen York permission to bring his Jolly Green into the Navy's area.

"Negative, Negative, the Navy takes care of its own." I can never forget that transmission.

The admiral may have thought differently, but Lt. Cmdr. Edney clearly understood how this time the North Vietnamese would not be caught sleeping. They'd be up and ready long before daybreak.

Dick was bait. The North Vietnamese expected a helicopter to come for the downed airman.

Bud Edney created a plan that relied more on heavy air-to-ground defenses for Big Mother than surprise. In darkness, with John Davis on his wing, Bud led the rescue force to the ridge. Bob Arnold and Barry Wood were to knock out any guns—they were assigned flak-suppression duties along with a number of other Magicstones and Old Salts. Locket A-1s with Barn Owl A-1s from USS Bon Homme Richard, bolstered the flak suppression force. F-8s wove overhead providing MiG defense, while other Magicstones patrolled with anti-radar Shrikes to counter the SAM-threat. There would be even more air-to-ground firepower at the scene when the Lockets escorting Big Mother arrived.

It was an operation the scale of an alpha strike. Bombs were dropped, pods of small rockets were fired in salvos, and big Zuni rockets pounded gun emplacements.

While the area was pummeled, Big Mother 67 navigated a 125-mile route in darkness. Then in the indigo light before dawn, the helicopter safely crossed the final valley, and the big rescue bird air-taxied down the ridge toward Dick's position.

The flak-suppression had been excellent. So far, so good. But there was one gun, a 37-mm double-barreled weapon that had not yet fired. Patiently, its disciplined crew waited.

"Someone shot a Zuni. It hit on the next ridge," Bud said. "Maybe Big Mother mistook that for Dick's smoke." For whatever reason, the big chopper began a turn out from the ridge.

"I called them. Others called, too. 'Don't turn!'" Bud's voice cracked.

It was too late. The arc carried Big Mother over the valley, out over waiting gunners, the disciplined gunners who'd held their fire until the helicopter was almost directly above them. Then they let loose.

Bud is almost whispering now. The huge bird erupted in orange flames, turned onto its back, and trailed a ghastly long stream of fire and smoke as it fell to the valley floor, he says. The loss took almost no time, seconds.

Bud's voice cracked as he told how, as he was departing and the helicopter was behind him burning at the base of the ridge, how Dick called over his handheld radio.

"Guys. Please don't leave me here."

Budney and I stood there in the passageway for a time. Quietly. Then he continued.

Barry Wood, low on fuel, headed for the water. John Davis was with him, and John's bird, too, was almost empty. John urged Barry on, telling him over the radio that he thought they'd make it; there was a tanker flying fast toward them. But Barry slowed, said he was getting out and ejected. "He's already back aboard Oriskany," Bud told me.

An aide appeared in the doorway. The admiral was ready to meet with Lt. Cmdr. Edney.

I eased myself onto the little couch, but now Grampaw Pettibone held no interest. I can't recall how long Bud was with the admiral. An hour, maybe. When he emerged, he appeared somber. I stood; we were once again face-to-face, speaking softly. If it was possible for Bud Edney to look even more distressed, even wearier than when he told me about Big Mother, he did now. But he spoke clearly, his voice sonorous and low.

"There won't be any more efforts."

He said more than this. I'm confident he explained the admiral's thinking, mentioning that too many lives had been lost already, that the defenses arrayed around Dick's ridge were overwhelming, that the calculus no longer worked.

I excused myself and turned. To keep my leg from buckling, I placed each step carefully—I remember the effort—favoring the knee as I moved down the glossy passageway until I reached the head. There I closed myself into a stall. Standing, I began to weep. Then sob. I reeled off wads of toilet paper, sobbing into handfuls to muffle any noise.

I was in there some while. At a white sink, I wiped my face.

## CHAPTER TWENTY-FIVE

# *Earthquake*

Budney flew back to Yankee Station. I don't recall what happened with me the rest of that afternoon. I was still wearing the Air Force pilot's gray flight-suit, and although I must have carried my torso harness, g-suit and survival vest, I had nothing else. For identification I had the Geneva Accords ID card we carried when flying in combat, and hanging under my t-shirt, my dog tags. But I had no money, so I didn't go into Saigon.

Someone shepherded me around, ensuring I was fed and so forth. What I do recall is a drive in a van at the end of that day. It was after dark, so I'd eaten dinner somewhere on the air base. Now I was to spend the night at a medical facility. The van carried me through heavy traffic out Cong Ly Avenue.

My folks had moved from the place I knew on Phon Dinh Phung to a more modern villa on Cong Ly—in 1960, after I left. It was from their balcony that they watched columns of troops march down Cong Ly during the first coup-d'etat—the first unsuccessful effort to rid South Vietnam of Ngo Dinh Diem. I thought about the letter Dad had written to me joking that he and our family were under Ti Ba's "house arrest" while battles were fought on this street.

The van turned onto Tan Son Hoa, the street on which the American Community School had been located. I strained to glimpse my school's five buildings or any familiar landmarks. But Saigon had changed so greatly in the six years since I lived there that I remained disoriented.

Did I see a doctor at this place? I don't think so. I was shown to a room set up to accommodate six or eight patients. I was the only occupant. Exhausted, I hit the rack immediately. Yet before I fell asleep, I had the eerie sense I was close to our old school. Very close.

The next day I somehow made my way from Saigon out to Yankee Station. I have a misty recollection of finding a seat on a COD, one of the twin-engine transporters that ferried mail and reels of movies to the ships. I did arrive aboard Oriskany riding in the jump-seat of a COD on the twentieth. I remember that unmistakably.

Once aboard Oriskany, I learned more details of my rescue, and once again adrenaline shot into my system. I learned that Big Mother 67's door-gunner, AX2 David Chatterton, had taken a round full in the chest as he was about to winch the hoist-cable down to me. His only hope for survival was immediate medical help.

As Big Mother raced toward the coast, a destroyer with a doctor aboard steamed toward Big Mother in an effort to close the distance and shorten time. My friend Hank Miller, a youthful Locket A-1 driver, I learned that day, had flown protection.

Chatterton lay on the floor of the helicopter near the pilots, bleeding. He told the pilots he didn't want to die, pleading with them to hurry. They had taken the shortest way to the coast, a dangerous rhumb line, a route that carried the helicopter and its Locket escort close to known flak sites. But the bold dash had not been enough, and before they got to the destroyer, the young second-class petty officer died on the helicopter's metal floor.

Perhaps the outcome could have been different had Big Mother 67 come for me earlier—before that shooter came up the hill to lurk with a rifle in the trees. Now I was hearing there had been a bureaucratic delay; the rescue chopper had been forced to loiter. During the minutes I spent sorting through my parachute seat pan, and then my time climbing the hill to camouflage myself as a log to wait for over an hour, the crew aboard Big Mother 67 was forced to wait for clearance to cross into North Vietnam.

They had orbited, burning precious time, waiting for permission. One of the great frustrations for the rescue community, I learned that afternoon, was a requirement that every rescue involving penetration into North Vietnam first needed approval from Washington, D.C.

Unbelievable.

So while I hid from North Vietnamese pursuers and while Sandys were being shot at and eventually were jumped by MiG jets, Red Crown patiently awaited permission from someone in Washington, D.C. to clear Big Mother 67 into North Vietnam. And while Red Crown waited for permission to attempt a feet-dry rescue, Big Mother 67 loitered, burning time and fuel, while half a world away, someone in the middle of the night held a meeting.

In addition to Chatterton, the crew assigned to SAR—sea-air rescue—duties that day were pilots Lt. John Bender and Lt. j.g. John Mike Schloz. I knew Schloz. He and I had been in preflight training together. Wayne Noah was the fourth crewmember.

After the evening meal in Oriskany's big wardroom, I stood at the front of the ready-room to recount—and relive—the events of two days earlier. Skipper Mow had asked me to, and he'd called an AOM—a mandatory all officers meeting—to ensure I'd have an audience.

One take-away, I told my fellow pilots, was that we should pay more respect to 37-mm guns. We hadn't always. "Just a little thirty-seven," we'd tell the debriefing officer after a mission. But now, I admitted, a single 37-mm gun terrified me as much as any SAM or radar-directed flak. And in that moment, standing before my buddies, I realized how badly my shoot-down had shaken me. Waves of fear rippled through me, churning my stomach and drying my mouth. I recalled Skipper Engel telling me to "press on," so I gathered my strength and went on, while what I wanted to do was to sit down.

I fleshed out the account with information I'd learned since my rescue. It had not only been Sandy and Locket A-1s protecting me. Roaring over my position, a dozen Spads were involved in my rescue, including Bon Homme Richard Barn Owls. Overhead, flying cover, was at least one F-8—the aircraft that first detected my beeper signal—several A-4s and perhaps even a big A-6 Intruder.

I had learned that two Air Force Spads, Sandys One and Two, were jumped by a pair of MiGs swooping down on them with airspeed galore, that the Spads out-turned the jets, while it nevertheless was still nowhere near an even fight. Sandy One, Maj. Bronczyk, was hit, but he did make it back to Udorn. When Air Force fighters appeared overhead, the attacking MiGs retreated. I described these events for my squadron, and my stomach churned.

I have a photograph from that evening, taken after the AOM finished. Five of us, all involved in ejections that week, are in the photograph. Larry Cunningham, Barry Wood and I are crouching. My right leg stretches stiffly out in front of me. We are grinning broadly, as if it had been nothing to be shot up and punch out. Standing behind us are the two parachute riggers, the skilled technicians who had properly packed the 'chutes that saved our lives. Raymond Slinky, who grew up in Gallup, NM, is on the left. He packed the one I used. It worked. We are both smiling in the photograph.

It was too soon to relive that day. That night, in a frightfully real nightmare, Dick and I were together on the ground in North Vietnam. We were lobbing hand grenades at barking troops coming for us. I woke tangled in sweaty sheets, wondering where the hand grenades had come from; I'd never even seen a real one.

Almost five decades after that night, Don Purdy and I visited Bob Arnold in a Southern California hospice facility. He was frail, no longer the robust guy who played handball with a vengeance into his 80s. An oxygen cannula's clear tubes looped from his nostrils to his ears and trailed off behind him. He was in striped pajamas. To see Bob—to see Hoser One—that day, it was a stretch to remember how this same guy flew 336 combat missions and racked up 1,265 arrested carrier landings during his Navy career.

Bob wanted to talk about July 19, that morning Bud lead the force to rescue Dick. He and Hoser Four, his wingman Barry Wood, were flak suppressors, and Bob had spotted an armed convoy.

"I rolled in on a half-a-dozen trucks that had come down off a hill," Bob recalled. "They were shooting at something, and then they saw me and were shooting at me. I had this piece of ordnance; it was a nineteen-shot rocket pod; they'd ripple off, all these rockets." He paused to take a few shallow breaths. "I hadn't fired one of these in God-knows-how-long, and I fired this. I'd forgotten how much noise they make. Scared the hell out of me. They roared off, nineteen of 'em. The trucks turned around. They went back."

Bob and Barry had separated—he didn't mention why—but they were both very low on fuel. Don and I remembered how Barry had gone out with John Davis, had run low on fuel and then ejected. Bob didn't mention any of that. What he wanted to relive in his time with Don and me was how he got back, how he flew 110 miles to the ship with a mere sip of fuel remaining. He followed an arc prescribed on a kneeboard chart. I still have my copy, and it dictates a climb at Mach 0.7, full power, until reaching a cruise-altitude of 30,000 feet. Flying that great arc, Bob would have been burning his precious fuel at max-power as he climbed to that altitude, yet test pilots and engineers had determined it was the most efficient way to cover the distance. He would have been fifty miles out from the ship, my cheat-sheet tells me, when he pulled his throttle to idle to set up a long glide at Mach 0.63.

It worked. While he was in that beautiful glide toward the carrier, Bob called Childplay to request priority. He had only enough fuel for a single pass—a straight-in approach. And that's what took place.

Bob was near the end of his life, yet he told us this as if it had taken place a week before. This is the power of memory etched for a lifetime by adrenaline.

It was the morning after I arrived back on Oriskany, less than twelve hours after Barry Wood, Larry Cunningham and I posed for the photo of guys who punched out, that Barry went to Skipper Mow's stateroom to hand in his wings. He was done.

He could have requested an administrative job somewhere, but he didn't. He wasn't afraid of combat, only of airplanes. He'd lost his confidence in them. Instead of a desk, though, Barry Wood requested orders to river patrol duty, a hazardous assignment in the delta area of South Vietnam. On river boats he excelled, earning a silver star. One of the news magazines featured him in a story.

Barry's wasn't the only Oriskany aircraft lost on the nineteenth. Commander Herb Hunter of VF-162, flying an F-8, was shot up that afternoon, and he needed to land somewhere. Right then. His Crusader was so badly damaged that most aviators would have kissed it goodbye and ejected. But Herb was a former member of the elite Blue Angels flight Demonstration Team. He was confident that he could get it aboard.

Hunter's battle-damage required he make a fast approach. Too fast. His fighter skidded across the deck and over the side. He ejected as his airplane rolled, but he was fatally blasted smack into the side of the ship. Herb Hunter had been a decade ahead of me at Austin High School in El Paso.

Ken Adams came within inches of dying that same day. He, too, had flown cover on the daybreak attempt to rescue Dick. After Big Mother was shot down, Ken still had unexpended rockets. He flew south toward Than Hoa to fire them off his plane. He knew of a target there. As he navigated into the dangerous area, a SAM came up. Ken told me he felt his tail lift and at the same moment saw a missile fly from under his airplane. He got rid of the rockets, then returned to the ship. As he taxied out of the arresting gear, he flashed a thumbs-up to a chief petty officer, but the chief disagreed, and showed a thumbs-down, meaning the bird was not flyable. The chief was looking at Ken's sliced-open centerline drop tank; the missile had hit his airplane, and had the detonating fuse on the SAM not misfired, Ken would have dropped our must-pump group's record to zero-for-three. The lethal range for an exploding SA-2 missile is hundreds of feet, yet Ken lived through intimate contact with one. Sometimes, for some guys, luck is boundless.

Losses began to amass at an alarming rate. In the early hours of the day before I returned aboard Oriskany, VF-162 had lost another, the squadron's third F-8. Lt. j.g. Jim Nunn's fighter had dribbled off the front end of the ship when his cat-shot didn't go as it should have. His aircraft settled into the water to explode not far ahead of the ship.

Still alive and in the cockpit, Jim saw ejection as his only way out of the sinking wreckage. Underwater ejections are not taught, never discussed or even mentioned in NATOPS manuals, yet his seat-rocket blasted him up through the canopy, which shattered as he went through. He found himself underwater, but alive, breathing oxygen from a little reserve bottle in his seat-pan. He struggled to swim under the burning surface of the water, but then realized his parachute had deployed and he was caught in sinking wreckage. It began pulling him deeper.

To free himself, Nunn shed his torso harness, and with it went his oxygen supply and his emergency hand-held radio. Nunn was an excellent athlete, a football player at the Naval Academy. He held his breath and swam beneath the surface until he was clear of the burning pool of jet fuel above him. Someone in the ship's plane-guard helicopter, perfunctorily circling what clearly should have been a fatal crash, spotted something illuminated by flames from the burning fuel—the reflective tape on Nunn's helmet. He was lifted to safety. Among Jim's injuries was a broken vertebra in his neck.

That same afternoon, the Saints lost an A-4. Lt. Russ Kuhl was hit by anti-aircraft gunfire near Cam Pha, an island off the coast of Haiphong. He ejected near the Northern SAR destroyer, but his ejection went badly, snapping him like a bullwhip. His brick-size hand-held radio broke loose and whacked him in the chin, snapping his head back. Russ also suffered a fractured neck—the same vertebra as Nunn's injury.

Counting the operational crash of an A-4 due to a bad cat shot two days before we arrived at Yankee Station, the losses in nine days totaled ten—more than one a day.

I slept aboard Oriskany three nights: July 20-22. On July 21st, the Vietnamese announced in a Hanoi radio broadcast that they had captured Lt. Cmdr. Richard Danner Hartman. It was my twenty-fifth birthday.

The morning of the twenty-third, I flew off Oriskany—again on the COD—to Cubi Point. I spent that night at the BOQ, and early the next day I made my way to the flight-line maintenance shack.

I asked if they had any birds that needed test hops flown. They did: Bureau Number 152048. They were happy to have a volunteer. I made my way slowly to the aircraft, carefully placing each step. Because my right leg was useless for climbing, I asked the plane captain, a young man from the maintenance crew, to help me up the ladder. He went ahead of me, and while he lifted on the collar of my torso harness, I went up backward, hopping with my good leg from step to step.

The test hop went splendidly, a magnificent flight in a jet aircraft, a pleasing memory that stays with me. One of the items on the test-flight form was to fly the aircraft to 40,000 feet. I did this, then I kept climbing, topping at around 44,000, where this A-4 reached its limit and struggled in the thin air. It was a clear morning, and from this great altitude I could see spread out toward the horizon hundreds of Philippine islands.

What a magnificent vista. I imagined I saw so far that I could discern the curvature of the earth. I ran through the remaining checks. It was a good bird. Although 402 had been through extensive maintenance, for many ills, the airplane performed flawlessly.

But I had not reckoned that my right leg would sabotage my landing. Cubi Point had a relatively short runway that demanded hard braking. My left foot worked fine, but I was unable to apply the right brake. To stop, I was forced to drop the tailhook and snag the mid-field arresting cable. The airplane and I were towed back to the maintenance shack.

"Bad brakes?" the maintenance chief asked. "Nope, the brakes are okay. Change the tailhook. Good bird."

This was a replacement aircraft, one new to our squadron and destined to replace the one I had lost, or Dick had lost or Barry Wood had lost. It needed only this test hop before delivery to the ship. Yet this 402 would itself be lost a couple months later, along with the life of Bud Edney's new roommate. Bud would finish this combat cruise having lost three roommates.

From the maintenance line, taking each step carefully, I made my way uphill to the Cubi Point hospital, one of the three medical facilities in which I'd spend the next ninety-eight days.

## CHAPTER TWENTY-SIX

# *Oak Knoll*

A young sailor wearing bell-bottom dungarees and a white t-shirt slathered my leg with brown ointment, wrapped it in layers of gauze and, finally, plaster. The cast ran from my ankle almost to my groin. I was in the cast room at Naval Hospital Cubi Point. A cylinder cast had been prescribed by a Navy doctor who examined me there that morning.

"Stand up, sir," the young sailor said. I did.

"What do you think?" he asked.

"I don't know," I said. "My first cast."

"Mine, too," the sailor said. He was smiling proudly.

I asked if he had recently finished corpsman school.

"No, I'm a patient here."

He could see I was perplexed, so he explained he was a torpedoman's-mate. While horsing around with some buddies on his ship, his Achilles tendon had been severed, an injury requiring months to heal. Someone at the hospital, someone with authority, had tired of seeing him idle.

"So I'm doing casts." His preparation for this assignment consisted of a single demonstration the day before.

Walking stiff-legged in my new cast, I was released from the hospital, convinced this would take care of my injury. In a few weeks, perhaps as long as a month, I'd be back in the cockpit. I was in excellent spirits when I arrived back at the BOQ. By 0100, however, my ankle and foot were so swollen that I was in throbbing pain. Two sleepless hours later I made my way up the hill to the hospital. The night-shift doctor, a civilian intern, refused to remove the cast. I explained that I could no longer fit my ballooning foot into my shoe. The pain was escalating. He was not authorized, he explained.

"Find someone who is."

"Not possible, sir." There was no one he could call. He was sorry.

I knew my way to the cast room. There, hanging from a hook on the wall, I located an electric tool that appeared made for the purpose. I had it in hand, when a nurse came into the room. She took it and trimmed away enough plaster to get me through the night. The next morning another nurse buzzed off the remainder. Then, with her nickel-steel bandage scissors, she slit away the gauze. When she peeled the gooey brown shell from my leg, we were both startled by the swarm of fluid-filled blisters. This swollen, weeping mess no longer looked like part of me. I had suffered a severe reaction to the brown stuff the torpedoman had so generously glopped onto it the day before.

By mid-morning I was wearing a thin gown with an open back and had been admitted as a patient. It didn't occur to me that my injury was severe enough to keep me down for months. And I couldn't know then that this was the launch of an ordeal that will add guilt to the mix of emotions that will torment me for decades to come.

And why would I think my leg had deteriorated enough to be serious? I was ambulatory until that morning. I had in fact been quite active since the shoot-down, flying out to the ship and back

as a passenger on a COD, a trip that entailed both an arrested landing and a catapult shot. I had even piloted an A-4 the previous
morning, flown it well; only the landing had been questionable.
And until last night, the pain was not excessive.

Days drifted by. I lay on the hospital bed at Naval Hospital Cubi
Point watching my knee swell. My ability to walk disappeared; I
now required a wheelchair. I woke each morning, had a nice breakfast, read Joseph Conrad novels, had a nice lunch and read until
evening meal arrived. After my recent ordeal, a rest should have
been welcome. But not boredom, not this. Not while my squadron
was so deep in war.

After several more days, Dave Dollarhide, an A-4 pilot from
USS Forrestal was moved into my room. Forrestal had exploded in
fire July 29, and Dave was among that ship's injured sailors now
jamming the small hospital. But unlike most of the patients, Dave
had not been burned. He'd been in his cockpit waiting to start his
aircraft, when an errant missile from another airplane (a safety pin
had been pulled early) struck the A-4 next to his, igniting a fire.

Dave narrowly escaped flames boiling up from under his airplane by clambering out to the end of his refueling probe and then
jumping over a pool of fire spreading on deck. Another A-4 pilot,
John McCain, was in the burning aircraft next to Dollarhide's. He
did the same.

The first bomb cooked off by the spreading fire had knocked
my hospital-roomie to Forrestal's deck. Shrapnel tore across his
foot and buttocks. With bombs detonating and flaming jet-fuel
pouring down to decks below, Forrestal's conflagration had become even more deadly than Oriskany's. A chief petty officer only
feet away from where Dollarhide had leaped to the deck, vanished
in the blast, the first of 134 sailors to die. My hospital roommate,
who'd also broken his hip and arm, was among the 161 injured.
Listening to Dave's account, re-ignited my memories of Oriskany's
inferno.

Before that, I had been dreaming nightly of being on the
ground with Dick Hartman. We were, in various scenarios, fighting

Vietnamese soldiers and trying to escape, but now, after talking with Dave about his ordeal, fires joined the mayhem in my nightmares.

When Oriskany finished her first line-period in early August and docked at Cubi Point, the ship with the call-sign Childplay had lost fourteen airplanes in thirty-eight days of combat flying. The air wing's flight surgeons left directly for the hospital to evaluate the ship's three hospitalized pilots. We weren't to be found.

A week earlier, Jim Nunn and Russ Kuhl, the two pilots with neck vertebrae fractures, had been in the hospital's other wing. I'd wheel to their room, where they were both in traction. We'd talk.

One day they were freed of the pulleys, cables and weights. Now ambulatory, they appeared in my room dressed in their khaki uniforms, both sported protective foam collars around their necks.

"We're outta here," Russ said. "They moved another guy into our room." He explained a young supply officer had been wheeled in on a bed the day before. The guy wouldn't talk to them, rolling over so his back was to Russ and Jim and ignoring them totally.

"Want to go with us?" Jim asked. "We ordered a staff car."

I've always been up for a lark, and escaping a stifling hospital, one with questionable medical proficiency, held promise. No one asked if a doctor had discharged us; we simply signed out.

When the car came, Jim and Russ wheeled me to the shiny black sedan in a wheelchair, which they dutifully returned to the hospital. At the Cubi BOQ, I waited while Russ and Jim checked us into rooms. They returned and each put a shoulder under an arm and helped me hop on my good leg to my main-floor room. Theirs was on the second floor, larger and with a good view. Since they still had use of the black car, they immediately headed to the Cubi O'Club, the historic alcohol-fueled playground for aviators.

And they forgot about me. Forgot about their third amigo.

During the long days while I waited for Russ and Jim to remember they had stashed me downstairs, I read more of Joseph Conrad's oeuvre—including *Lord Jim* and *Heart of Darkness*. My right knee continued to swell, puffing to the size of a soccer ball. I was able to hop on my left leg from my bed to the adjacent head, so that issue was solved. But the idea of slipping on a uniform—my swollen leg would not have fit into my pants—and then hopping down a long passageway to the dining room was daunting. Impossible. The first night I skipped dinner. By the time the room steward arrived around 0900 the next morning, I was hungry. I handed him some bills and asked him to go to the bar and bring back ten hot dogs—the little six-inch dogs cooked on a vertical conveyor belt in one of those appliances then common in barrooms.

"Oh, and ten gin-tonics, please," I added. I knew that they, like the dogs, would be small. He brought them to me on a metal tray. By late afternoon I was munching on the last, now room-temperature, soggy hotdog and sipping a final tepid and diluted gin-tonic. I repeated the request the next morning, and every morning for the best part of a week. (This restricted diet, interestingly, didn't ruin my fondness for a good hot dog and a refreshing gin-tonic. I still love them both.)

The Oriskany flight surgeons couldn't locate their patients at the Cubi hospital, and staff there was unable to explain where they'd gone. No one had any idea. Eventually, Doc Adeeb, the Saint's flying doctor, thought to check the BOQ.

We were brought back to the hospital and readmitted There we learned that the supply officer dumped into Russ and Jim's room, the guy who refused to talk to them, was supposed to have been on a suicide watch. No one had bothered to say anything to Russ or Jim, and chillingly, no one on the hospital staff had been properly checking on him. Alone in the room, the despondent young officer used a call-button cord to hang himself.

The hospital was demonstrably dysfunctional. Our air wing flight surgeons decided Russ, Jim and I should go back to the States. Arrangements were being made.

Before I left the Cubi hospital, a series of squadron-mates dropped by. Skipper Mow was among the first, and he said he'd recommended an air medal for my few minutes orbiting overhead Dick—for my failed effort as on-scene rescue coordinator. Later in the day, Jim Waldron and Roger Duter showed up with something more substantial—a fifth of bourbon they smuggled in. The bottle went around only once. I wasn't up for it.

From Cubi, I was flown to Yokota, Japan, and from there a C-141 Starlifter, a flying ambulance, carried some 140 wounded Army and Marine soldiers—and me—to Travis Air Force Base in California. Stretchers three-high lined the sides of the big bird, with another triple stack down the centerline. At the heads of a number of the stretchers, IV-bags hung from steel poles. Some guys dozed, so heavily drugged they were out all nine hours of the flight.

Medical technicians and flight nurses walked the aisles and tenderly cared for us, changing the saline and glucose for the patients with those, cutting the meat on dinner plates into bite-size bits for men who no longer had use of their hands, or bringing cups of water when we asked.

Most of the young men on the flight were badly damaged. A distressing number were missing limbs. A kid directly across from me had a broken back: quadriplegic. "Stepped on a mine," he told me. He smiled easily. He believed he'd get better.

While the aircraft was refueling in Guam, volunteering wives of servicemen stationed on the island came aboard with trays of cookies. Tropical heat poured into the airplane. One of the volunteers offered to rub my back. The lotion felt cool.

When we landed at Travis, it was an overcast morning. A procession of gray buses that had been converted to stretcher-carriers lined up, along with a handful of black ambulances for the most grimly maimed. I looked around to see if I recognized the terminal building where three of us, almost giddy with anticipation, boarded an airliner to fly off to the Vietnam air-war ten months ago. Of us three must-pumps, only Ken Adams was still flying.

I was back in the States for an operation on my knee, a procedure I believed would return me to flight status in six weeks—an illusion I picked up somewhere along the way. My destination was Oak Knoll Naval Hospital set on an Oakland hillside overlooking San Francisco Bay. Its buildings spread across what had once been an opulent Roaring Twenties country club—something straight

230

out of a F. Scott Fitzgerald novel. After its Gatsby days, however, the Great Depression's hard times shuttered the club. It had gained its new life as a hospital early in World War II.

I was wheeled into an old wooden building of two-by-fours and cheap siding, one of the many wings slapped together to accommodate the stream of wounded men flowing stateside from brutal Pacific Theater battles in 1942. The old structures were maintained to the Navy's high standards, yet a faint odor of dry-rot wafted up from corners.

At Oak Knoll, I was examined for the first time by a doctor trained in orthopedics. His report was sharply disappointing: the time for corrective surgery had passed. To mend, my knee required time, nothing else, meaning medical treatment would be comprised of numbing days in the hospital ward. I'd convalesce—while on Yankee Station, Air Wing Sixteen continued its hellish work. And I missed that, I missed the intoxication of combat flying.

My parents drove up from Palo Alto to see me. Mom couldn't conceal her worry, yet she summoned energy to cheer me. Dad hovered behind her, quiet. I couldn't decide if his slim smile meant that he was worried or happy I was away from peril for a spell.

## CHAPTER TWENTY-SEVEN

# Tissue-Thin Letters

A motley collection of patients—mostly long-term guys—gathered in the day-room to watch three bachelors throw out their lines. For a brief morning spell, the silly show offered escape. A breather from the wretched news flowing from Oriskany.

"From Hollywood, the dating capital of the world. In color. It's *The Dating Game!*" The host, Jim Lange, strode onto the cheesy set. "Thank you. Thank you. Oh boy. Thank you." His teeth, white and big, flashed through his smile. "Welcome to romance on the air!"

Not everyone in the ward joined our little group to watch the inane show. Some were unable to leave their beds. Others, like a Marine first lieutenant who had a room to himself, did not interact with the rest of us in any way. Once I stopped my wheelchair at his doorway. His plaster cast, ash-gray, spread up from his hips, wrapped his torso and then swept up and over each shoulder. On his cast he balanced an Olivetti portable typewriter, robin's-egg

233

blue. Two pillows craned his head forward so he could see his work. He was typing rapidly when I interrupted.

I introduced myself, then asked a few questions, trying to ignite a conversation. He didn't invite me to enter his room. From his cryptic answers I learned that, yes, he had been wounded in a firefight. He offered no details. He was in no mood for chitchat. Not that day, or ever. His anger filled the room. I turned my wheelchair toward the day-room and the inane daytime television show about to come on.

Today it would be called depression, but fifty-three years ago it was more commonly called melancholy. It was fueled by news from Oriskany. It arrived in letters scrawled with a splotchy ball-point pen on tissue-thin paper, many from Jim Waldron. The stationery, a single pale-blue sheet, had been folded along dotted lines to create its own lightweight envelope. "Air Mail/Par Avion" was printed in the corner. Insubstantial. Yet such heavy news.

One of the Saints, Don Davis, had been hit with small arms fire: killed in action. In another thin letter, I learned a KA-3B like the Whale that ferried me to Oriskany in 1966 had gone down. The pilot attempted to top a fierce thunderstorm, but failed. Sometimes a cell is too high and too fierce. Two of the three aboard were killed.

Three days after the Whale fell, Charlie Zuhoski, a Crusader pilot with VF-111, was bagged. The Vietnamese announced he was a prisoner. "arrested," was their term. Then Ralph Bisz, a young Saints pilot, was nailed by a SAM. Don Purdy witnessed it: no 'chute. Ralph was KIA. He roomed with Ken Adams, who would lose three of his roomies on this cruise

Then there was a lull; weeks went by, and Air Wing Sixteen lost no pilots. But it wouldn't last. In September a letter arrived, telling me Dick Perry had been hit by a SAM on a particularly bad alpha strike at the end of August. They had been inbound to a target at Haiphong. Someone transmitted, "Magicstones, break, break," and Mike Mullane, Dick's wingie, broke one direction while Dick pulled hard the other way. Then the massive blast. John Davis was in trail behind Dick when the SAM came up, so Davis and his wingman, George Schindelar, watched Dick's airplane turn for the coast.

John transmitted that he and George would accompany Dick, and that Mike should continue to the target.

His airplane was streaming fluids, but Dick continued toward the water, flying evenly. Over the coast, however, the wounded A-4 began to burn. Then it rolled. When Dick ejected, he was over islands in a bay. To John and George, it appeared Dick was in a good place for a rescue. John had a SAR helicopter on its way.

But then George transmitted, "Shouldn't he have his radio out? We should be hearing from him."

John slowed and lowered his flaps, then circled in close. Dick hung limply beneath the shrouds. He went into the water and the parachute floated down over him. The SAR chopper arrived, and a rescue-swimmer went into the water. Dick Perry was dead, tangled in the 'chute, the swimmer reported. A massive chest wound. The helicopter came under fire, so Dick's body was left in the jade waters of Ha Long Bay.

Dick Perry, the guy who managed to bring a heavily damaged A-4 aboard a carrier in a spectacular feat of airmanship, the man who organized a group of us to escape our ready-room while Oriskany burned, that man had died? It was hard to visualize; he was a man so filled with life.

There was more.

Minutes after Dick Perry was hit, two more missiles came up, these stalking a section of Saints. One detonated as Dave Carey tried to do a barrel-roll over the missile—often an effective evasive maneuver—but the missile split the difference between Dave and Al Stafford, to detonate between them and take them both out. Now they were POWs, the letter said. Dave and I had spent hours together on the platform as LSO trainees.

When the letter arrived describing Dick Perry's death and the captured Saints, I sat alone on my bed at Oak Knoll Naval Hospital. I felt hollow, as if any capacity for emotion was draining from me. I crawled back under the covers.

Some evenings I'd join a few others in the day-room and watch

*The Huntley-Brinkley Report.* Their fifteen-minute broadcasts offered a way to follow the war's progress. General William Westmoreland, Brinkley reported more than once, announced we were slowly winning the war. Westmoreland said the "enemy's hopes are bankrupt" and that he could "see light at the end of the tunnel." I wanted to believe that. Later I'd learn that General Henri Navarre, the general in charge of the French fighting the Viet Minh in Vietnam had, in 1953, used the same metaphor. The French were defeated by the Viet Minh in 1954.

Following the losses of Perry, Stafford and Carey, it seemed Oriskany's appalling luck in combat might change. During September, while I wasted days in the Oak Knoll Naval Hospital, no Air Wing Sixteen aircraft or pilots were downed over Vietnam. But three airplanes did splash into the water due to operational issues.

Two were F-8 Crusaders and one was a Saints A-4. All pilots were recovered. On a peacetime cruise, losing three airplanes in a single month would have been shocking, but the pilots were okay. I was becoming hardened to all the dreadful information.

I read novels and any magazines I could find at the hospital. In the day-room one day, I came across an *Atlantic Monthly*, and in it was a piece by General David M. Shoup. The general had finished his career as Commandant of the Marine Corps, and during WWII, he'd earned a medal-of-honor fighting Japanese at Tarawa. He was therefore, in my mind, both brave and sharp. The article stunned me.

The retired general challenged our strategy, our basic assumptions about the Vietnam conflict, even the air war—my air war. We were not going to defeat communism fighting against nationalism, the general argued. He said foreign influence was unwelcome in the South as well as the North, so our participation was providing a rallying focus. He wrote that corporations and the CIA were improperly influencing the war—in a wrong-headed way. He said we should ". . . keep our dirty, bloody, dollar-soaked fingers out of the business of these nations so full of depressed, exploited people."

I was astounded. There was a growing anti-war movement afoot in the United States. I knew about that. And I dismissed so-called peaceniks as uninformed. But the general, a hero and a man whose life as a warrior I admired, was challenging my participation in this war.

I bought *The Two Viet-Nams*, a book by Bernard Fall, a journalist who had marched with the French in their war in Vietnam. We were not going to win, he wrote, because we did not understand the dynamics of the country—in the same way the French did not. Jim Waldron, YDK, had given me Fall's *Street Without Joy*, and I read it, too.

This reading did nothing to lift my spirits and left me even more conflicted.

My convalescence stretched on. For exercise—and to break the boredom—I'd race down the ward's passageway fast on my crutches, throwing the tips out ahead, skipping once on my good leg before planting the tips way forward for the next big skip. I'd spin on one crutch tip and race back. But the exercise was not energizing; I was sliding further into depression, weighted with guilt for watching daytime television while Air Wing Sixteen bore such violence.

An officer with a clipboard came to my room one quiet day. He wanted to know what I'd like for my next assignment. I had given this question my attention. Why not; I had nothing but time to think and reason. Yet I remained conflicted. General Shoup thought our war was senseless. So did Bernard Fall. They both made sense.

On the other hand, I felt an obligation to the Navy—and a bone-deep commitment to my country. To my squadron-mates, too. I'd be abandoning them if I asked for some other duty; I'd be leaving them with the heavy lifting, while I skated. And there was the matter of survivor's guilt.

Another A-4 pilot in the hospital had asked for orders to a patrol-plane squadron. He wanted to fly the P-3 Orion, he said, a sub-hunter with four engines. It was safe; you could drink coffee while you flew an Orion.

And you did not kill people when you were searching the ocean for Soviet submarines. I was initially critical of his request—it seemed he was dodging something. Yet when I thought more about it, I realized his new duty would fulfill those obligations I was fretting over; his was an honorable request. It might even be enjoyable to walk the length of a fuselage and talk to technicians seated at screens or wearing headphones as they searched for elusive prey, all the while carefully balancing your mug of hot Navy coffee.

So with a list of pros and cons swirling in my head, I used my days of quiet convalescence to ponder. By the time this officer showed up, I'd come to an answer. I was prepared. He stood in my room and asked, and I responded quickly.

"Back to my old squadron, VA-164," I answered.

I wanted to go back to fight because of my affection for the South Vietnamese people—Domino, Mssr. Ich and Ti Ba and their children and grandchildren. I thought about them and people like the rice-farmers next to our school and Joe's curbside motorcycle mechanic. They deserved good lives.

I was no longer gung-ho—this I understood about myself—and my conviction that we would win this war was teetering. Yet I still bought and accepted, without question, the official line about dominoes—the theory that if we didn't stop communists in Southeast Asia, other nations would topple one-after-another to the cruel rulers painted so vividly by Dr. Dooley while I was in high school. I hadn't forgotten about the French yacht club member who had his head handed to his wife. Yes, I believed there was still strong rationale, even though General Shoup and Bernard Fall had outlined the folly.

I harbored another motive, an emotional one I don't like to acknowledge these days. Flying combat was—I've tried to find a better word for this, but cannot—flying combat missions was exhilarating. The surge of adrenaline that infused me as the beach and safety receded under my wings made me feel more alive than I'd ever known. Adrenaline was dope—as alluring and addictive as any of the drugs my peers were discovering in the late 1960s.

Deny Weichman was the poster-boy for this, but I was an addict, too. We all were; why else would we keep doing it, when the out was as simple as taking the wings off a uniform and handing them to the skipper?

Toward the end of my days in the musty ward at Oak Knoll, another officer entered my room. Without ceremony he handed me a small black case. Inside, resting on yellow silk, was a Purple Heart. He handed me a certificate, and after a perfunctory handshake, he left. It was as if he was running an errand, delivering a package.

It never occurred to me I'd receive an award for a knee injury. I sat on my bed thinking about those young men—eighteen, nineteen and perhaps a few seventeen-year-olds in the mix—lying on those stretchers on the C-141. Kids. The young man across from me with the spinal injury, the boys with the IV-bags flopping on poles at the head of their stretchers. I snapped the case shut.

Each morning, a doctor—rarely the same one—would peek in my room, say hello, then continue on his rounds. But one day the doc took a few minutes with me, then told me I was to start physical therapy the next morning.

My leg, after almost three months of inactivity, had atrophied, with thigh muscles so thin and skin so pale it looked like a young boy's. That first day of P.T, lying face-down on a padded table, I was unable to move my leg. "Try to lift it," the corpsman said. It was as if the signal from my brain to the leg had become lost. Nothing.

After a few days, though, I was working the leg hard. I let the corpsman know I wanted to get back onto flight status, I wanted him to push me.

"Sir, can you lift this?" the corpsman would ask after affixing a weight-belt to my ankle.

I'd do the reps and challenge him to strap on more.

In the physical-therapy building the patients were not separated into officers and enlisted. Everyone worked in the same gym-like room. One day I watched a young man, a kid not over nineteen, test his new prosthetic. He supported himself on two parallel bars, and gingerly took a step. His face showed fierce concentration. Then another. Clearly this was painful. Excruciating. A nurse hovered behind him, one hand on a belt around his waist.

"You're doing so well. Great job."

I held my breath until the kid crossed the dozen feet to the far end of the bars. He arrived and he was spent, sweating. He grimaced as he eased down into his wheelchair.

The thin blue letters came sporadically, and whenever one arrived it required care. It had to be opened in a certain way, since the envelope, once carefully unfolded and spread out, became the letter itself. And each one required psychic preparation, too, since they were so loaded with emotion-ripping flak.

In early October havoc returned from its holiday. Dave Matheny, a cherub-faced F-8 pilot with a quick smile, had been shot down by triple-A. He'd been a roommate in the junior-officers bunkroom with Don Purdy, Roger Duter and me. He ejected and was captured, the letter informed me.

By this time I had mended enough to walk with a cane, and was upgraded to outpatient status, which permitted me to move to my folks' house for some of each week. From Palo Alto I commuted forty miles up San Francisco Bay to physical therapy sessions at Oak Knoll. For a brief interlude, the warmth of my family and the freedom to move about in society cheered me.

Weekends were mine, and I had an idea. I owned a small airplane which was tied down at the Palo Alto Airport. I believed I could fly it. After a short test, I made the hour-and-fifteen-minute flight to a small crop-duster's strip not far from an apartment complex where many of the young Lemoore pilots lived.

Walking slowly, heavily dependent on my cane, I made my way the few blocks from the little strip to a buddy's place. There my high spirits were dashed. Within a few minutes of arriving, I learned that Rock Hodges had been hit by a SAM near Hanoi. No parachute.

Rock was an intelligent man, a studious yet aggressive attack pilot, who sometimes waltzed perilously close to disrespect—career-damaging—yet he never crossed the line and balanced his behavior with competence.

We junior pilots admired his skill and bravery; he was a pilot you wanted to fly with, and we loved, too, that he could come so close to mocking senior officers without crossing the line. I reeled that afternoon when I was told he was dead. If pilots with the abilities of Rock Hodges and Dick Perry could be killed...why, any of us could.

There was to be a service at the air-station's chapel the next day. I borrowed a uniform and attended. I was leaning on my cane when his widow, Lisa, took my free hand in both of hers and thanked me for being there. I did control my tears. I think.

A day after Rock was hit, Larry Cunningham made it to the water and ejected, his second punch-out of the cruise. He was picked up by a destroyer.

Occasionally the pale-blue letters brought encouraging news. I heard about successes, raids that went flawlessly. And there were reports of the rollicking fun ashore during off-line-periods, when pilots would unwind.

But the sad news wouldn't disappear. Ten days after Cunningham's second ejection, John Barr went down in AH-402, that airplane I took up on a test-hop at Cubi Point the day I went to the hospital. John was a wiry bundle of energy, a man constantly in motion, either studying charts and target photos for upcoming missions or conferring with the chief petty-officer leading the division he was responsible for. Once again, no parachute. His was the third VA-164 KIA.

Another pilot in the Oak Knoll hospital was also receiving letters from Yankee Station, and he reported that Denny Earl, a particularly nice Saints pilot, had been hit. He was another of the guys in our junior-officers bunkroom. He'd been near The Hourglass when a 12.7-mm anti-aircraft round blasted into his cockpit. Aimed a fraction of a degree higher, it would certainly have killed him. Instead, it hit his rudder pedal and split in half. One part went through his left foot and the other shattered his right tibia. Doc

Adeeb, the Saints flight surgeon who had earned aviator wings, was airborne at the time, and he advised Denny to manually inflate his g-suit, which squeezed his legs and slowed the bleeding. In a display of beautiful airmanship, Denny Earl successfully brought his A-4 back aboard the ship.

This was followed by a more distressing report. On another strike, a SAM streaked up as the group neared Haiphong. It destroyed Jim Dooley's airplane, killing the young Saints pilot. Jim and I had agreed to ski together when we returned from the cruise in January. He had raced in college. I was an intermediate, so I looked forward to hitting the slopes with someone who could help me progress.

Two days passed, and Oriskany lost another airplane, this one piloted by Skip Foulks, another Saint. He'd been downed by anti-aircraft guns and rescued. Three days after that, October 25th, the Saints lost J.M. Krommenhoek, who was being listed as MIA—though his chance of survival was slim.

Next, Charlie Rice, a fighter pilot with VF-162 was shot down and now a POW. Then John McCain, another Saint, punched out and was captured after nearly drowning in a downtown Hanoi lake. McCain had been flying with the Saints only a short time. He'd transferred as a replacement pilot to Oriskany from the burned USS Forrestal—orders he requested.

There was a brief respite, and then a letter from Waldron told me a Ghostrider replacement pilot I never met, Woody Knapp, had been killed. Woody was a must-pump, replacing one of us who was gone. And, like the must-pump Mike Confer, Woody died on a night strafing run. So many deaths.

Even with my freedom as an outpatient, despondency once more settled over me. Reading books and magazines no longer brought pleasure. There were mornings I'd go back to bed after breakfast.

Learning of the combat losses from SAMs and guns was torture, but it didn't stop there. Air Wing Sixteen's accidents and system failures were claiming way too many airplanes. Equipment was wearing down. Pilots too. They endured fatigue beyond limit. Loss of the Whale in the storm back in July was listed as operational and may have been related to fatigue.

Now in October, another KA-3B was lost, this one attributed to systems failure. Then an E-1B Tracer, one of the twin-engine radar-airplanes employed to warn us of MiGs, flew into a mountain, killing all five aboard. The Saints lost two A-4s in operational accidents, and fortunately both pilots were recovered. VF-162 lost two airplanes this way, recovering both pilots. The other Crusader squadron, VF-111, also suffered two operational losses. One pilot was killed, the other recovered.

I had freedom, sure, and it was good to be staying with my folks. But at Oak Knoll, when I went for sessions in the big physical-therapy room, I was in with broken Marines, all of them too young, and most with a tough life ahead. So much frightful damage in the room: missing limbs, disfigured faces, spinal injuries. My gloom deepened.

One day a nurse wheeled in a blond kid—he appeared to be about eighteen. His legs were gone at the hips—no way to affix prosthetics—and his left arm was gone. Completely. As she wheeled him closer, I got a better look. My heart knocked. All the digits on his right hand, except his index finger, were also missing. That's all he had for the rest of his life: one finger. The young nurse leaned in over his shoulder, talking to him as she pushed his wheelchair at a quick pace. She was upbeat, perky, and as she bent forward, her hair touched his cheek. He was smiling at whatever she was saying.

This poignant moment, the image of the nurse with her hair falling onto the smooth face of the shattered young man, this boy...it stays with me. What could his life be like going forward?

## CHAPTER TWENTY-EIGHT

# Airborne Again

In early November I drove away from the Naval Hospital at Oak Knoll with a clearance for flight and orders to the RAG for some touch-up training.

A few days later, an instructor and I waited through the morning for Lemoore's winter Tule fog to burn away. It was my first flight in 101 days, and with the fog lifting, he and I taxied two A-4s out for a formation take-off. As we accelerated down the long runway, it felt as if I had flown the day before, like nothing had been lost. Our airplanes lifted free of the earth, the concrete runway fell away with its stripe-dashes flashing beneath us, and we accelerated rapidly. I matched his climb-angle and settled in close. He was a smooth pilot, and flying tight formation on his wing was liberation; it was as if I'd never been in a hospital.

The loud hiss in my cockpit and the whining rumble behind me provided the only hint of all this thrust powering my bird into this fine steep climb. The Central Valley's farmland retreated under us to form a puzzle of winter-hued squares as we turned toward the bright snow-capped Sierras. We climbed under a fine blue sky in the cold air, and the earth below shifted to pastel colors in haze as we leveled at our altitude. I once more felt whole.

By now I'd received orders to rejoin the Ghostriders, when Air Wing Sixteen returned to Lemoore in January. While waiting, I tuned my skills at VA-125, flying thirty-two hops, all of them good. My energy returned.

One afternoon, after I had flown and changed back into uniform, I sat down with a couple instructors at the front of VA-125's big ready-room. I had a question for a lieutenant about to leave the Navy. While in the hospital I'd had time to think about my future—specifically, whether to stay in the Navy or sign on with one of the airlines, the only career courses I saw available. Bill might have insight.

"What airline are you going to?"

"I'm not going to an airline," he answered.

I was stunned. "What will you do?"

"I'm going to medical school."

"Wait, you must be, what, twenty-seven?" I said. "Won't you be thirty when you finish?" Thirty seemed so old.

He smiled as he explained he faced a far longer slog. He'd first attend undergraduate classes to complete science requirements he needed before he could even apply to medical schools. If he was admitted, a long process followed—academics, internship, residency and then more training for specialization. "I'll be well past thirty by the time I'm practicing," He told me.

I knew he was married. "How can you think this way?"

He answered with a parable. "You know how when you're on a road trip on two-lane roads, how you work to get around those slow cars, maybe a bus? You know how you feel when you've passed them and they're behind you?"

I did.

"Then you start seeing signs. 'See the Caverns, See the Really Interesting Caverns.' You don't want to turn off, because those cars and that bus will get ahead of you." He paused for effect. "Larry, I'm going to see the caverns."

In coming years, I'd think about that afternoon, how as we relaxed after our flights that day and chatted, how with a simple parable, Lt. Bond explained life for me. His message: no matter how far along you are on the long continuum, possibilities abound.

William Bond, who did become a doctor, a neurologist, showed me with his folksy parable that life never presents binary choices; always there are many.

News from Yankee Station arrived at the RAG daily and swirled around the ready-room. Oriskany's losses continued to build. I'd hear truncated versions in the ready-room, then days, even weeks later, a pale blue letter from someone aboard Oriskany would furnish details.

In early December, a fighter pilot I didn't know took a hit from anti-aircraft guns, ejected and was rescued. The air wing took a breather, and Oriskany steamed to Hong Kong for the Christmas holidays. When the ship was headed back to Yankee Station, Jim Waldron penned a note to me. For once it was all upbeat. He met a Scottish girl. The squadron rented a room in a fine hotel and set up a wonderful bar. Food was terrific, especially at a place they found in Kowloon. At a dealership, Jim found a new BSA motorcycle priced so sweetly he had to buy it. Sailors helped him wrestle it up the steep gangway.

Air Wing Sixteen's final line-period began the last day of December. Right away, another Crusader was hit with anti-aircraft guns. The pilot ejected and was recovered. Two days after that a Saint, Rick Minnich, was bore-sighted by a SAM, and now he was listed MIA. The next day, Skip Foulks was hit again, but this time fatally—another KIA for the Saints.

The Ghostriders were not spared. In January, George Schindelar experienced total electrical failure. It threw him into darkness, and control problems followed. He punched out near the ship. A few days later, January 11, Deny Weichman, flying his 400th mission, took a hit from small-arms fire over Laos. He flew the disintegrating A-4 east across Vietnam, heading for the Gulf of Tonkin. But before making it feet-wet, his aircraft began to burn. Tom LeMay, who was on his wing, saw the flames and began calling for Deny to eject from the uncontrollable airplane. But Deny hung with it, riding helplessly, as the dying A-4 soared through death-rolls, one after another. He was over clouds, unable to determine his position, and the barrel-rolls were describing larger and larger looping arcs, each time carrying him closer to the earth at the bottoms. Later Deny said he was not going to eject unless he saw water. For him, capture was not an option.

"They know me," he explained, referring to his 1964 missions with the CIA outfit.

A final roll took him into and then under the cloud layer. Water. Deny's leg was broken as he ejected from the cockpit. It was Oriskany's last day of combat.

My squadron was headed home to Lemoore. I'd met a lieutenant-commander at the RAG who had orders to VA-164. Together, he and I made it a project to see that the Ghostriders' hangar and office spaces were spruced up and ready for our squadron's return. Lt. Cmdr. Roger Meyers and I worked well together. He was an excellent leader, and I liked him. I was pleased when he told me that he was to be VA-164's maintenance officer. "I'm going to ask that you work for me," he told me one day.

Our squadron's color was orange. The departing squadron had painted blue stripes and trim all over the ready-room and hangar. Roger and I made it a mission to replace all the blue paint we could find with the proper orange color. A skeleton crew of enlisted men and petty officers were also waiting to join the squadron, so we had plenty of help. I located an artist among them, and he painted a seven-foot diameter version of our squadron patch onto a wall at the top of a stairway. Roger and I wanted to ensure the squadron felt welcome when it arrived home at Lemoore, for it had been a hellish cruise.

In 122 days of combat operations, Oriskany lost thirty-nine airplanes, about one every third day—the highest losses of any carrier in the Vietnam Air War. On a daily basis, airplanes would land with battle damage, some with hits that—a few millimeters one way or another—would have brought the airplane down. At least one aircraft returned so battle-damaged that, after its pilot, Mike Mullane, managed to land aboard, it burst into flames. Mike escaped and the fire was extinguished, but so little of that A-4 remained useful, it was stripped of a few workable parts and then pushed over the side.

## CHAPTER TWENTY-NINE

# One More Try

Precisely one year after I had been shot down, USS Hancock, CVA-19, departed for Yankee Station. The Ghostrider squadron, now part of Air Wing Twenty-One, was aboard.

Roger Duter, Don Purdy and I, the three NAVCADs, along with a new guy, Mike Norwood, qualified for a stateroom, one located directly beneath the port catapult—not highly desired real estate. With every launch, we'd experience a shuddering, slamming blow to our small space, like a colossal hammer hitting steel right over our heads. You felt the jolt in your skeleton. Otherwise, it was a great stateroom. We each had a small safe, which happened to have the same dimensions as a fifth of whiskey—whiskey supposedly never found aboard a Navy vessel. That was a plus.

In Honolulu, we bought spray cans of psychedelic colors and painted our door Haight-Ashbury orange, electric-blue and snow-white. Breaking with the customary practice of stenciling ranks, initials and last names, we mimicked a Jefferson Airplane poster and painted our full names in huge, ballooning script. Above the door we painted "Alice's Restaurant," honoring Arlo Guthrie's mild war-protest song. We expected to be ordered to repaint everything gray and follow the traditional stenciling protocol. Instead our room became party central for the Ghostriders.

In early August, we arrived on Yankee Station to face restrictive rules of engagement. McNamara's robust Rolling Thunder bombing campaign had fizzled, and we were now limited to soft targets. Attacks above the nineteenth parallel were no longer allowed, meaning Hanoi, Haiphong, Phu Ly and the MiG bases were now off limits.

Vinh and equally hostile Than Hoa were below the nineteenth, and still in our operating area, but most target assignments would be easier and less hazardous than last cruise.

The idea, we were informed, was to lure the North Vietnamese to a bargaining table. Somehow our bombing of their country had distorted into a form of communication.

Safer for us, but frustrating. It felt as though we were no longer fighting to win the air war, but instead were subjecting ourselves to dangers for little good effect. It was hollow work. The air wing's morale fell. I can vividly remember only a few of the ninety-two missions I flew that cruise.

One I recall in vivid detail was above Vinh. With Don Purdy on my wing, I was to provide Shrike-missile protection for a section of Old Salts. They were to run a road recce mission a few miles south of us in a well-defended region just north of Vinh. Although it was a night assignment, the mission outline could not have been sweeter.

We were each armed with two Shrikes and four bombs, and Don and I were to—this part I had trouble believing—remain feet wet, safely over water for the entire mission. We were to set up a race-track pattern of three-minute legs, so that one of us would have his airplane—and Shrikes—pointed at the Vinh-area threats while the other aircraft was flying the outbound leg. It was a form of communication with the operators of the nearby SAM-sites.

The message was: we'll fire Shrikes at you if we hear your acquisition-radars come up. They understood and kept their Fan

Song units silent. Everyone involved understood. Yet the North Vietnamese did keep running their search-radars. Round and round Don and I went, hearing only the voop-voop sounds of search-radar in our headsets.

The Saints cleared the area and it was time for Don and me to head back to the ship. It was forbidden to come back aboard carrying bombs (but not missiles), so we were to disarm the bombs and dump them three miles off the coast. I called Don telling him that we were done and I was dumping my bombs. He was inbound and almost at the coastline. "I'm going feet dry to take a peek," he transmitted. As he did, my earphones came alive with fire-control-radar noise—the radars used to aim big guns—and at the same moment, the most flak I'd ever seen at night filled the sky near the coast. "Yikes!" he transmitted.

"Turn around," I called.

"I can't, I can't turn," he transmitted.

Airbursts followed at his altitude as he dodged inland, trying to get away from it.

I watched in horror, as my friend's path was traced by the flashes in the sky. He eventually swung south and out over the water. Purdy had come way too close to buying the farm on one of the safest night missions we'd draw for the entire cruise.

Over a shot of single-malt whisky, whenever we're together these days, we retell that story. Don's never been able to adequately explain why. The answers he usually comes up with are either, "I didn't want to drop bombs in the water." Or, "I thought I might find a truck."

Crazy. Had a bomb fallen above the nineteenth parallel—and on that black night it was unclear just where that might be—the result would have been a court martial, maybe two. Plainly, it was his need for a hit of adrenaline to punch up a serene mission—proof I wasn't the only one addicted.

For the Ghostriders, in terms of losses, the '68-'69 cruise went better than the previous two deployments. Combat took only one pilot: Don Erwin, our executive officer. He and I had flown together on a road-recce, and we'd found some barges tucked under a line of trees along a small tributary river. We made multiple passes; we were causing secondary explosions with each good hit. When we debriefed, I reminded him that what we had done was dangerous, bordering on folly. Making multiple passes at a target was a good way to get shot down—and against operating rules. Not many days later, Don Irwin took a 37-mm hit near Vinh. He managed to keep his aircraft flying some twenty miles until he was feet-wet. Mike Mullane and his wingie, Mike Williams, arrived overhead not long after Erwin ejected. Mullane went down for a closer look, and saw the parachute deployed underwater. After a search of the area, Mullane spotted an empty helmet floating. But no sign of our executive officer. I asked; he had not been making multiple runs. Don Irwin's remains came home in 1990.

My collateral job—unlike the Air Force, Navy pilots had a secondary duty—was as power plants officer in Roger Meyers's Maintenance Department. It turned out to be an easy task, since I had a competent chief petty officer under me in that department. I'd meet with him, mainly to sign off paperwork. On one visit, he pointed to his number-two, a first-class petty officer.

"Does that bother you, sir?" the chief asked me.

I looked more closely. The man had grown a huge afro, and perched on top was a ballcap. We all wore ballcaps aboard ship—and most of us had a squadron patch on the front. But the patch on his was an upraised fist—the defiant symbol of Tommie Smith and John Carlos at the Olympics that summer—one of the early expressions of Black Power.

"How's his work going?" I asked the chief.

"Working his ass off, sir," the chief said. "He and two guys did a full engine-change overnight. Book says it's a 24-hour job."

"You see anything wrong with the haircut or the ballcap?"

"No sir. So long as he keeps up his work."

"I don't see a thing," I said.

In late January, Roger Meyers gathered both of his lieutenants and told us a message had come in instructing that our maintenance department replace pins in the nose-gear struts of all our

squadron's A-4s. There had been a failure, and a nose-gear had collapsed on an airplane in another squadron.

Our deployment was almost finished, and the entire maintenance department—from chiefs down—had been putting in long
hours without letup. I suggested that changing out the pins would
be a good task for the crews as we steamed back toward the States.

"I know it's a lot to add this job, too," Roger said, "but it's a
safety issue. I'd like to see it done now."

Our final day on Yankee Station was Feb. 9, 1969. My combat-
flying would be finished with a final hop that night. Hancock was
on the noon-to-midnight operations schedule, and I was slated to
fly on the final launch. It would be my 137th mission, well short of
the numbers racked up by Duter, Purdy, Schindelar, Cunningham,
Mullane and the other Ghostriders who completed two full cruises.
They had all blown well past the so-called 200-mission combat
limit.

Roger Meyers donned flight gear with me in the locker-room.
My boss and I were both in bright spirits. As we cinched our torso
harnesses and strapped on our survival vests, I kidded him about
my lucky tanker assignment. He told me he was headed out on an
armed-road-reconnaissance mission—an easy road-recce in a relatively benign area.

"You don't need to win any wars tonight," I said to him.

"Don't worry, I have to get home to meet this guy."

He unzipped the small pocket on the shoulder of his flight-suit,
the same pocket where Dick Hartman carried his Saint Christopher
medal. Roger carefully slipped a photo of his infant son from the
small pocket. His boy had been born during the cruise. Roger
passed the color-print to me. The baby appeared pink and vulnerable. I told him the kid looked terrific. We headed to the flight-deck
together.

Mine was the first aircraft launched, as tankers customarily
were. I entered a climbing arc around the ship, looking for the off-
going tanker. The routine was for the bird coming on station to
draw any extra fuel from the off-going bird to replace fuel used in
the climb to altitude. I was still climbing, when a flash of light below

caught my attention. A sheet of flame spread across the water ahead of the ship.

No! No! Not on the last launch! My stomach began to churn. Surely whoever lost the airplane had ejected. I heard nothing about it over the radio, and worried throughout the tanker sortie. After I landed, after my aircraft was chained to the deck and after the plane captain came up the ladder to help me unstrap, I asked.

"Which squadron lost the airplane?"

"I heard it was Mr. Meyers," he answered.

It was the replacement pins that were bad. Roger's airplane had one that our department's guys, who had worked overtime on this project, replaced. It broke. His nose-strut splayed out in front of his airplane during the final few feet of his last catapult launch of the cruise. His A-4 pointed viciously down as it shot off the end of the ship, and he slammed toward the black water at a sharp angle, not even a quarter-second to eject. Unlike the F-8, it is impossible to eject underwater in an A-4. No chance.

My last memory of Roger is his joyous smile, wide and genuine, as he slipped his infant son's photo back into the shoulder pocket on his flight-suit.

Hancock docked March 3, 1969, at North Island near San Diego. I took leave and flew to Palo Alto to see my folks.

Joy in the house was palpable. All of us understood war was behind me. I had written to them about my decision to leave the Navy. I wanted to see the caverns. But there was sadness, too. Anne, my grandmother, had died two days before. Her funeral was to be in San Diego, where she would be buried at Fort Rosecrans National Cemetery and share a headstone with my grandfather, the man from whom she had run away to join a barnstorming flying-circus, when my father was eight, and the man to whom she ultimately returned a year later to love and bicker with—in equal passionate measures—for the rest of their lives together.

My folks flew down to San Diego to take care of the arrangements. I followed in their new Chrysler with my three younger sisters. We caught up with constant chatter, but I recall little else of that drive, except that we were stopped for speeding. I wasn't accustomed to how quiet the big car was at speed. I was freshly returned from the long deployment, so my driving skills needed honing. I didn't realize the car would go so fast.

The highway-patrol officer continued to write the ticket as I ticked off these exonerating facts for him.

My grandmother's services were at a modest gray-stucco funeral home. Words were said, and then the funeral director came near my father and whispered quietly. Dad stood. So did Mom, and I understood it was time for the family to file by and view Anne's open casket. I remained on the pew. I'd had enough with death. I didn't want a close look.

Dad came back to the pew quietly weeping, Mom looked stricken and conflicted. Stricken because she loved Anne, and had taken care of her during the past two years while Anne's renal disease ran its course. Conflicted because, as she had confided to me years before, Anne could be difficult. My sisters were sad, of course, and all three came back to the pew with tears streaking their cheeks. Dad sat next to me, now crying openly.

I felt empty.

I loved Anne, loved the stories she could tell, and I loved her sense of adventure. My first thrilling ride in an airplane was with Anne, my grandmother, at the controls. We flew from the airport toward my neighborhood, and then she did something terrifying—she banked to the right and circled tightly over our house.

It unnerved me because she had opened what served as a canopy on that airplane; I was on the low side of a steep bank, and with only clear air between me and the green roof of our home far below, I thought I might fall out. I'd forgotten she had snugged a seatbelt around my hips before we took off. A glance over to see her smiling, was enough to make it all fun.

She was piloting the Ercoupe she had purchased new in Maryland. With Pop, she'd flown it from the factory to El Paso a few weeks earlier. Anne was the first licensed woman pilot in Texas, she claimed. This was the summer I turned five.

Later that year, we went to California—only the two of us. We rode the Southern Pacific, slept in a compartment, and we ate off fine china in the dining-car. In the parlor-car, she read stories to me and told me of her childhood adventures growing up in British Columbia.

I did; I loved Anne. Now I felt nothing. What was the matter with me? She was the grandmother I adored, but on this day I could not cry for this outsized presence in my little-boy life.

In the stucco funeral home, with Anne's body ten feet away, I understood then that I had lost something—something that had at one time made me tender and sensitive.

# PART VI

RETURN TO SAIGON

The cave you fear to enter holds the treasure you seek.

—*Joseph Campbell*

Vu Thi May led the author into a cave on the karst ridge behind her. The cavern is above the white outcropping. Afterward, Duthie and his friend Richard Turner sat at her table to eat their lunches.

CHAPTER THIRTY

# *See the Caverns*

My final assignment in the Navy was as a utility pilot with the RAG. There was limited flight-instructing involved, but lots of great flying, ferrying failing airplanes to a major maintenance facility in Florida and refurbished A-4s back to Lemoore. The time went quickly, and in mid-August, 1969, I drew my final pay and drove to my apartment to pack my stuff.

From my sock drawer, I lifted my pistol and turned it over in my hands. As always, I admired its flawless blue-black steel, the beautiful machine-work, the slick action of the slide and, especially, the pistol's balance. My 9-mm Beretta Modello-1951, a pristine example, had been crafted by an Italian company with a heritage going back to the sixteenth century. I owned it because it was a gorgeous example of art in steel and also because I grew up in Texas, where it was understood a man should own, at minimum, a pistol.

Now, handling it, I thought about its intended use. I set it aside and didn't box it up with my other stuff. A day or two later I sold it to one of the guys in the apartment complex.

By Christmas that year, I was working thirty-hour weeks at the *Aspen Times* and living the life of a ski-bum in an ancient aluminum trailer next door to Hunter S. Thompson's place. Caverns, maybe, but I'd quickly become bored; I needed to do something productive. One more go at college?

I was accepted into the University of Colorado's journalism school in January, 1970. The G.I. Bill supplied enough to buy books and live on, and my savings covered out-of-state tuition.

My first day on the Boulder campus, I found myself standing in a long registration line looking out over a vast sea of children. Kids. Perhaps at twenty-seven, I was a bit too far along life's continuum for a do-over on a campus. But there ahead of me in that line stood a cute girl, a petite hippie co-ed. She wore a white linen tunic, embroidered in flowers. Emerging from her bell-bottoms were leather hiking boots, an indication she was into the outdoor-culture of this university. Her dark hair, silky and smooth, hung to her waist. Her name was Roz.

Our wedding took place six months later, a small affair in the backyard of her parents' home—a garden ceremony, her mother called it. We honeymooned backpacking in the Rockies, and it was Roz who caught all the fat trout we ate for dinners. In Boulder we moved into a cozy apartment near campus, a love-nest above a red-brick carriage-house behind the stately Victorian home of a prominent Boulder judge. Steep steel steps, a ladder almost, took us up to a tiny landing leading into the apartment.

Four months after our wedding, I waited for our newspaper-delivery-girl to climb those steps. The Associated Press promised to print a story I wanted to read.

After a morning final-exam, I had ridden my bike back to our apartment. If our paper-girl was punctual, I'd have time to read it in Boulder's afternoon newspaper, *The Daily Camera*, then ride quickly—it was all downhill—back to campus for my afternoon final.

Until this day, the Vietnamese had never provided names of the captured men they held. Nor had they allowed many of their prisoners to write to their families. Dick Hartman's mother, for instance, had never received a letter from him. Now, finally, a full accounting of the POWs held in North Vietnam.

Right on time I heard light footfalls on the steel steps. I met the delivery-girl on the landing and thanked her. Leaning on the steel platform's railing, I read the lead-story. It jumped to page three. Columns of names, hundreds, dominated the page. The names of guys I had flown with jumped from the columns: George McSwain, the ensign I replaced in 1966; Dave Carey and Al Stafford, taken down by the same SAM; two Oriskany fighter pilots, both named Charlie—Zuhoski and Rice; John McCain, a future senator and Dale Osborne, a VA-55 pilot I knew from USS Hancock. A handful of other names on the long list—guys I had known in flight training—jumped from the page.

But where was Dick Hartman?

I ran my finger down each column, reading carefully. My watch told me it was time to be on my bike; I could not miss the final. I continued searching.

Then I noticed.

At the bottom of the page, tucked in a corner, was a smaller box with a shorter list. Richard Danner Hartman's name flashed at me. He had died in captivity. It was as if I had been punched hard. In the chest. Until now, all this time, I thought we'd see each other again. That I'd be there to welcome Dick back to the States, to freedom. That we'd meet again for a quiet breakfast.

Roz and I graduated in June and headed to Europe for three months of cavern-seeking, riding bicycles and living in a tent. Less than a year after that, we veered from the path most traveled, and purchased the smallest newspaper in Colorado—a weekly in the Alps-like San Juan Range of the Colorado Rockies. And during the time we lived at 9,300 feet elevation in the Rockies, our daughter let us know she was about to be born.

There were no doctors in Silverton, so with Roz in the passenger seat, grimacing in labor, I drove our old Jeepster fifty miles over two mountain passes—each with summits approaching 11,000-

feet—to Durango. It was February, the dead of winter, and the Jeepster's heater puffed air no warmer than a puppy's breath. Bundled in plaid woolen shirts and down-filled jackets, we looked more like mountaineers than a young couple on their first trip to a maternity ward.

Five days after our little girl's birth, Hanoi began its release of POWs. With dignity they marched out in order of their shoot-down dates. At the air base at Gia Lam, which some of these pilots had bombed, they boarded American C-141s, these fitted with airline seats instead of stretchers. The Vietnam War, for America, was done; a treaty had been signed.

I thought it was done for me, as well. I had a family, completed when our son was born while we briefly owned three weekly newspapers at the foot of Mount Shasta in Northern California. It was all behind me; I had community journalism, not Vietnam, on my mind.

In 1978, Roz and I, with our infant son and daughter in tow, took another risk and purchased a failing newspaper located on an island at the top of Puget Sound. This was what I had wanted, here we'd truly see the caverns. After a struggle, we turned it around financially and won awards for our journalism. I loved this one, because it was much like the *Aspen Times*, my model for a perfect community newspaper. And I loved our insular life.

From our house, our children could walk to and from school or down to a beach. My daughter had a horse. We cherished our islander neighbors. We restored a small cabin-cruiser—wooden, built in 1928—and aboard we'd cruise the waters among San Juan County's hundreds of islands. We never tired of watching bald eagles soaring over the sound, orcas spyhopping, and almost always, harbor seals pacing our old classic boat.

For occasional trips to the mainland, we'd board Washington State's handsome white ferries that would thread green-water passages among some of the most beautiful islands on the planet. Spectacular journeys every time, and social events, too, because we knew many of the other passengers aboard. Our life in the islands was magnificent.

Until seventeen years after my shoot-down.

I began to wake up angry. I'd start every day that way. Nothing was right. In the beginning it wasn't an explosive anger, only a murky overcast in my life, a rumbling issue deep inside I couldn't quite identify. And could not fix.

So it had to be Roz. I began to argue with her.

Looking back at this distressing period, I'm sure I initiated most of the verbal battles. We didn't fight in front of our two kids. We still loved each other. We still made love. But we fought. My anger escalated. And we both felt dreadful.

About this time my fear of fire flared. My daughter says she remembers when we traveled that I'd ask for a room on the ground-floor of the motel—to make escape easier. And if we took an upstairs room, I'd brief the family on routes to at least two exits—neither of which could involve the elevator. I didn't allow use of the little catch that allows motel doors to be cracked but not fully opened. It might slow an escape. In restaurants I wanted a seat where my back was to a wall, no one behind me.

None of this sounds like the guy I had been, a pilot who would saunter confidently out to his aircraft knowing that people he had never met would soon be shooting at him. What was with this new caution, this near-phobia? And this fresh desire for control in a relationship founded on shared decisions: what was with that?

It wasn't the stress of owning a small business fueling my fears and anger. The troubled days of sleep deprivation and marginal cash-flows were behind us. I loved my work as a community newspaper publisher. Life was good on San Juan Island, about as perfect as I could have imagined. And as each day passed, I became more and more agitated. A coal-black miasma settled over me, over our beautiful life.

I found it hard to do my work, impossible to concentrate for more than a few moments. One afternoon I jumped up from my desk. On my way out the front door, I told the office manager I'd be back. I didn't know when. I found myself walking rapidly down the street, marching toward the office of one of the shrinks on the island. I stormed in.

"I need to talk with Lance," I said to the receptionist. She let me go through, and I settled into the patient's chair in the small office of Dr. Lance Sobel, a PhD psychologist.

"What's up?"

Sitting rigidly on the front edge of a cushion, I leaned forward and began to unload. In anguish I spilled out to Lance all the exasperation I was feeling. After a few minutes, he asked this:

"You were in Vietnam, weren't you?"

I answered that I'd been there.

"You never talk about it."

Lance knew this because during our many days crewing together on racing sailboats, I had barely mentioned the nearly seven years I spent in the Navy.

"I think you need to," he told me.

There was no break-through, but slowly, week-by-week, I felt Lance's questions and observations lifting me, by inches, out of the deep well. The short questions—often, "How does that make you feel?" or "Can we talk a little more about that?"—prompted long responses.

He listened carefully as I detailed troubling memories: the fire, days and nights flying over an enemy land and, eventually, the vivid image of Dick alone on that ridge gathering in his 'chute. I told him of the regrets, the *shoulda, coulda, wouldas.*

And the guilt.

Guilt from my recent behavior, yes, but largely the old guilt. I don't recall if I ever spoke of watching *The Dating Game* while my Childplay buddies were dying—that guilt—but I tried to tell it all.

Oriskany—Childplay—that aircraft carrier left over from the Second World War had played such an outsized role in my life. Aboard this ship I was introduced to combat flying and the accompanying losses. I made it through a terrible fire, while so many airwing buddies died. When it seemed it would be better, Dick and I were promptly shot down. There was that submerged guilt of having killed, because I had never fully rationalized what we were up to—really up to—with that Shalt-Not commandment. Some of my weapons had crossed that line. Bombs and cluster-bomblets dropped on gun sites headed the list.

The guilt wouldn't stop. I could not free my mind of an image—all those terribly maimed boys on the flying ambulance—most were never going to be better; nor were the teenagers in the big physical therapy room at Oak Knoll. I was going to be okay, I knew it, but so many of them would not.

All the deaths and all the guys imprisoned for years and years enduring brutality—that guilt, the contrition of one who somehow skirted it. And that companion to survivor's guilt, too, haunting me that my friends were going through true hell, while I shuffled around in a peaceful hospital, reading and watching television. Dick Hartman's capture and death. All that guilt. Layers.

Lance helped me put it into some sort of perspective. It wasn't going to go away; that could never happen. The memories were seared in—adrenaline. But he helped.

Also, I was past my fortieth birthday by a couple years.

"Nobody gets to their fifth decade," Lance told me one day, "without causing harm."

During this period, I took care to avoid arguments with Roz. We talked nicely to each other. We hugged. We made love. We weren't fixed yet; my anger still smoldered. But the heat was down, the ember was cooling, much of it turning into historical white ash.

I began to feel again. Numbness was slipping away.

Then one day Lance told me I was through. Done. He had taken me as far as he was able. I left the office feeling slightly abandoned. I had looked forward to those afternoons, anticipated them.

As I walked up the hill toward my newspaper, I realized the black miasma, the gloomiest haze at least, was lifting. I was once again growing close to and happy with my soulmate, the sweet hippie girl I'd met in the college registration line.

I understood, too, that I needed to see Vietnam—North and South—at least one more time. I had some unfinished emotional business there.

CHAPTER THIRTY-ONE

# *Incense and a Prayer*

 T he aircraft entered a gentle descent, crossing the coastline at a recognizable place south of The Hourglass. So familiar. Off the right wing, through the ragged bottom of the overcast we had broken through, I glimpsed the rivers, right where they should be.We were feet-dry now and headed to Hanoi. But the butterflies were not there, nor the chilling adrenaline. I was comfortable in the window-seat of an ATR-72, a new Vietnam Airlines turbo-prop. It was early March, 1996.

Seated next to me was Richard Turner, my high-school buddy, one of the Clods. It had been almost twenty-eight years since I'd last glimpsed this coastline. It looked the same.

A week earlier, Roz and I had flown to Saigon, checking in at The Hotel Majestic, the same hotel my family lived in during our first month in Vietnam. Looking at it from the street, it was thrilling to see it retained the same classical French Riviera style I remembered. Even the same color, although the paint was now fresh. The interior was all new and elegantly improved. Gone was the creaking birdcage elevator my sisters had loved to operate, and gone were the musky odors of tropical decay. Now it was sparkling clean, air-conditioned and posh, having recently undergone an $11-million refurbishment by the current owner: the communist government of Vietnam.

Outside the hotel: another change. No longer was the street we knew as Rue Catinat and then Tu Do, tree-lined and quiet. A river of bicycles, motorbikes, and cars gushed toward us, generating a turbulent racket.

This was now Dong Khoi Street, and the torrent of bikes and cars was a visual clue to the burgeoning population of Ho Chi Minh City. In 1959 there had been one million people living in Saigon's metropolitan area. The official figure in 1996 was six million.

Roz and I stepped out of the hotel after breakfast our first day there, and we found it impossible to find an opening in the traffic. The technique, demonstrated in pantomime by a kindly woman who had watched us frozen on a corner, was to step slowly and purposefully off the curb and into traffic, and then to keep a steady pace as we crossed the street. The theory is that the bikes and motorcycles and cars judge your rate of crossing and like water in a stream flow around you. It worked.

Showing Roz my old haunts was exciting and invigorating. We went to Cercle Sportif, converted from private club to one for the people. The pool was packed and somewhat dingy, but familiar.

Up the street from the Majestic, we walked past what had once been the opera house and in our time a government building. It has undergone a restoration and today is gorgeous. We walked further up Dong Khoi to the stately post office building, which had also been spruced up. It now displayed a huge painting of Uncle Ho.

That afternoon we walked a couple blocks to the Continental, built in 1880 and still a handsome hotel. We took a table in the cool and tranquil inner courtyard, shaded by manicured trees. Lovely. As we sipped gin-tonics, we were shielded from the noise and heat of the asphalt streets bordering the hotel on two sides, and we imagined Graham Greene writing at one of the nearby tables. He had lived in Room 214 while working as a foreign correspondent, and it was here, maybe even at our table, that he began writing his great novel, *The Quiet American*. I read the book during my high-school year in Saigon, not quite understanding that Greene was predicting tragedy for Americans meddling in the affairs of this complicated, divided country.

The Vietnamese people were as friendly as I remembered them. Their wars, the long one with France and the longer one with us, were not mentioned. Only once did we detect animosity. An aging cyclo driver, his feet resting on the pedals, told us in good English that he had been a major in the South Vietnamese Army. There was bitterness in his voice when he reminded us that the U.S. had left; now this was the only job he could get. But then he smiled.

One morning Roz and I walked to the top of the former Rue Catinat, took a right turn at Phon Dinh Phung and headed toward my old home, the villa my family moved into after our stay across from the opera house. Our old street was still tree-lined and beautiful, and the French Colonial homes along it were smartly maintained. But when we arrived at the corner where our villa should have been, I became disoriented. On our corner stood a three-story building occupied by an Australian engineering firm.

No luck finding the house, so I'd show her our old school. We directed a taxi-driver to Tan Son Hoa Street, where we'd find the American Community School. But the area was now developed so heavily, I recognized nothing. Up and down the Tan Son Hoa we went. Roz sensed my growing frustration. "We don't need to see it," she said. "We're enjoying ourselves."

Richard arrived in Saigon at the end of the week, the day before Roz was due to return home to her teaching duties. The three of us dined that evening at one of the newer establishments catering to Western tourists. The next morning I accompanied Roz to the airport.

That day Richard and I resumed the hunt for our school. Again, a taxi-driver was asked to cruise up and down Tan Son Hoa. Eventually Richard spotted familiar roofs tucked between more modern structures. The former American Community School was now part of a Vietnamese government compound of some sort.

We found the man in charge, a military officer, and he and Richard conversed in French. Our school had been transformed into a hospital, operated at first by the Seventh Day Adventist mission—the kind folks who stitched a teenager's fight wound. When the last of the American civilians left, the U.S. military had taken over the hospital. Now this officer, a French-trained M.D. who had served with the Viet Minh was in charge. He'd been placed there after the fall of Saigon. But, analogous to our own civil war, because he had been born in the South, he was not trusted by his northern comrades. He retained his rank as colonel and drew a salary, but he was allowed no staff, no budget and no patients. For decades he had been in charge of a ghost hospital. He gave us a tour.

There was a newer building several stories high, built on land I'd watched being planted with rice in 1959. Still stenciled in large letters on the building was: "Ambulances Park Here." Under the awning over a walkway, the colonel had collected war implements, creating a sort of museum. He showed us one of the famous beefed-up bicycles used to transport war materiel down the Ho Chi Minh Trail. Bamboo sheaves reinforced wheels. The front fork had been doubled, and plywood gussets strengthened each tube-junction of the frame. An acetylene lamp—something that appeared to be from the 1890s—was affixed to the handlebar. There was no seat, for the bike was pushed by a man or woman walking beside it and steering with a bamboo pole tied to one of the handlebars with a band of rubber cut from a section of old inner tube. This bike had a capacity of 200 kilos, the doctor told us, but there were some that could carry up to 400. I marveled. This bit of nineteenth-century technology helped defeat the strongest military on earth.

Richard and I went over to inspect what had once been our classrooms. Both of us, at about the same moment, recognized the painted tiles on the floor. This indeed was our school, these small buildings at the core of the complex.

Another memory struck. After I had been rescued and then taken from Udorn to Saigon—the day I learned there would be no more efforts to rescue Dick Hartman—I was brought here. I had slept fitfully in one of our old classrooms.

Richard and I headed to Hanoi the following day.

The ancient Volga sedan jounced wildly on the packed red laterite dirt-road. Not only, we were discovering, did the old car need to be pushed to start, but its tires had long-ago worn smooth as a green mango's skin. Also, it no longer had shock absorbers. Richard and I were thrown about in the back seat, while our middle-aged driver, along with Xuan, our twenty-one-year-old guide/translator, seemed not to notice the wild gyrations.

My mission this morning was to find the ridge—Dick Hartman's ridge. The potholed red-clay trail hardly merited its title: Hai-Muoi-Mot—Highway-21. Our route threaded through a valley created by karst ridges jutting up sharply. From time to time we stopped. I consulted a map. "This looks like the place," I'd tell Richard. "That ridge could be it."

We'd travel further southwest, and stop again. "Now this looks like it," I'd tell him.

The morning wore on. It was overcast, but no rain yet. Every steep karst ridge looked like it, like the right one. We got around a bus, a frightening maneuver on the narrow dirt road, and we were making good time when we passed a sign made of concrete, its intaglio letters distinct.

I asked Xuan what it said. "See the grotto," he answered. Then he asked if we'd like to see the cave.

"See the caverns? Why, yes. Yes!"

The Volga and its bald tires handled the path to the base of the cliff okay, although it was far worse than the Hai-Muoi-Mot. We arrived at a small temple and a hamlet comprised of five tiny houses with thatch roofs. Otherwise this bucolic valley at the base of a cliff appeared empty. We parked, left the Volga running (so we would not have to push-start it later) and walked to the temple.

There Xuan laid a few coins on a table and took up sticks of incense. I should do the same, he indicated. Under the tiled roof at the front of the temple, an older woman acting as a priestess sat cross-legged on an open platform. She faced a small gathering, mostly older people, who were kneeling or sitting cross-legged on the concrete platform. She chanted. And as part of her ritual, a bell was struck from time to time, piercing the morning air with a clear ringing peal.

I followed Xuan into an enclosed room behind the prayer-platform. In the smoky and dark little space, he placed his incense sticks into sand-filled vases. Before each one, he bowed and appeared to pray. I did the same, saying to myself *Bless Dick Hartman* as I inserted each smoking stick gently into the sand. Dick was so religiously Christian; what would he think of this?

When I emerged from the tiny room, I asked Xuan if there was a way to have the priestess say a prayer for someone. He showed me to a wooden box, and I slipped some bills, my offering, through its slot. Then I entered his name into the open book next to it. I wrote in the Vietnamese manner of one syllable at a time: DICK HART MAN. And, as I stepped away and thought about this Vietnamese priestess chanting his name to heaven at the base of a ridge so like the last place I had seen Dick, I was overwhelmed. I began to cry.

"It's okay," Richard said. "That's what you came here for."

"Do you want to go to the grotto?" Xuan asked.

"Yes, Xuan. Please."

A woman named Vu Thi May was hired to lead us. She smiled easily. We struck out for the ridge, following a footpath that ran along rice paddies and toward the karst. As we padded along, it occurred to me that this woman, May, might know some old timer who remembered the day the airplanes were shot down. Xuan asked her, and an animated exchange followed.

She remembered, yes, and she gave him the date in July. She remembered because she had just turned seventeen. Her brother had been in charge of the gun emplacement. He had been the man giving the orders to fire.

I was stunned. "Could I talk to her brother?"

"No, he was now head of a commune three kilometers away," Xuan translated. "These country people think everything is three kilometers away," he added.

"What about the pilot?"

"He hid in a grotto," she told Xuan. "Two nights. Then he was arrested."

"Did he die?"

"Oh no," she said through Xuan. "He was taken by authorities out of the district."

We walked through the timeless scenery and eventually arrived at the base of the steep ridge. It was daunting. In fact, it appeared impossible. May handed walking-sticks to Richard and me.

The trail traversed the face, doubling back every few hundred meters. Climbing on the crumbling limestone was taxing, but patches of red clay made it worse. We slipped on it, and had to grab small bushes to keep from falling down the sheer slope. Several times Richard and I asked May to allow us to stop; we needed to catch our breath. This amused her.

We gained maybe 700-feet in the steep climb up the switchbacks. We arrived at the mouth of the cavern, both winded. A priest, wearing a traditional black robe, greeted us. Two acolytes seated us at a wooden table with a view out the cave's mouth. They poured astonishingly strong black coffee into tall glasses. Before us spread the green valley, the safe valley we flew over on raids to Hanoi. At the edge of one of the rice fields below, I pointed to a line of small round ponds.

"Bomb craters," I explained to Richard. "Maybe from that day."

Behind us, about thirty feet into the cave was an altar made of rough-cast concrete. Xuan explained that two years earlier, the people of May's hamlet had discovered this cavern. They reasoned tourists might come if they developed it as a sacred destination. Religious icons adorned the altar, and near the entrance hung a bronze bell that Xuan informed us weighed 170 kilograms. The priest had been hired. Additionally, that temple just outside the hamlet had been built. The incense and fake money (to be ritually burned) being sold to pilgrims generated income. Guiding groups to the caverns became another component of the hamlet's economy. It was working out well.

Word was spreading about the sacred grotto and pilgrims were coming. The group we had seen worshiping in the temple, Xuan explained, had traveled all the way from Haiphong. As an aside, he informed us that Richard and I were the first foreigners to visit. It was worth the climb, we told him; the cavern was impressive.

"You want to see more?" Xuan asked.

We were surprised to learn the cavern continued beyond the concrete altar. We'd need to make a donation to fuel the tiny Honda generator that powered the lights, Xuan explained. Our cost: the equivalent of a dime.

The generator was somewhere outside the cave's mouth, so we heard only a purr. We followed one of the priest's assistants around the end of the concrete altar and into the cool moist air of the cavern. Clear dim lightbulbs strung from stalactites cast a magical spell, throwing a yellow glow onto the flowing rocks. Minute crystals sparkled, having never been soiled by the oily hands of tourists. Xuan translated our guide's spiel as he paused to point a flashlight at a structure.

"Ho Chi Minh sitting." Then to another formation: "Ho Chi Minh praying." And so on.

Deeper and deeper we went, at times balancing with care as we gingerly stepped across planks spanning deep black crevasses. May was with us, and it seemed as if this was her first venture so deep into the cavern. She examined individual stalagmites with intensity.

It was disorienting, so I didn't realize we were headed out. But in the distance we caught the blue glow of the cave's opening to the valley.

"Hey, Larry, look at the end of the tunnel," Richard said. Yes, General Westmoreland's light at the end of the tunnel. I finally got to see it.

We politely declined another round of the bitter coffee, and then May led us down the steep ridge, pointing out slick patches of red clay that might cause us trouble. We left our walking sticks at the bottom. Some other out-of-shape pilgrims might need them. The return trek along the path toward the hamlet seemed to take longer. We walked single-file...in silence.

Along the way we came upon an elderly man coming toward us. He wore a clean gray tunic formally buttoned at his neck. A wispy beard, just a few white strands, trailed down from his chin. Xuan and May spoke with him. The conversation gathered energy.

Xuan turned to me with excitement. "He was a gunner." Then he rejoined the conversation in his language.

The three of them—Xuan, May and the elderly gentleman—continued. Eventually, Xuan turned to me with a correction. The man had not shot at our airplanes; he had been a gunner the year before. He had shot down an airplane then, but not mine or Dick's.

I asked Xuan to tell the gentleman I was pleased that he had made it through the war. He came back with the same. We shook hands, and then we stood together. Richard snapped a photo with my camera: two old adversaries side-by-side on a red dirt path not too far from Phu Ly.

May invited us into her home, so at the end of the trek back, the four of us—Richard, our driver, Xuan and I—went in. The floor was packed earth. The walls were whitewashed mud over thatch—which brightened the tidy place. Stabbed into the floor in a corner was a carefully trimmed tree-branch that forked three ways. It had been cut to securely cradle a small plastic pan: a wash basin. She gestured, so Richard and I washed our hands in it. Then she motioned for us to take seats at her oilcloth-covered table. We broke out our lunches. May smiled as we ate.

Did any of my bombs kill people like May? Some did fall short, a few soared long. Had they hit sweet people like this woman, or possibly nice young college students like Xuan, or perchance hard-working men like our driver? Or like the priest in the cave or his assistants? I hoped to God not.

But the man in the gray tunic we met on the trail? Gunners like he had been?

I had flown flak-suppression missions, watched my bombs—rigged for an airburst with extensions that put the fuse out front—

watched these air-burst bombs march across emplacements. And I had dropped CBUs, those cruel anti-personnel devices that rained bomblets—I had dropped them onto gun sites. It's a thought that will not stay tucked away. It visits without warning.

Now, sitting here in May's home—she's over there smiling at us—I am comfortable. I'm enjoying my lunch in her company and the company of young Xuan and Richard and our driver. I like being here. But my thoughts sabotage the moment, doubling back to the gunner on the path. To other men like him. Men who would not be enjoying that wish—*The Wish*—the one where you live to die old and of "natural causes."

Then, stinging. In the bridge of my nose. And a chuff-chuff deep in my chest. I turn as if I am inspecting something in the corner of her little home. The chuffing comes heavier. Then the tears, unexpected and warm; they flood my eyes. At the oilcloth-covered table in the home of Vu Thi May.

# Afterword

T he bravest aviator was granted *The Wish*, the gift we all wanted, the outcome where our prayers would be answered and someday we'd die of natural causes. Instead of in the sky over Vietnam. Which at the time was so implausible. Back then, none of us could have agreed on precisely what "natural causes" might actually mean, though we can tell you now.

Glen York, the bravest, lived eight-and-a-half decades before his final sortie into the sunset. From what he told me when we spoke on the phone toward the end, he wasn't particularly enthused about the final months of those eighty-five years.

We surviving Ghostriders, like Glen, have dodged what at one time seemed inevitable and gained that ephemeral wish. We find ourselves close to the prize, and we're amazed we got through, made it to now. But one by one we're being picked off. Deny Weichman, the guy who survived 625 combat missions, died on his sixtieth birthday. Stroke. He's buried at Chattanooga National Cemetery in Tennessee. A heart attack in 1998 got Doug Mow, our skipper on the ruthless '67 cruise. Roger Duter, my roomie on Hancock, went on to become Deputy Assistant Secretary of the Navy, but he died at sixty-seven. Another heart attack. Too soon. Too soon for all three. Though, back in the day, when we were being shot at, we'd have considered winning a few extra decades as the big door-prize.

Roz and I knew Glen was failing—though failing may not be the correct word, since he was still sharp; it was his physical health letting him down. We had asked his oldest daughter to alert us in the event "anything happened." And in the spring of 2014, "anything" did. The funeral was to take place in the fall, she told us, at Arlington National Cemetery. I alerted the Ghostriders. We look for reasons to get together, and funerals work. Glen's was set for October 15 that year. I dusted off my dark suit and a couple dated ties and booked airline tickets.

The day remains so vivid. Rain pounds hard as five of us make our way from Alexandria to Arlington. The car's wipers won't keep up, so the highway goes blurry. Jim Waldron is driving, and despite his running commentary on his challenge, he's doing a good job. We arrive as the rain eases enough for us to make our sprints to the administration building.

I've been here before, and what comes back to me is the way this place doesn't so much feel like a government building as a quiet funeral parlor. I find it settling. The patter of rain on the concrete sidewalk outside and the way those soft sounds add to the murmur of folks already here—that's calming, too.

There are hugs and smiles as Roz and I find Glen's family. The other Ghostriders are scattered. Over there is Larry Cunningham talking quietly with Don Purdy. Jim Waldron is with one of Glen's children. Mike Mullane is off with someone I don't know.

They remember that Glen earned the Air Force Cross, recognition only 197 others in the service have ever merited, and they know the other three on his crew—Billy Privette, Ted Zerbe and Randy McComb—each was awarded a Silver Star for their actions the day of one of the Air Force's most valorous rescues. These Ghostriders are themselves brave and decorated men. Yet they've come to honor the breathtaking courage of Glen York, a man they've never met, and I love them for this. But I think they've not only come for this, but also to recognize what the Jolly Greens meant to us all.

Glen's co-pilot, Billy, the guy who spotted me on the ground, is here. He's staying in the same hotel we are, and last night, while we talked, Billy told Roz about sticking his head out the Jolly Green's side-window, searching the jungle for me. He told her the guys around me were shooting so rapidly it sounded like popping-corn on a skillet. Hot shooting all around, and thank God he spotted me. I, however, remember only the pounding of the chopper's rotor blades and the crashing noise when they slashed off the top of a tree.

Someone tells me Paul Engel, my first skipper, my wingman, the man who showed me the dauntless meaning of "Press On," has arrived. He's driven here with his wife Tan in a cherry-red pickup through cells of torrential rain. Yes, today they pressed on from their home on the Potomac, a custom house Paul named "Final Landing." I keep my eye out for him, but it will turn out he and Tan are waiting in the red truck for the motorcade to form. Admiral Engel knows this drill.

Ted Zerbe arrived with his family—the van was full—not long after we did. They've driven down from Pennsylvania. He and I haven't seen each other since that day forty-seven years ago. I find Ted, and I'd like to continue my chat with him, but an officer in full-dress-uniform has given the signal. It's time. The storm has eased, and we're to follow in our cars to the columbarium. It would be good to walk instead.

If we walked, we could detour along Eisenhower Drive to where Dick Perry is buried. We all thought Dick would rise to the top, but he'd only had time to make it half way to admiral —to lieutenant commander—when a helicopter was forced by flak to leave his body in the warm waters of the Tonkin Gulf. His remains were eventually returned, and he was buried here at Arlington National Cemetery in April, 1987. It was almost twenty years after his shootdown, yet a solid showing of Ghostriders attended.

The three men flying on Dick Perry's wing the day he died— John Davis, Mike Mullane and George Schindelar—were there. So were Cunningham, Duter, Purdy, Waldron and Deny Weichman. Jimmy Seeley, a junior officer with the Ghostriders on the '66 cruise and the first man I knew to outfly a SAM, served as one of Dick's honor guards.

Dick's widow, Margot, sat in the front pew along with their son Steve, deprived of his father while he was a little boy.

Roz had come with me to Arlington. Paul and Tan Engel both were there. Doug Mow, our skipper at the time Dick was downed, and his wife Rosalie attended. Magnolia also attended. All three— Magnolia, Doug and Paul—had by then risen to the rank of Admiral. Someone counted eleven flag-rank officers honoring Dick that cold morning.

This was my first experience with a full-honors burial at our national cemetery, so I wasn't prepared to see his flag-draped casket on a caisson. It was hitched to six dark horses, riders on three— all on the left side, for a symbolic reason. Symbolism abounded, right down to the number of folds in that flag—thirteen—after it was lifted from the casket.

I knew there was to be a four-plane flyover of the gravesite, the traditional salute to a fallen pilot—so steeped in symbolism. I'd witnessed this before, and waited to hear the formation approach. I knew to expect that one jet, the section leader, would pitch up as the four came into view, then zoom-climb heavenward. But what I hadn't anticipated was tears, the damn blurry clouding of vision as the remaining three arrived overhead, over Dick's grave. It was the gap in the formation, that got me. The missing-man.

If we were walking today, it wouldn't be much further down the hillside to Section 11. Dick Hartman was buried there in May of 1974—almost seven years after he died. I didn't attend. I received notice only a week before; maybe that was my reason—or perhaps because Roz and I were struggling with cash-flow at our first newspaper, and couldn't afford it. At the time, possibly I convinced myself those were my reasons. Later though, when Lance-the-shrink helped me see things honestly, I'd understand I was hiding.

Beginning with my retreat to Aspen, and for many years after that, I'd tried to make Vietnam disappear. I wore my hair long and grew a gun-fighter's moustache so no one would mistake me for a vet. And most acquaintances—even close friends—had no clue that I'd ever been to Vietnam. Not to Vietnam the first time with my family, and certainly not the next three ventures to the country as an attack pilot. I was flying below the radar... and among vets, I wasn't alone.

A letter I had received from Dick's mother earlier that year quoted a report from the Navy stating that Dick arrived in Hanoi unconscious with a flesh wound on his right foot. It said he died the next day of "acute inflammation of the lungs and physical deterioration."

On Dick's death-certificate, the Vietnamese claim that my section leader died in a military hospital on July 22. The day before, my birthday, a Hanoi radio station had announced Richard Hartman had been arrested. So, he died twenty hours after they captured him, they say, claiming he wasn't killed on the ridge or even en route to the POW prison, as I imagined. The document says he perished in a hospital, one founded by the French in 1894 as Lanessan Hospital. It became Military Central Hospital 108 under the communists, and at the time of Dick's death, it was reserved for senior officials.

Truly? Did doctors at Military Central Hospital 108 try to save Dick?

Or was he already dead when he was brought in? In fact, I wonder if he ever made it to any hospital. We have only the stark information on U.S. Army Form AR 638-40, and it tells so little.

The Vietnamese say his remains were among twelve Americans disinterred from the Ba Huyen cemetery in Ha Bac Province twenty-five miles northeast of Hanoi. But in reality, there were twenty-three American POWs buried there—or reburied there, since most had first been interred at a cemetery closer to Hanoi.

Dick Hartman was denied the wish. He rests now beneath the sloping grass in Section 11 at Arlington National Cemetery. Throughout 1967 and the remainder of my Navy days and my time as a ski-bum and then marriage and those many months in college—during all that living of life—I was so very sure Dick was imprisoned in Hanoi. That I'd see him again.

It would be good if we could stand quietly before Dick Hartman's white marker for a few minutes. But there isn't the time or the weather today.

With time and sunshine, we could walk to Doug Mow's grave. His headstone is about halfway between Hartman and Perry. And we might then go on a bit farther to where Roger Meyers rests. And Clyde Welch, who died in Oriskany's fire—the one I escaped—we could find him nearby. Don Irwin, too, killed on our final deployment. I know he lies close to Roger. Rod Carter, the air wing commander who dove with me against a flak site at Vinh—he's in Section 13.

In Section 60, where Dick Perry rests, we might also look out on that open place where in the summer the grass will be so green and where in 2013, in May, Roz and I and several Ghostriders stood in warm sun for another ceremony. If we made our way down there today, we'd see the large headstone marking a single coffin. Just one, yet it cradles the remains of four brave men, the four who fell with Big Mother 67 in their attempt to pluck Dick from that karst ridge. They're in one box because their bones and dog-tags and dust had comingled in the earth for so many years at their crash-site that their families agreed they should continue on together.

But we don't walk.

With Jim Waldron driving, we join the long line of cars, the five of us, and we follow Skipper Engel and Tan in the red truck, and Jim parks when the motorcade stops at the columbarium. Though we're outdoors, we stand sheltered beneath a handsome flat-roofed structure.

Proper words are said. The rain lifts somewhat. Seven riflemen fire three volleys in perfect unison, and then far in the distance, almost obscured by lavender-gray sheets of mist, a lone bugler begins taps, mournful and desolate as always, and tears, the goddamn tears surprise me. Again.

Glen's honor guard, six servicemen, ceremoniously begin to fold his American flag—they make the thirteen folds, finishing with a final crisp turn to create a taut parcel. An officer kneels and passes the sad triangle, cobalt field, white stars, to Glen's oldest daughter. She sits somberly in the first row beside her sister and brother.

For the walk to Glen's niche, the rain generously lightens. Scattered splashes of sunlight warm the path. Moving briskly, the small crowd follows the daughter carrying the flag triangle in both her hands.

Roz and I hold back. We accompany Ted Zerbe, the brave crewman who hoisted me to safety and then gave me his box-lunch. He's sliding a walker along in a slow shuffle—he and his wife are both struggling.

Then sooner than I expected, it's over. Glen's remains have been slipped into his vault next to his wife's urn. I'm still teary, but I smile, too, because Major Glen York pulled it off. By God, he fulfilled *The Wish*. Natural causes.

We have agreed to gather a little while later for a reception back at our hotel. We want more time with Glen's family, with Ted and his and more time with Billy.

Yet, before we leave the columbarium, we agree we should visit Roger Duter, our roomie in the stateroom we called Alice's Restaurant. His niche is a couple rows over. And we do this.

The sun is out when we arrive, and Roz snaps a photo as four Ghostriders place their hands onto Roger's vault.

After the reception, it will be us old Ghostriders, along with Billy, in Alexandria for dinner. There, with all the somberness behind us, we'll laugh and brag about our kids and grandkids and have a few drinks. We'll talk of plans we have, upcoming travel, and inevitably we'll talk about flying.

It will be the good stuff, fine tales of camaraderie and cerulean skies and making contrails at high altitudes, of sunsets seen from 40,000 feet and of traps and cat-shots on aircraft carriers steaming across tranquil seas. And all the good guys; we cannot forget friendships so strong and tight they could have been annealed in no other way...only in the chaotic heat of combat in the skies.

# Acknowledgments

I've made a strong effort to achieve accuracy in this book, calling on my decades of experience as a journalist as I endeavored to verify facts. I've checked multiple sources, and whenever possible, instead of memory, I've turned to military records, including the official histories of VA-164 and Carrier Air Wing 16.

My flight logbook has, of course, been a primary resource. Also, I was privileged to have at hand Roger Duter's meticulous daily journal from our 1967 combat deployment, entrusted to me by his widow Cheryl. His powerful diary, more than any other document, helped clarify details of the morning Dick and I were shot down.

Squadron-mate Chuck Nelson provided pages from his personal journal detailing the night Frank Elkins was shot down.

Hugh Lynch, a retired Navy captain, generously shared documents, including official histories, from a trove of material he amassed over the years for a book he was working on. I also called on his deep experience as a career naval aviator to answer a number of questions.

Over the years, I spoke often with Glen York, the heroic Jolly Green rescue pilot, to compare notes. His equally brave co-pilot, Billy Privette, contributed details of the day they rescued me. The late Ted Zerbe, the crewman who gave me his lunch, also answered some questions.

We remaining Ghostriders stay in touch. I'm indebted to my former roomie on both Oriskany and Hancock (and fly-fishing buddy), Don Purdy. He patiently answered many hundreds of questions as I wrote this, and then he generously designed this book's cover. Our squadron intelligence officer, Jim Waldron— gifted with a sharp memory for dates and details—has been a solid resource. So has Mike Mullane, a keen observer who once used our ship's shootdown data to calculate precisely which day his time would be up (a date he lived past and now celebrates each October). Mike also painted for me a vivid image of the SAM explosion that fatally damaged Dick Perry's aircraft.

Larry Cunningham provided a written recollection of his first mission and shootdown. And because he flew on Deny Weichman's wing, he helped me understand the practical joker who set an American record for combat missions flown. John Davis has been a steadfast resource, and he, too, helped me understand the shootdown of Dick Perry. Bill Span, who retired as a captain, supplied the coordinates and a helpful chart of the Co Trai bridges.

Retired Rear Admiral Paul Engel, my first skipper and a man I admired for courage and grace, stayed in touch over the years. He supplied or verified many of the details in this book. I have likewise stayed in contact with Leon Edney, who retired as a full admiral. He too has been very helpful.

More than the assistance they provide, I appreciate the friendship of my squadron mates. No one, except my wife, understands me better than the old Ghostriders—and I love them for this.

A number of VA-163's Saints also assisted. Retired Rear Admiral Bryan Compton, who led the strike to the Co Trai Bridge, cleared up some fine points, including how we accomplished our rendezvous over the ship. Ken Adams, fellow must-pump, helped with details of our trek out to Yankee Station and of the day a SAM sliced open his centerline drop tank (yet failed to explode). I spoke at length with Dave Carey at a joint-squadron reunion, and then I learned even more from his inspirational book, *The Ways We Choose: Lessons for life from a POW's experience.*

John Bender and John Schloz, pilots of Big Mother, the first helicopter to come for me, were very helpful. They each poignantly related details of their futile attempt to save the life of door-gunner David Chatterton. Hank Miller, the Locket A-1 pilot who escorted their helicopter on its valiant dash for help, provided additional details.

Two other A-1 pilots who assisted in my rescue—Jim Harmon, a Navy Locket driver, and Air Force Sandy pilot Jimmy Kilbourne—also helped me understand that morning. Big Mother Pilot Neil Sparks, who rescued an F-8 pilot from the same karst area, further expanded my understanding of the Big Mother operations.

Tom Phillips, co-author of the definitive helicopter-rescue book *Leave No Man Behind* was a fine resource (as was his book).

Peter Fey, a meticulous researcher and author of *Bloody Sixteen: The USS Oriskany and Air Wing 16 during the Vietnam War,* was a great help. I checked many facts against his book—which is one of the most accurate depictions of the air war over Vietnam. Rene J. Francillion's *Tonkin Gulf Yacht Club: U.S. carrier operations off Vietnam* is another book I turned to for statistics and facts.

To better understand the strategies of some of the leaders involved in prosecuting that war, I turned to Robert McNamara's *In Retrospect* and to biographies of Ho Chi Minh and General Vo Nguyen Giap, and I read books about Ngo Dinh Diem and his sister-in-law, Madam Nhu. I also reread Bernard Fall's *The Two Viet-Nams: A Political and Military Analysis* (first published in 1963, early enough to have helped, had McNamara and the rest of the Whiz Kids heeded his warnings).

I turned to retired Navy captain Wynn F. Foster's book about the Oriskany conflagration—*Fire on the Hangar Deck*—to cross-check my memory of that grim October day.

Perhaps the best books about the cascade of bad decisions and national hubris that that sucked our nation into the first war it lost are Stanley Karnow's *Vietnam: A History* and Neil Sheehan's *A Bright Shining Lie: John Paul Vann and America in Vietnam.* I reread portions of both, some sections many times.

I want to thank three of the Clods from my Saigon high school days for their help: Paul Christensen, Dick Plagge and Richard Turner.

Richard was with me in North Vietnam for the scene I describe in the Afterword. He filmed much of that day, and the recording helped me recover details I'd have forgotten. Years later, Paul, Richard and I spent a weekend in Vermont rehashing everything we could recall, and both men read from their notes and journals.

I also want to express gratitude to the Dogs.

For more than three decades I've been part of a small writing group—The Wet Dogs—and they have patiently helped with many versions of this book. Lynn Thompson, who first organized our little assemblage, was always honest in her gentle criticism, as was Marjorie Hillson. Scott Sparling was our group's first to publish (a fine novel, *Wire to Wire)* and he was always insightful. In the gentlest manner he would "wonder" where I was going, and then guide me back on track. Steven Wing also afforded valuable criticism and went a step further. He combed through an earlier version, then outlined a reorganization. I took his advice to heart.

I am grateful to literary agent Robert Wilson, who suggested a number of revisions and expansions. His advice led me to a more cohesive rewrite, and he helped me make this into a better, more focused read. He also suggested the current title, *Return to Saigon.*

Similarly, author John Shore (*Everywhere She's Not*, winner of the Best New Fiction, 2020 American Fiction Award), provided valuable advice that helped me further tighten and focus this memoir.

Nevertheless, even with all this help, there may be errors, and oversights. I accept full responsibility and in advance, apologize. Likely there are others who have contributed to this history, and if I have failed to thank them here, please forgive those omissions.

I want to thank my children, Kassie and Forrest, for urging me to finally get some of this on paper.

I am thankful to all, but I am most grateful to my wife.

Roz has been over every word in many renderings of this book, catching errors, typos and questionable sequences. She is my first reader. It is to her I turn for valuable thoughts on content, typography and then final editing.

*Return to Saigon* is as much Roz's, as it is mine, for without her love and support, it would not have been written.

Thank you, Rozzie. I do.

# About the Author:

**Larry Duthie** is a retired newspaper publisher who lives with his wife, Roz, on a small hay-farm in Eastern Washington. In addition to writing, he spends his time rebuilding old sailboats, trucks, cars, motorcycles and very old tractors.

He still loves aviation.

Over the years he's owned a series of light airplanes, including part-interest in a floatplane. There is nothing better for the soul, he will tell you, than landing on the still surface of a clear mountain lake and then fishing from its pontoon.

OK-3
PUBLISHING
Annapolis, MD

Made in the USA
Monee, IL
09 April 2023